SHERLOCK HOLMES & MORIARTY
Associates

Author: CED   **Illustrator**: Boutanox   **Colors**: Damien Gay   **Translation**: JF Gagné
This book is a translation of the original *Sherlock Holmes & Moriarty: Associates* © Makaka Editions
© Van Ryder Games 2019

Van Ryder Games and Graphic Novel Adventures are Trademarks of Van Ryder Games LLC
ISBN : 978-0-9997698-5-0   Library of Congress Control Number: 2019903160

Published by Van Ryder Games and printed in China by Avenue 4. First Printing.

Find printable investigation sheets and other Graphic Novel Adventures at www.vanrydergames.com

1 – THE MERYSEYSIDE RIVER

Who is the murderer?

(Suspect list in 37)

2 – THE FALL OF THE LELAND BANK

Who caused the death
of Ernest Leland?

(Supect list in 64)

3 – THE MISSING PRINCESS

Who made the princess
disappear?

(Suspect list in 41)

Number of precious stones found:

Dear reader, the only accessories you need are a pen and a sheet of paper to note anything interesting found during your investigation.

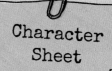

Character Sheet

Throughout the investigations you will take on the role of one of three characters, each with their own unique abilities.

Doctor Watson is Sherlock Holmes's trusted friend. He recently started taking things into his own hands by investigating his own cases.

He may ask up to four questions during interrogations, ask Holmes for tips, and inspect a victim's corpse using his medical knowledge. Playing with him will make the cases somewhat easier.

Sherlock Holmes is London's most famous consulting detective.

He may only ask up to three questions during interrogations, but his keen deduction skills allow you to ask the right questions and make insights others can't.

Careful, some questions may frustrate the individuals you meet and make them unwilling to answer any further inquiries.

Starting with the second investigation, you can take on the role of Professor Moriarty, the Napoleon of Crime.

Like Holmes, he may only ask three questions during an interrogation. If he deems that a question may frustrate the suspect, he can insist and threaten the suspect. Once threatened, the suspect will eventually reveal a secret. This will end the interrogation, regardless of how many questions were asked.

Note: showing an object to a suspect is not considered "asking a question."

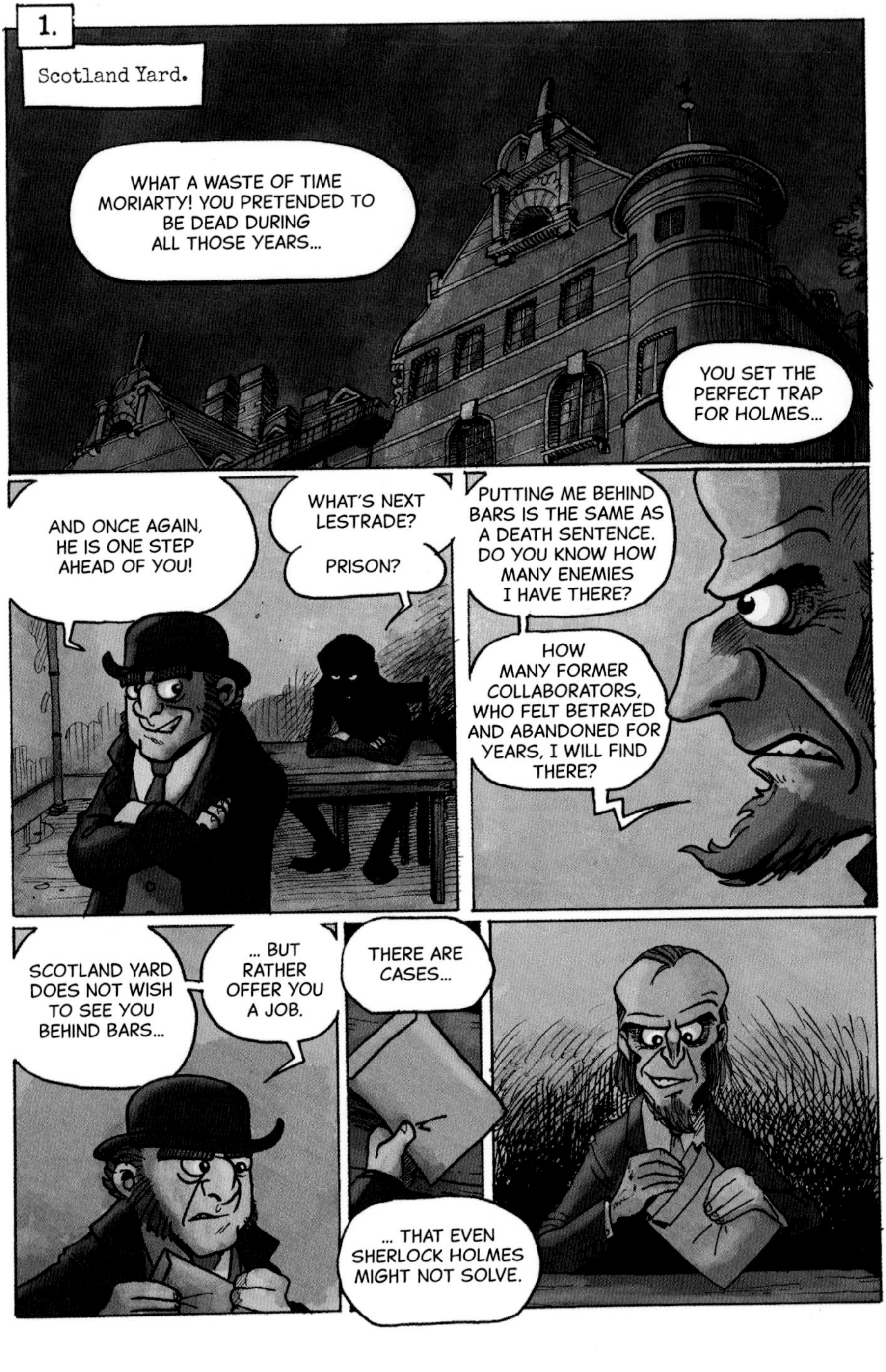
1.
Scotland Yard.
WHAT A WASTE OF TIME MORIARTY! YOU PRETENDED TO BE DEAD DURING ALL THOSE YEARS...
YOU SET THE PERFECT TRAP FOR HOLMES...
AND ONCE AGAIN, HE IS ONE STEP AHEAD OF YOU!
WHAT'S NEXT LESTRADE?
PRISON?
PUTTING ME BEHIND BARS IS THE SAME AS A DEATH SENTENCE. DO YOU KNOW HOW MANY ENEMIES I HAVE THERE?
HOW MANY FORMER COLLABORATORS, WHO FELT BETRAYED AND ABANDONED FOR YEARS, I WILL FIND THERE?
SCOTLAND YARD DOES NOT WISH TO SEE YOU BEHIND BARS...
... BUT RATHER OFFER YOU A JOB.
THERE ARE CASES...
... THAT EVEN SHERLOCK HOLMES MIGHT NOT SOLVE.

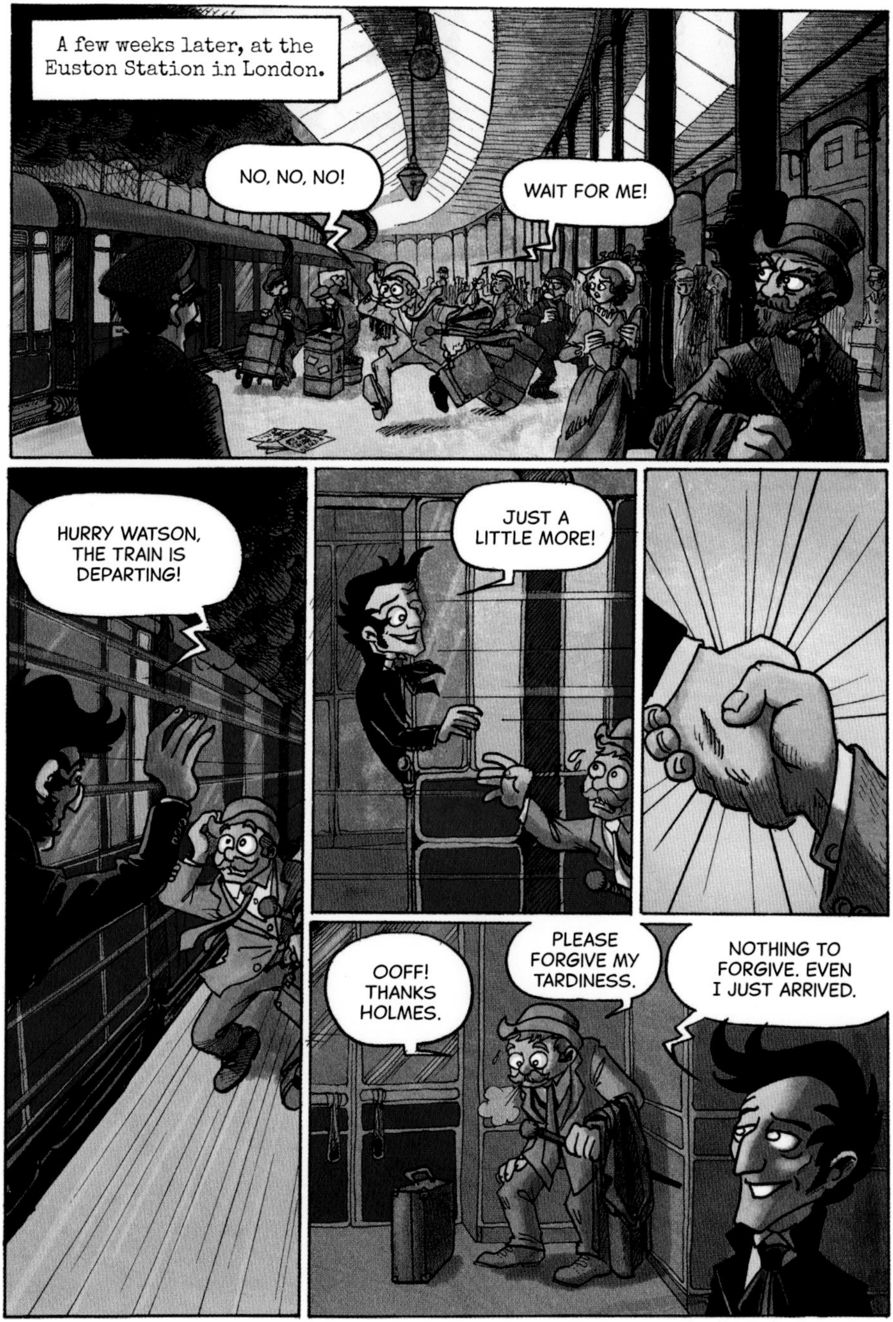
A few weeks later, at the Euston Station in London.
NO, NO, NO!
WAIT FOR ME!
HURRY WATSON, THE TRAIN IS DEPARTING!
JUST A LITTLE MORE!
OOFF! THANKS HOLMES.
PLEASE FORGIVE MY TARDINESS.
NOTHING TO FORGIVE. EVEN I JUST ARRIVED.

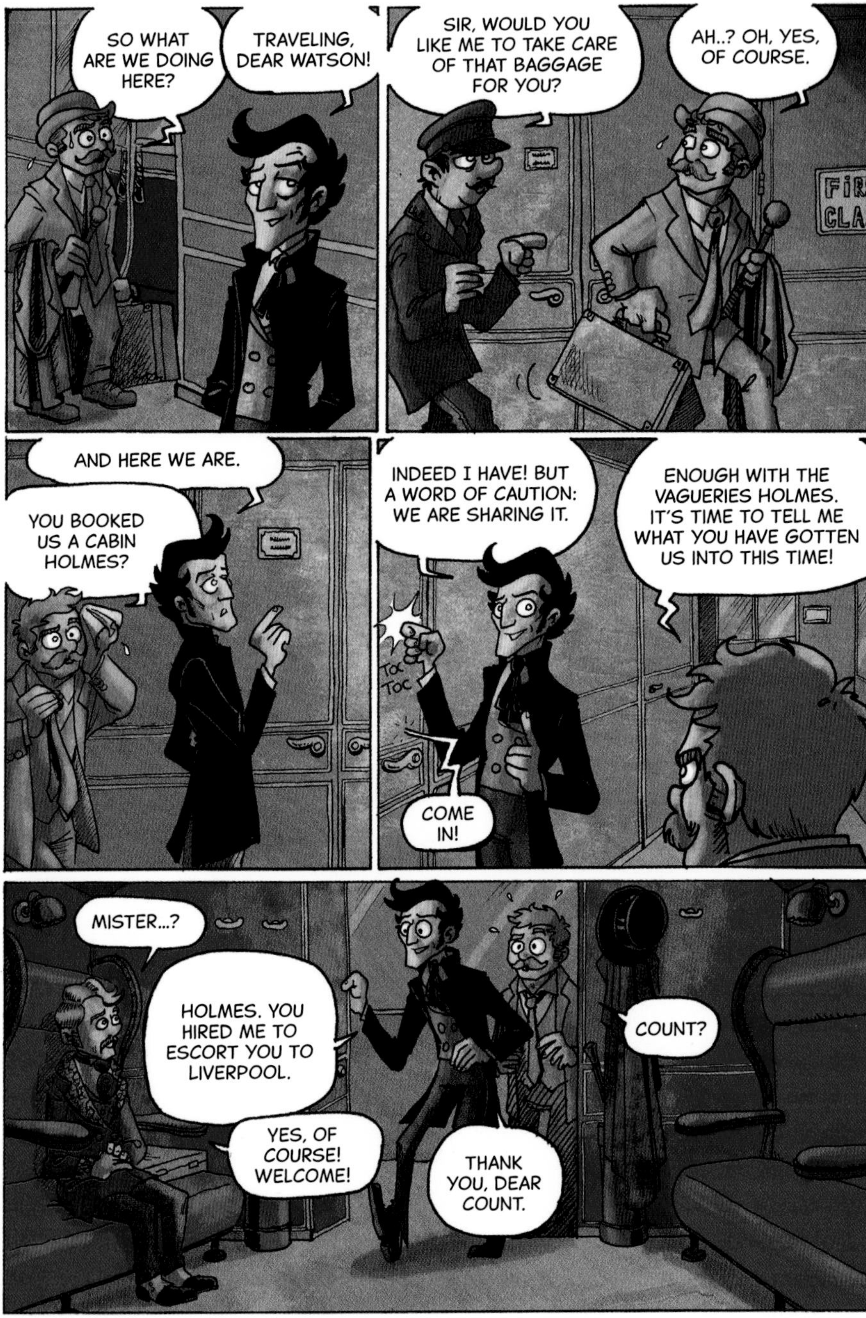
SO WHAT ARE WE DOING HERE?
TRAVELING, DEAR WATSON!
SIR, WOULD YOU LIKE ME TO TAKE CARE OF THAT BAGGAGE FOR YOU?
AH..? OH, YES, OF COURSE.
FIRS
CLAS
AND HERE WE ARE.
YOU BOOKED US A CABIN HOLMES?
INDEED I HAVE! BUT A WORD OF CAUTION: WE ARE SHARING IT.
TOC TOC
COME IN!
ENOUGH WITH THE VAGUERIES HOLMES. IT'S TIME TO TELL ME WHAT YOU HAVE GOTTEN US INTO THIS TIME!
MISTER...?
HOLMES. YOU HIRED ME TO ESCORT YOU TO LIVERPOOL.
YES, OF COURSE! WELCOME!
THANK YOU, DEAR COUNT.
COUNT?

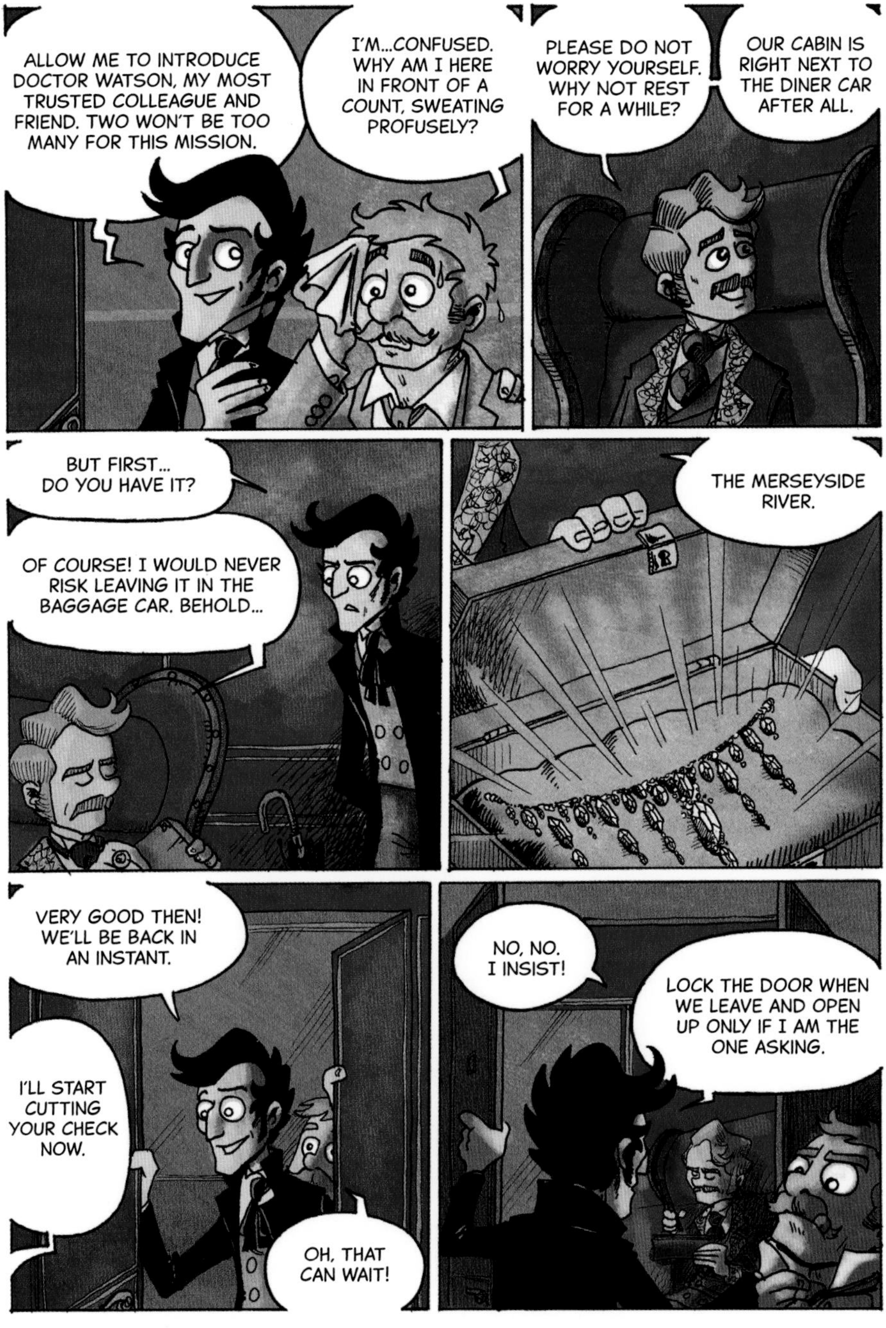
ALLOW ME TO INTRODUCE DOCTOR WATSON, MY MOST TRUSTED COLLEAGUE AND FRIEND. TWO WON'T BE TOO MANY FOR THIS MISSION.
I'M...CONFUSED. WHY AM I HERE IN FRONT OF A COUNT, SWEATING PROFUSELY?
PLEASE DO NOT WORRY YOURSELF. WHY NOT REST FOR A WHILE?
OUR CABIN IS RIGHT NEXT TO THE DINER CAR AFTER ALL.
BUT FIRST... DO YOU HAVE IT?
OF COURSE! I WOULD NEVER RISK LEAVING IT IN THE BAGGAGE CAR. BEHOLD...
THE MERSEYSIDE RIVER.
VERY GOOD THEN! WE'LL BE BACK IN AN INSTANT.
I'LL START CUTTING YOUR CHECK NOW.
OH, THAT CAN WAIT!
NO, NO. I INSIST!
LOCK THE DOOR WHEN WE LEAVE AND OPEN UP ONLY IF I AM THE ONE ASKING.

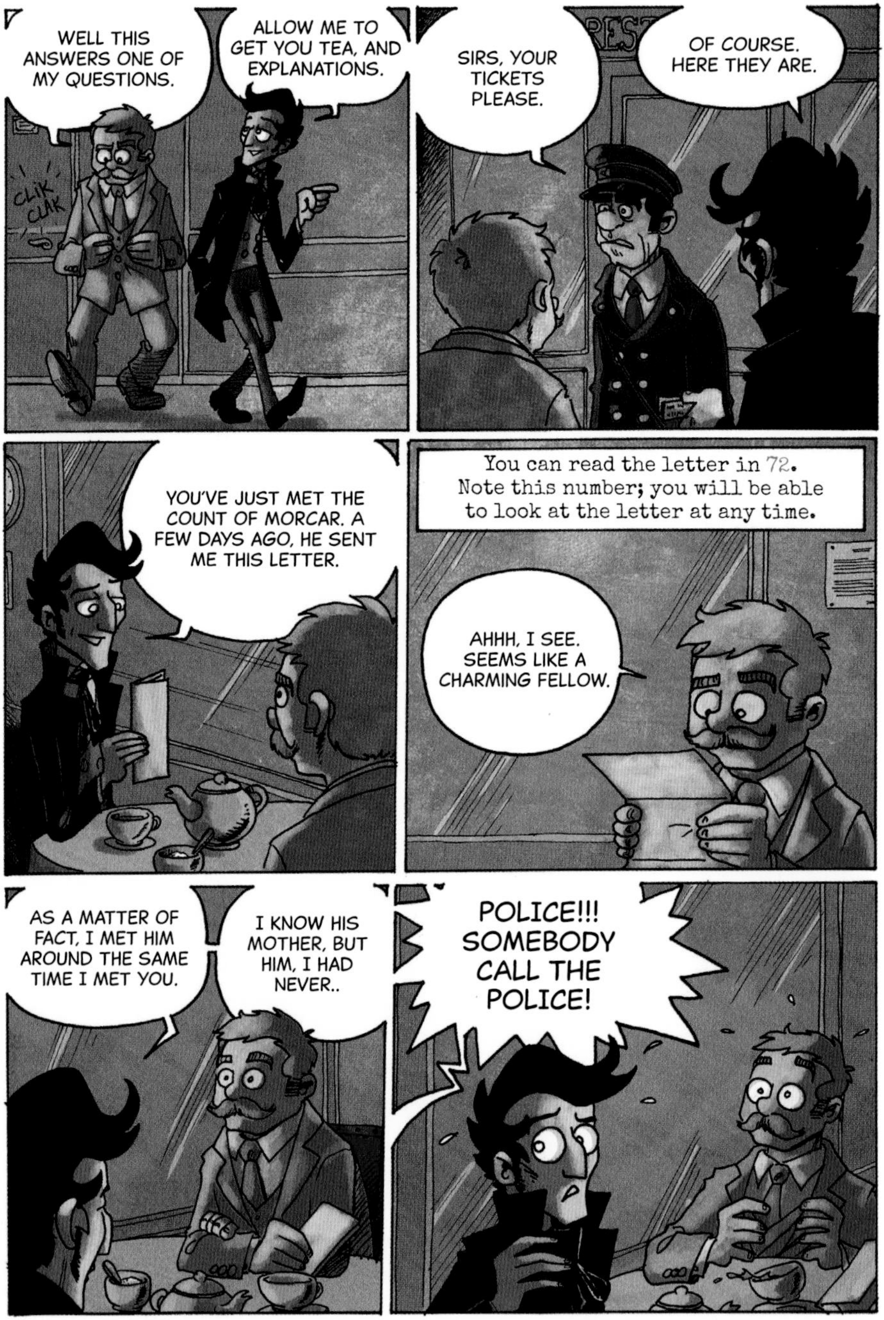
WELL THIS ANSWERS ONE OF MY QUESTIONS.
ALLOW ME TO GET YOU TEA, AND EXPLANATIONS.
CLIK CLIK
SIRS, YOUR TICKETS PLEASE.
OF COURSE. HERE THEY ARE.
YOU'VE JUST MET THE COUNT OF MORCAR. A FEW DAYS AGO, HE SENT ME THIS LETTER.
You can read the letter in 72. Note this number; you will be able to look at the letter at any time.
AHHH, I SEE. SEEMS LIKE A CHARMING FELLOW.
AS A MATTER OF FACT, I MET HIM AROUND THE SAME TIME I MET YOU.
I KNOW HIS MOTHER, BUT HIM, I HAD NEVER..
POLICE!!! SOMEBODY CALL THE POLICE!

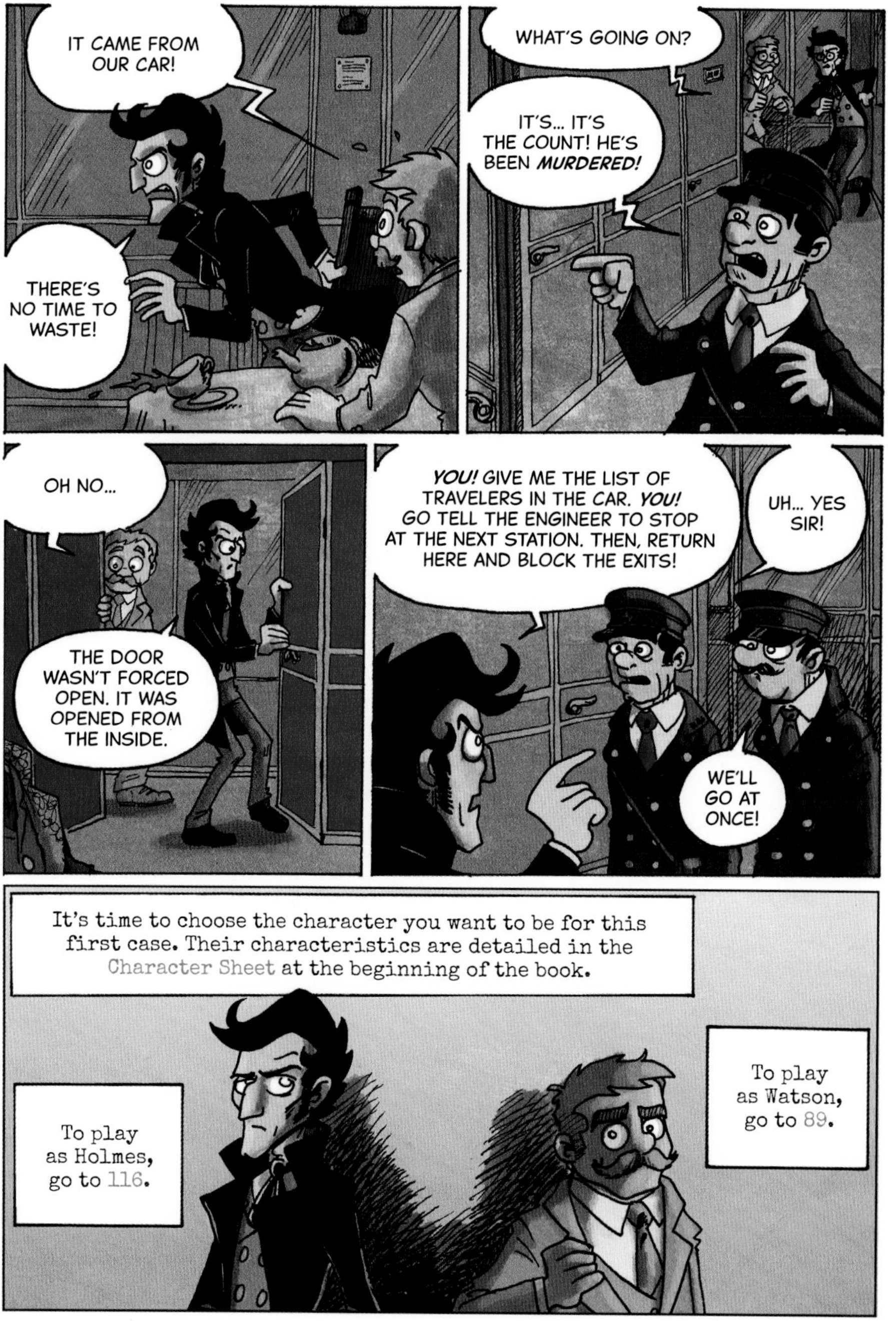
IT CAME FROM OUR CAR!
THERE'S NO TIME TO WASTE!
WHAT'S GOING ON?
IT'S... IT'S THE COUNT! HE'S BEEN *MURDERED!*
OH NO...
THE DOOR WASN'T FORCED OPEN. IT WAS OPENED FROM THE INSIDE.
YOU! GIVE ME THE LIST OF TRAVELERS IN THE CAR. *YOU!* GO TELL THE ENGINEER TO STOP AT THE NEXT STATION. THEN, RETURN HERE AND BLOCK THE EXITS!
UH... YES SIR!
WE'LL GO AT ONCE!
It's time to choose the character you want to be for this first case. Their characteristics are detailed in the Character Sheet at the beginning of the book.
To play as Holmes, go to 116.
To play as Watson, go to 89.

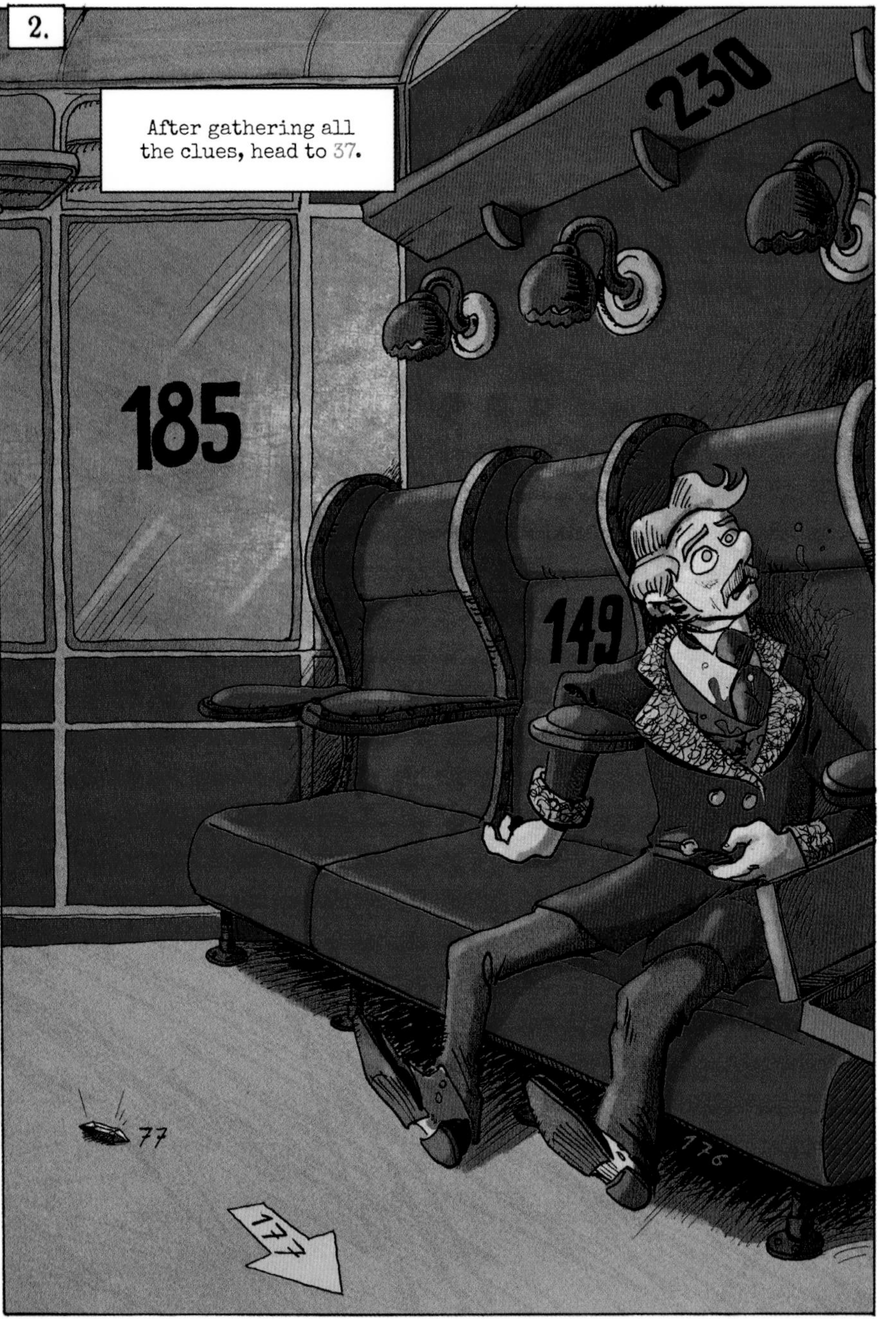
2.
After gathering all
the clues, head to 37.
230
185
149
77
176
177

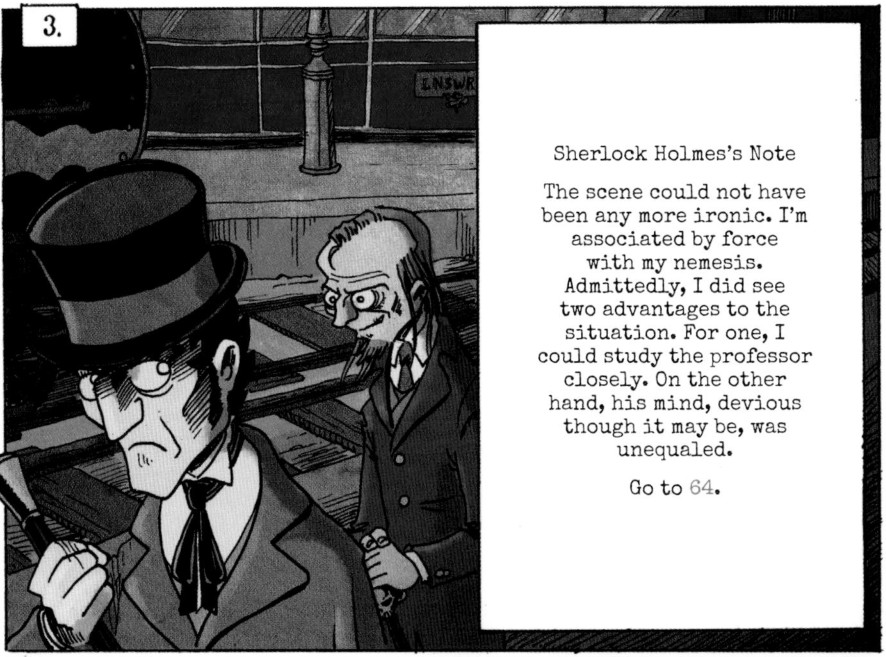
3.
LNSWR
Sherlock Holmes's Note
The scene could not have been any more ironic. I'm associated by force with my nemesis. Admittedly, I did see two advantages to the situation. For one, I could study the professor closely. On the other hand, his mind, devious though it may be, was unequaled.
Go to 64.

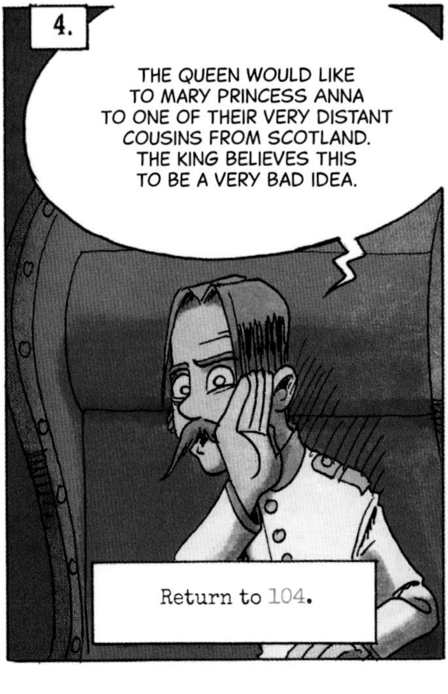
4.
THE QUEEN WOULD LIKE TO MARY PRINCESS ANNA TO ONE OF THEIR VERY DISTANT COUSINS FROM SCOTLAND. THE KING BELIEVES THIS TO BE A VERY BAD IDEA.
Return to 104.

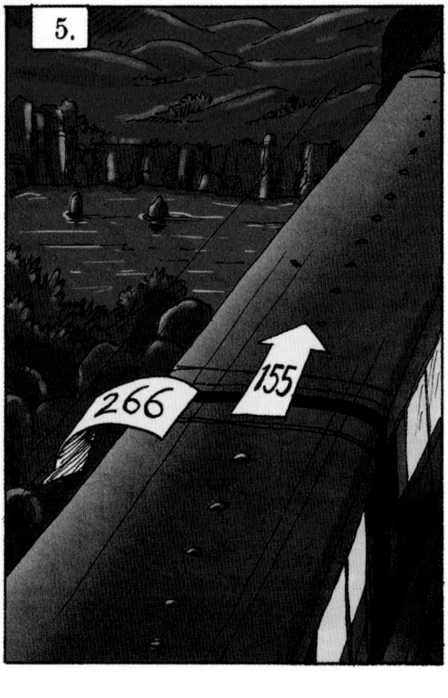
5.
266
155

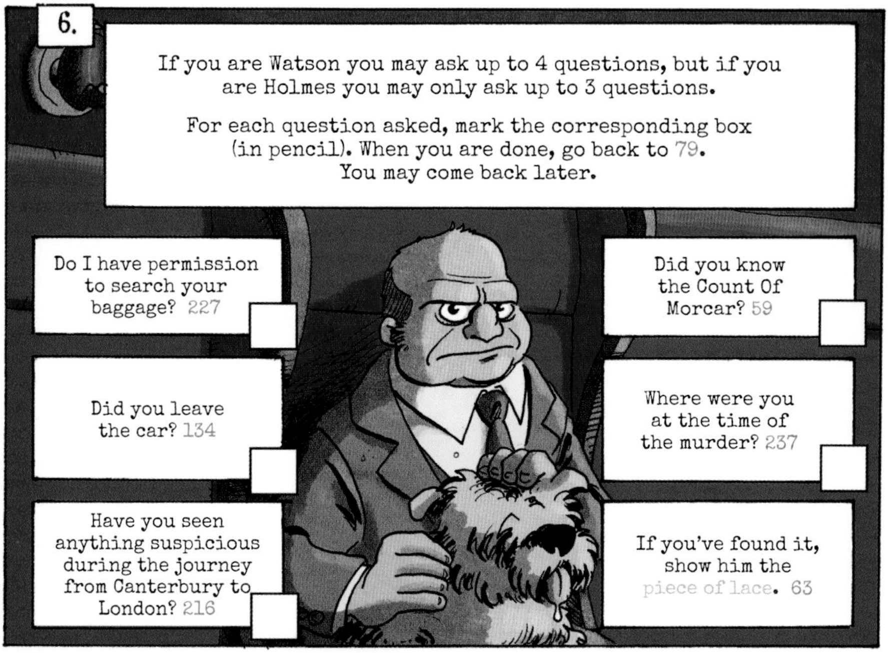
6.
If you are Watson you may ask up to 4 questions, but if you are Holmes you may only ask up to 3 questions.
For each question asked, mark the corresponding box (in pencil). When you are done, go back to 79. You may come back later.
Do I have permission to search your baggage? 227
Did you leave the car? 134
Have you seen anything suspicious during the journey from Canterbury to London? 216
Did you know the Count Of Morcar? 59
Where were you at the time of the murder? 237
If you've found it, show him the piece of lace. 63

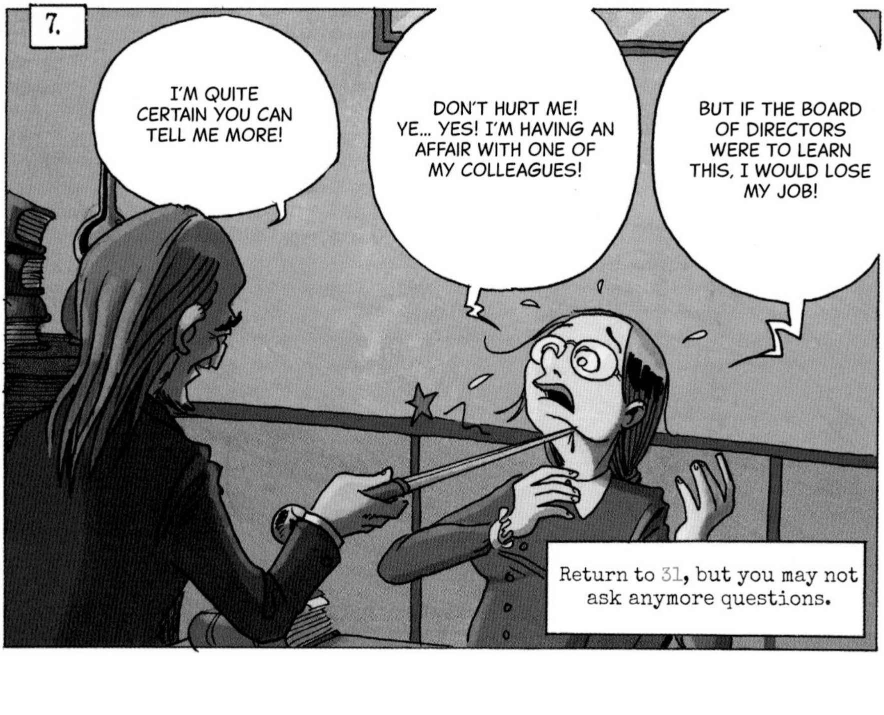
7.
I'M QUITE CERTAIN YOU CAN TELL ME MORE!
DON'T HURT ME! YE... YES! I'M HAVING AN AFFAIR WITH ONE OF MY COLLEAGUES!
BUT IF THE BOARD OF DIRECTORS WERE TO LEARN THIS, I WOULD LOSE MY JOB!
Return to 31, but you may not ask anymore questions.

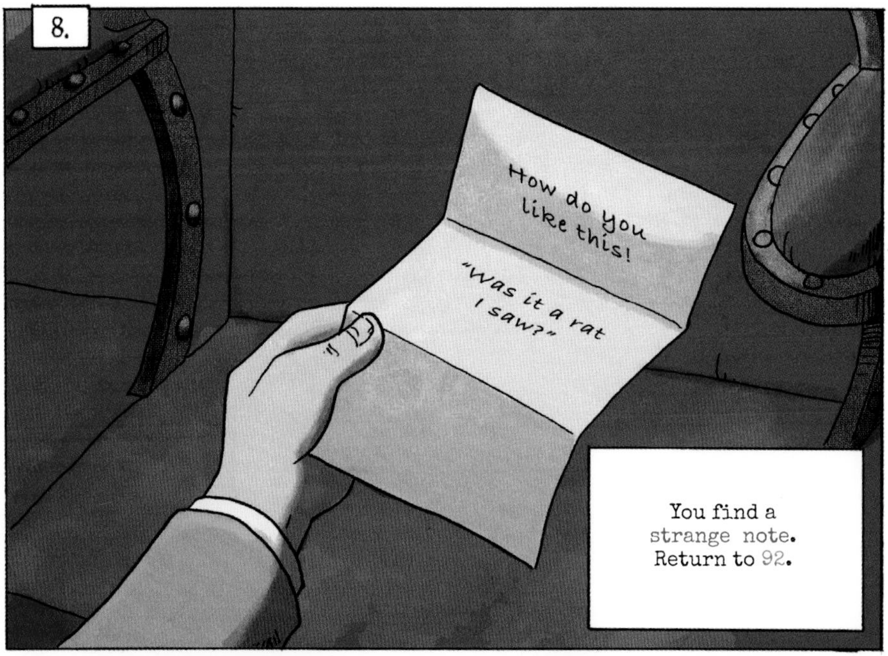
8.
How do you like this!
"Was it a rat I saw?"
You find a strange note. Return to 92.

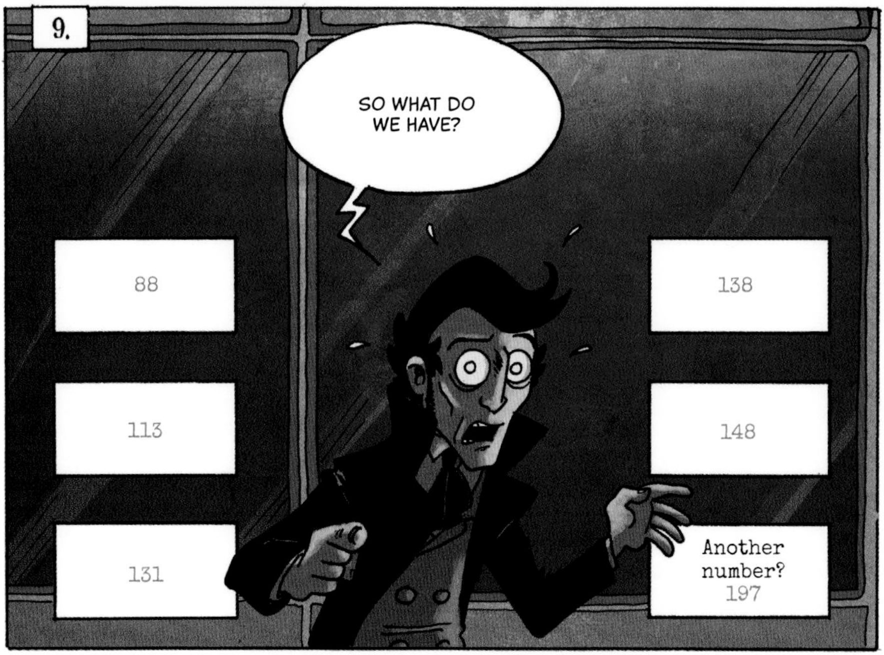
9.
SO WHAT DO WE HAVE?
88
113
131
138
148
Another number? 197

10.

SINCE BIRMINGHAM. I SNEAKED THROUGH THAT BIG DOOR OVER THERE. THERE'S A CHAIN, BUT I'M SMALL ENOUGH TO SQUEEZE THROUGH WITHOUT A PROBLEM.

Return to 73.

11.

MYSELF, AS WELL AS ALL OF THE TRAIN CONDUCTORS.

Return to 51.

12.

WOW!

49

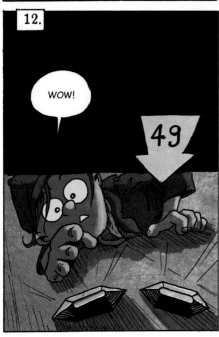

13.

Nothing interesting here.
Return to 153.

14.

The briefcase where the jewel was stored.
You notice the chain is still there. The thief must have
pulled on it and only taken the precious stones.

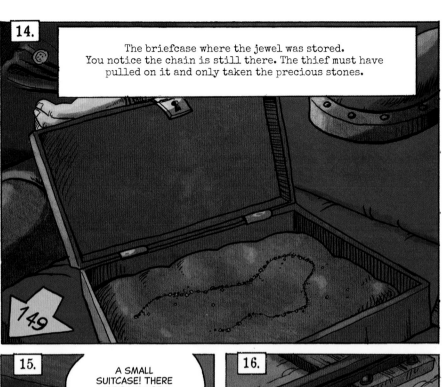

15.

A SMALL
SUITCASE! THERE
ARE BANDAGES
INSIDE!

16.

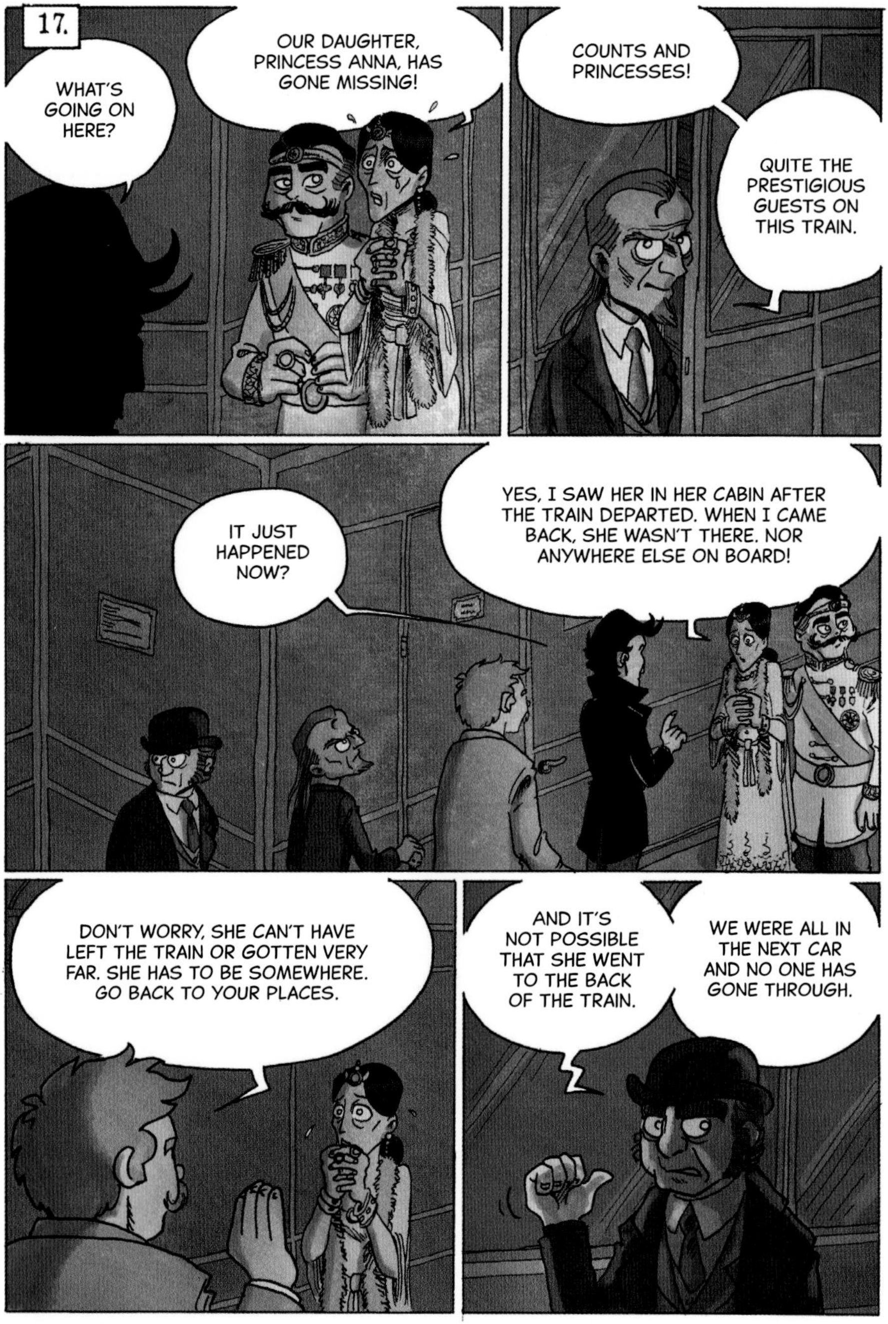
17.
WHAT'S GOING ON HERE?
OUR DAUGHTER, PRINCESS ANNA, HAS GONE MISSING!
COUNTS AND PRINCESSES!
QUITE THE PRESTIGIOUS GUESTS ON THIS TRAIN.
IT JUST HAPPENED NOW?
YES, I SAW HER IN HER CABIN AFTER THE TRAIN DEPARTED. WHEN I CAME BACK, SHE WASN'T THERE. NOR ANYWHERE ELSE ON BOARD!
DON'T WORRY, SHE CAN'T HAVE LEFT THE TRAIN OR GOTTEN VERY FAR. SHE HAS TO BE SOMEWHERE. GO BACK TO YOUR PLACES.
AND IT'S NOT POSSIBLE THAT SHE WENT TO THE BACK OF THE TRAIN.
WE WERE ALL IN THE NEXT CAR AND NO ONE HAS GONE THROUGH.

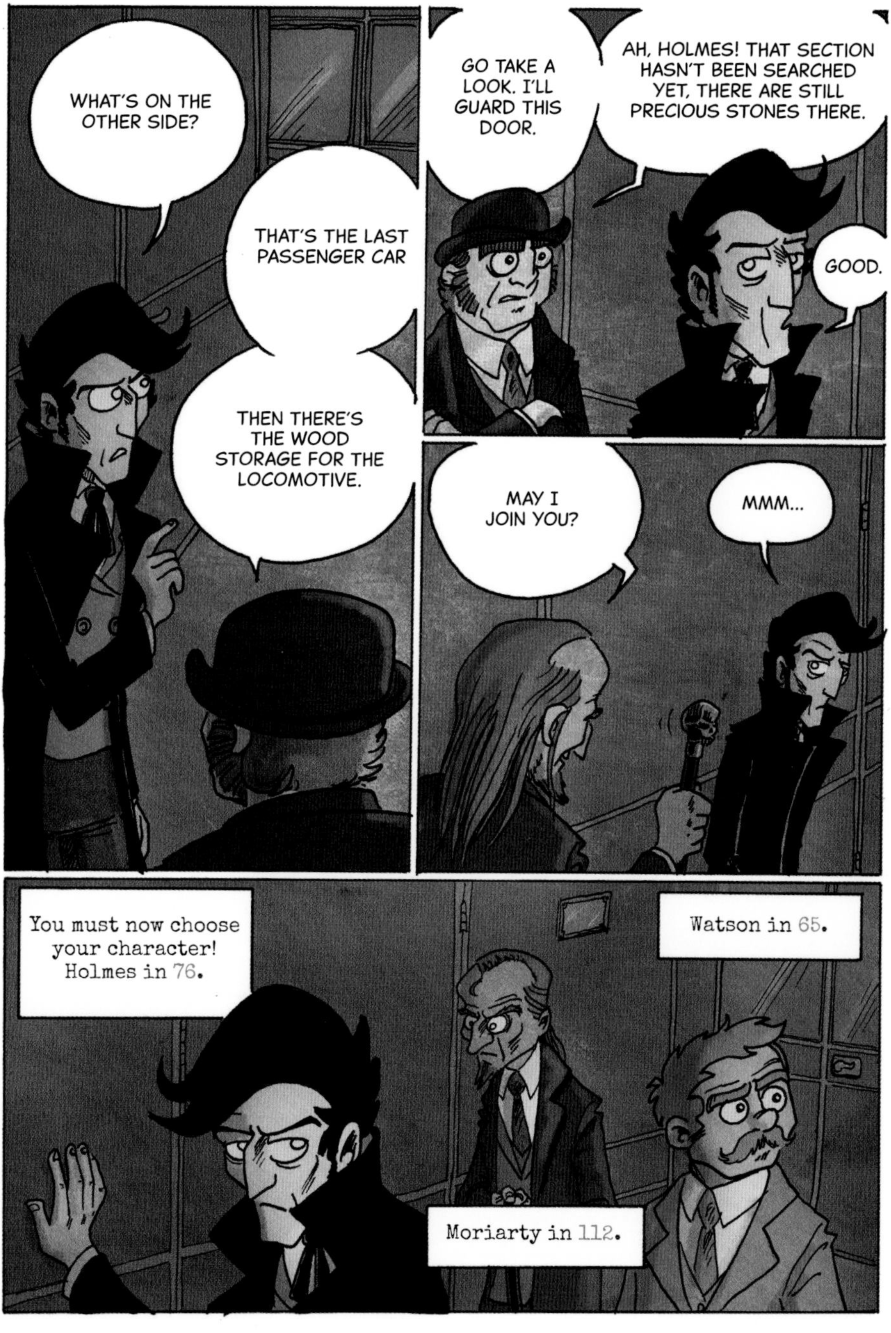
WHAT'S ON THE OTHER SIDE?
THAT'S THE LAST PASSENGER CAR
THEN THERE'S THE WOOD STORAGE FOR THE LOCOMOTIVE.
GO TAKE A LOOK. I'LL GUARD THIS DOOR.
AH, HOLMES! THAT SECTION HASN'T BEEN SEARCHED YET, THERE ARE STILL PRECIOUS STONES THERE.
GOOD.
MAY I JOIN YOU?
MMM...
You must now choose your character! Holmes in 76.
Watson in 65.
Moriarty in 112.

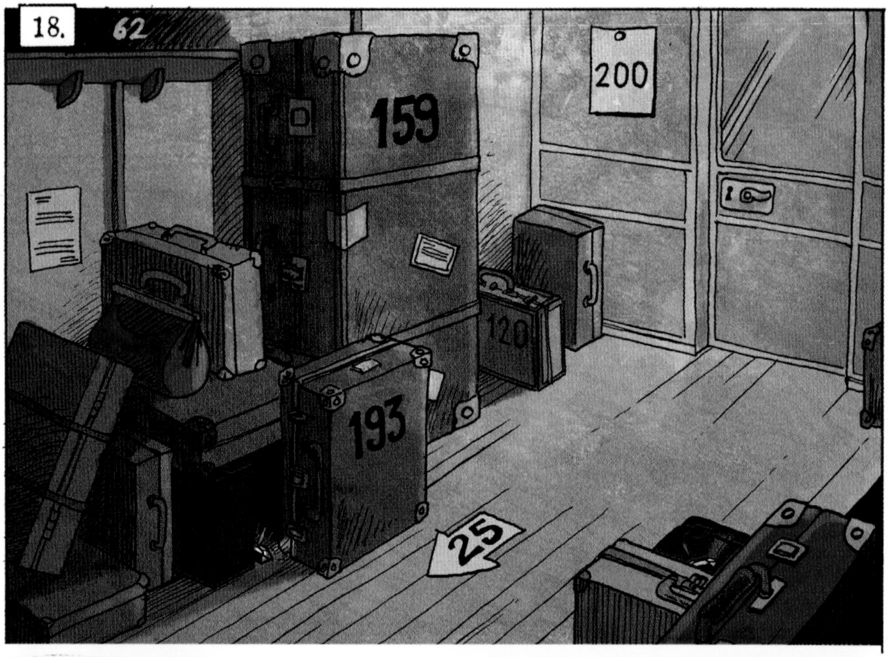
18.
62
159
200
120
193
25

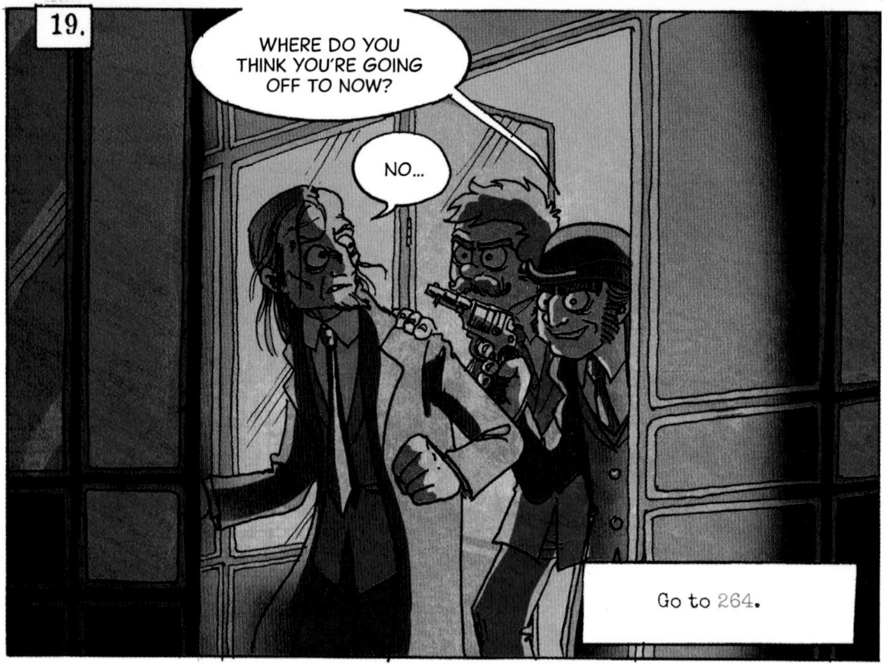
19.
WHERE DO YOU THINK YOU'RE GOING OFF TO NOW?
NO...
Go to 264.

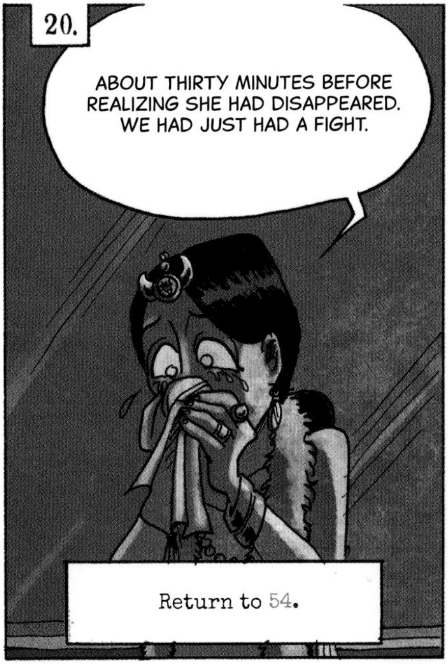
20.
ABOUT THIRTY MINUTES BEFORE REALIZING SHE HAD DISAPPEARED. WE HAD JUST HAD A FIGHT.
Return to 54.

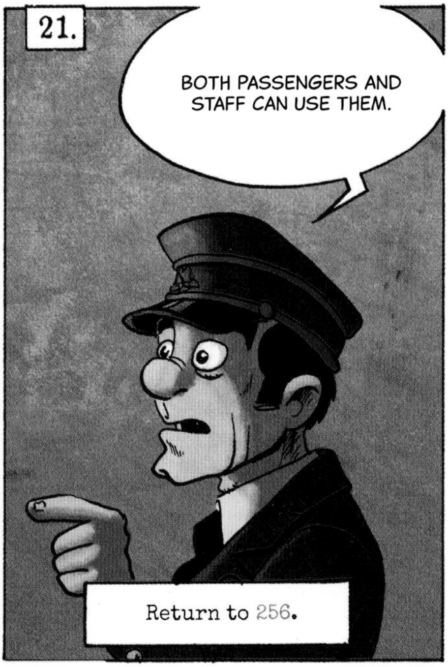
21.
BOTH PASSENGERS AND STAFF CAN USE THEM.
Return to 256.

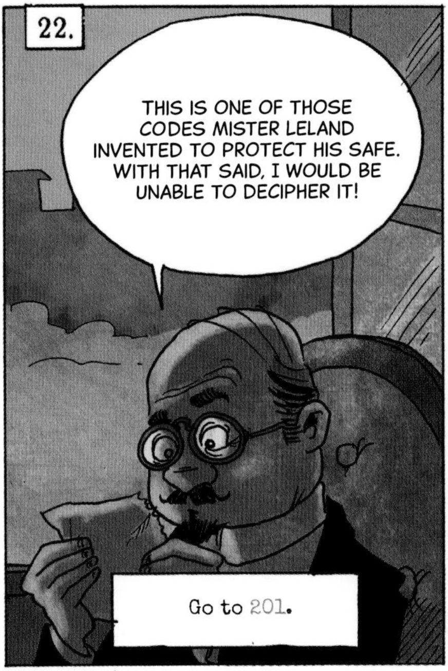
22.
THIS IS ONE OF THOSE CODES MISTER LELAND INVENTED TO PROTECT HIS SAFE. WITH THAT SAID, I WOULD BE UNABLE TO DECIPHER IT!
Go to 201.

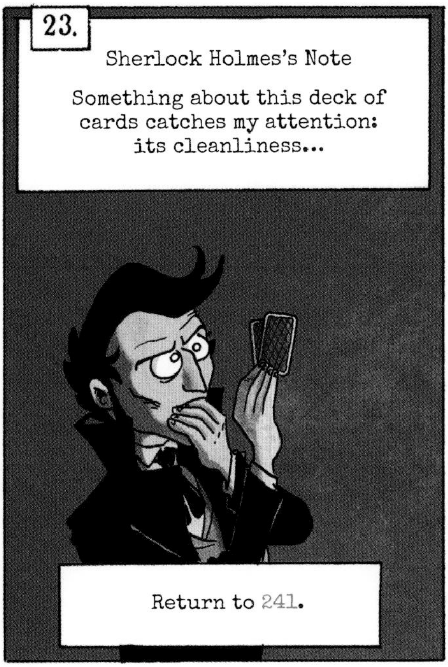
23.
Sherlock Holmes's Note
Something about this deck of cards catches my attention: its cleanliness...
Return to 241.

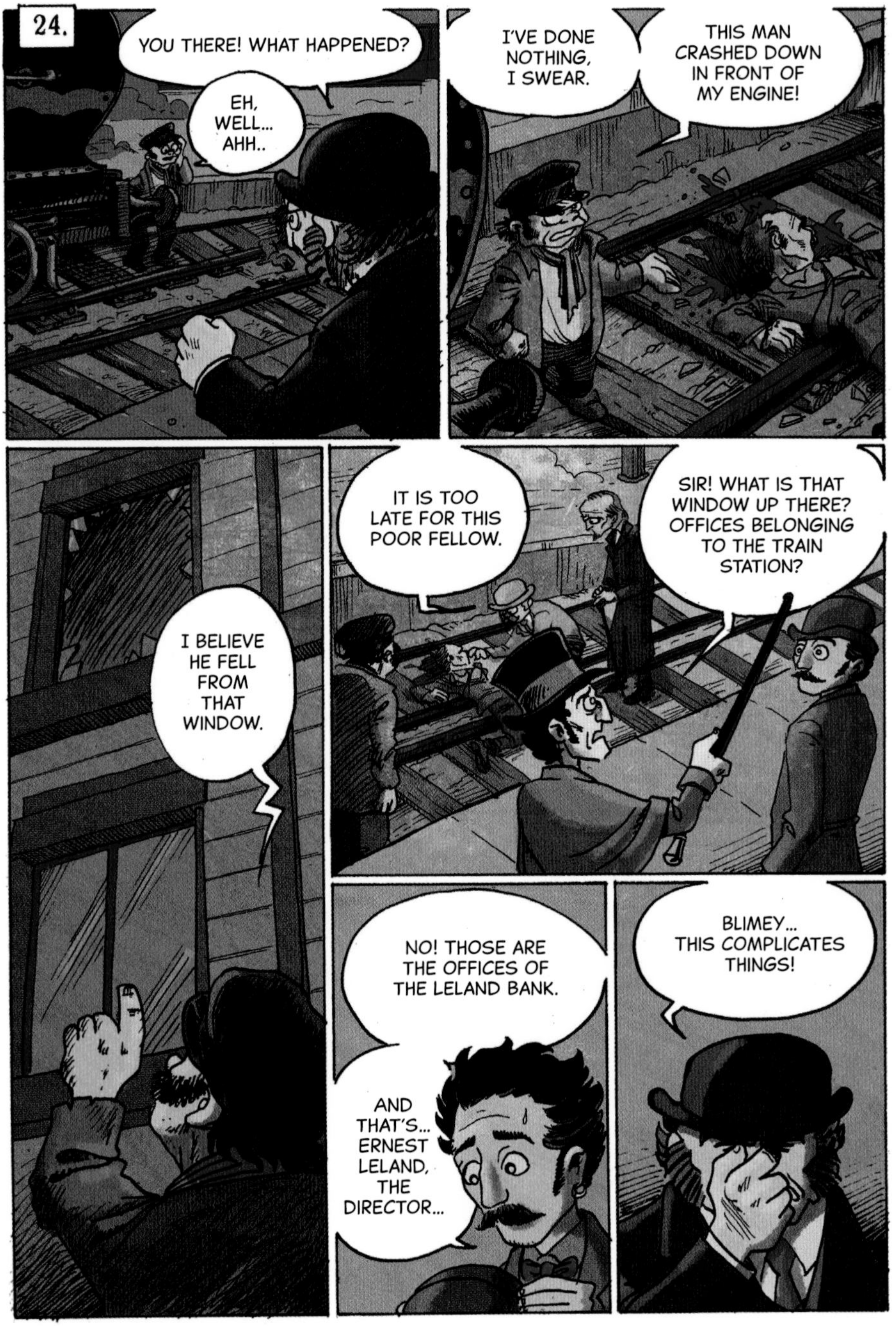
24.
YOU THERE! WHAT HAPPENED?
EH, WELL... AHH..
I'VE DONE NOTHING, I SWEAR.
THIS MAN CRASHED DOWN IN FRONT OF MY ENGINE!
I BELIEVE HE FELL FROM THAT WINDOW.
IT IS TOO LATE FOR THIS POOR FELLOW.
SIR! WHAT IS THAT WINDOW UP THERE? OFFICES BELONGING TO THE TRAIN STATION?
NO! THOSE ARE THE OFFICES OF THE LELAND BANK.
AND THAT'S... ERNEST LELAND, THE DIRECTOR...
BLIMEY... THIS COMPLICATES THINGS!

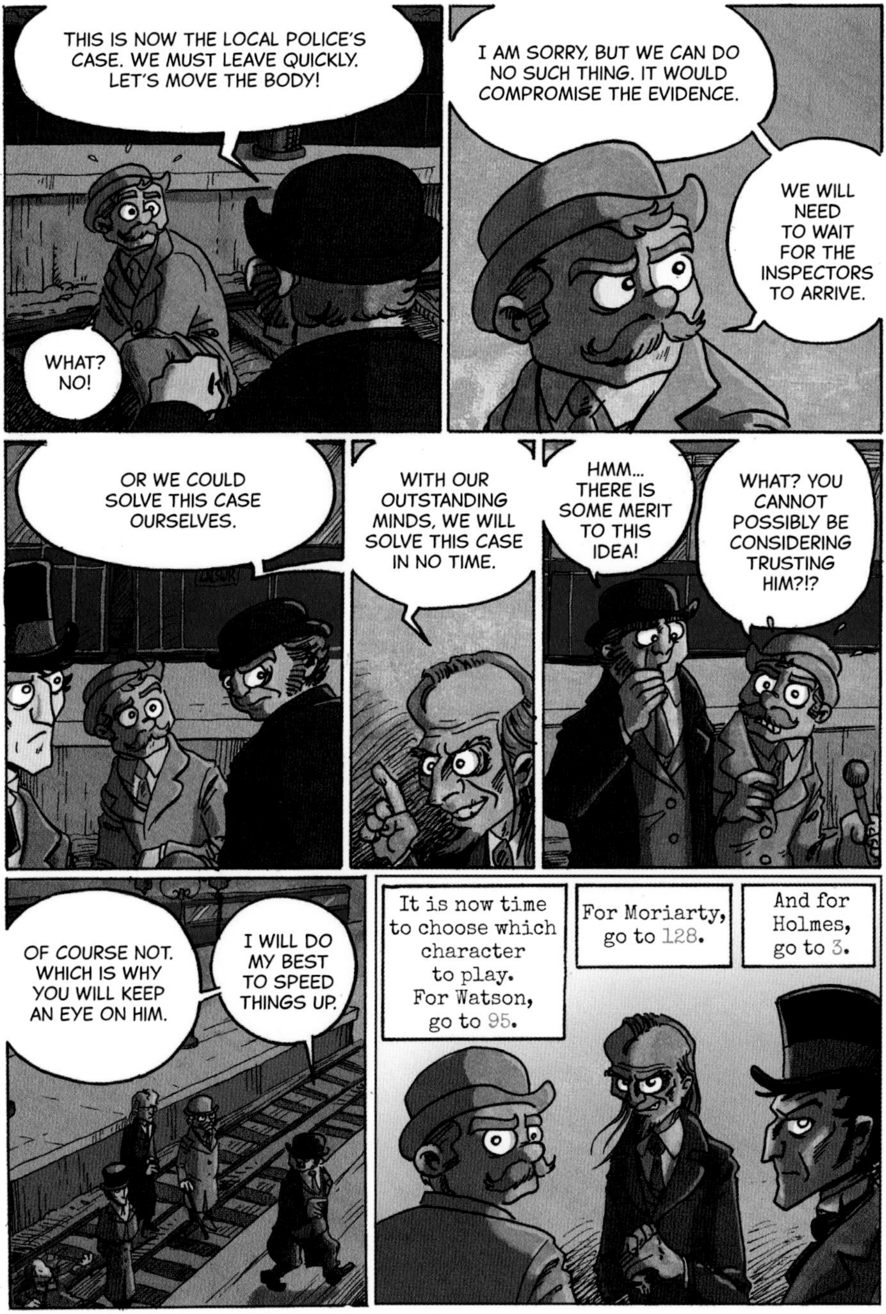
THIS IS NOW THE LOCAL POLICE'S CASE. WE MUST LEAVE QUICKLY. LET'S MOVE THE BODY!
WHAT? NO!
I AM SORRY, BUT WE CAN DO NO SUCH THING. IT WOULD COMPROMISE THE EVIDENCE.
WE WILL NEED TO WAIT FOR THE INSPECTORS TO ARRIVE.
OR WE COULD SOLVE THIS CASE OURSELVES.
WITH OUR OUTSTANDING MINDS, WE WILL SOLVE THIS CASE IN NO TIME.
HMM... THERE IS SOME MERIT TO THIS IDEA!
WHAT? YOU CANNOT POSSIBLY BE CONSIDERING TRUSTING HIM?!?
OF COURSE NOT. WHICH IS WHY YOU WILL KEEP AN EYE ON HIM.
I WILL DO MY BEST TO SPEED THINGS UP.
It is now time to choose which character to play. For Watson, go to 95.
For Moriarty, go to 128.
And for Holmes, go to 3.

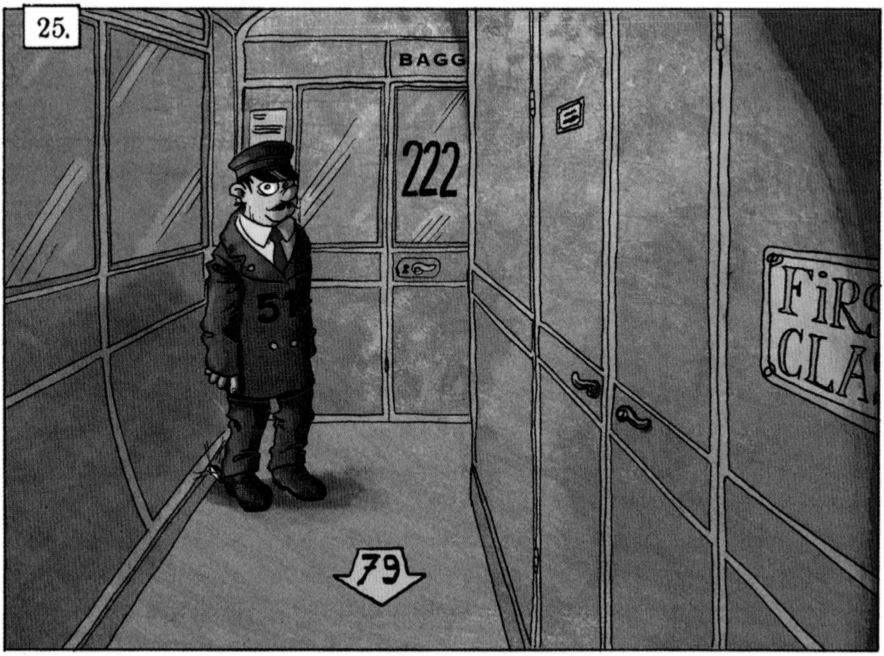
25.
BAGG
222
79

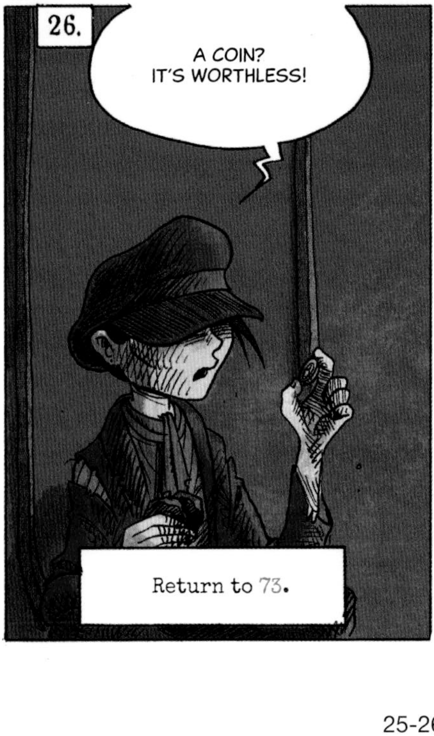
26.
A COIN?
IT'S WORTHLESS!
Return to 73.

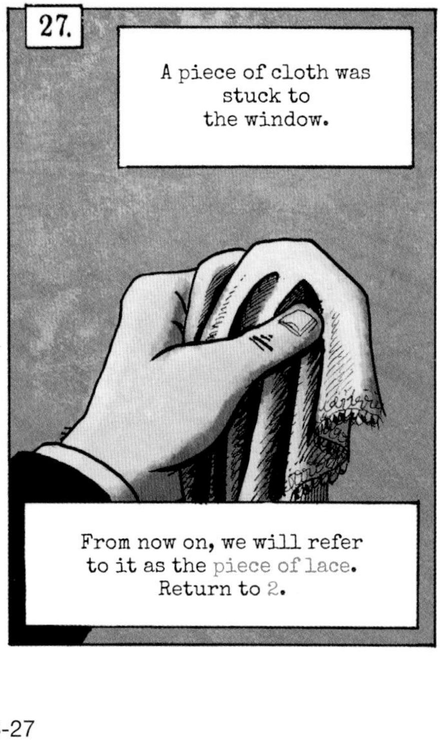
27.
A piece of cloth was stuck to the window.
From now on, we will refer to it as the piece of lace.
Return to 2.

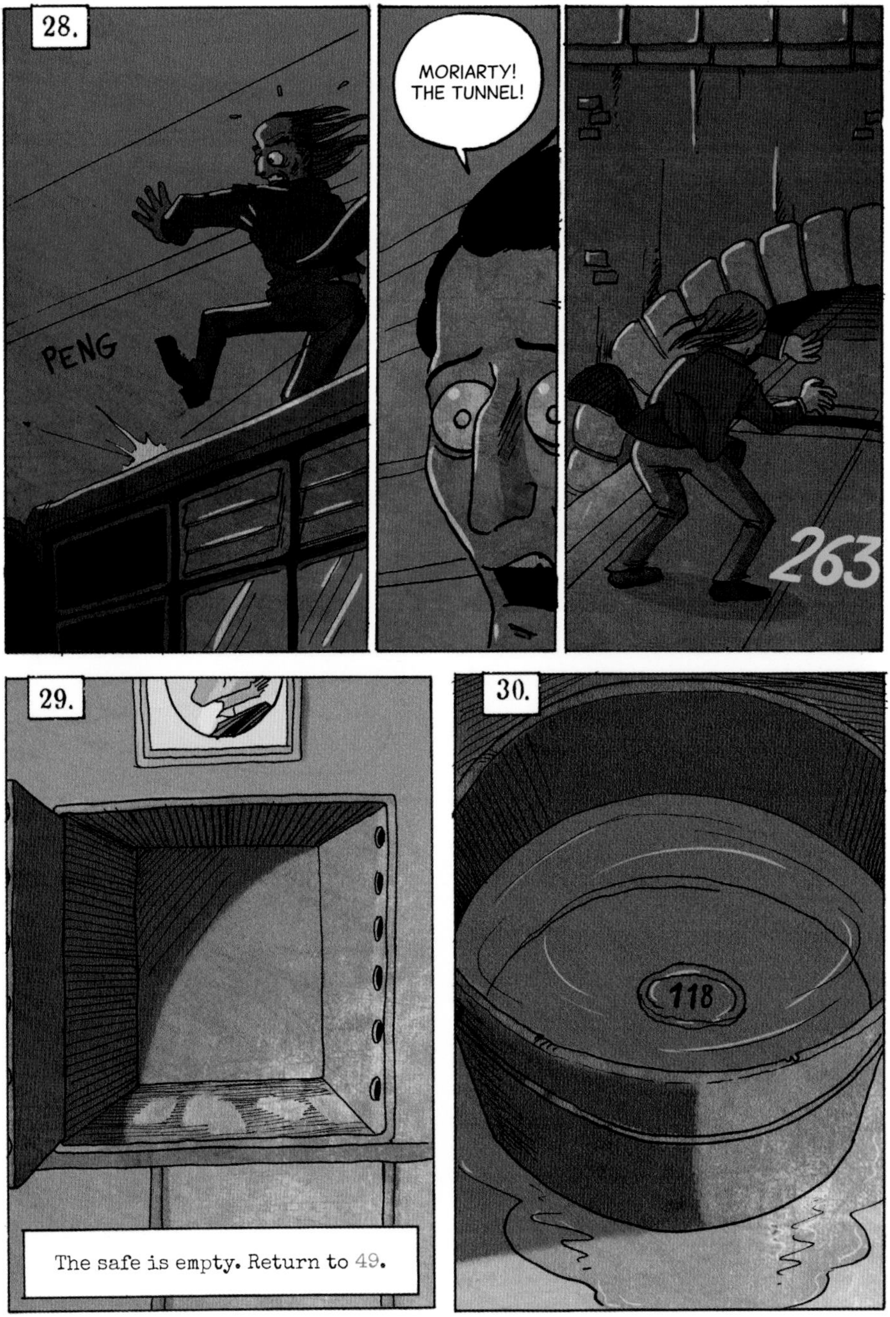
28.
PENG
MORIARTY!
THE TUNNEL!
263
29.
The safe is empty. Return to 49.
30.
118

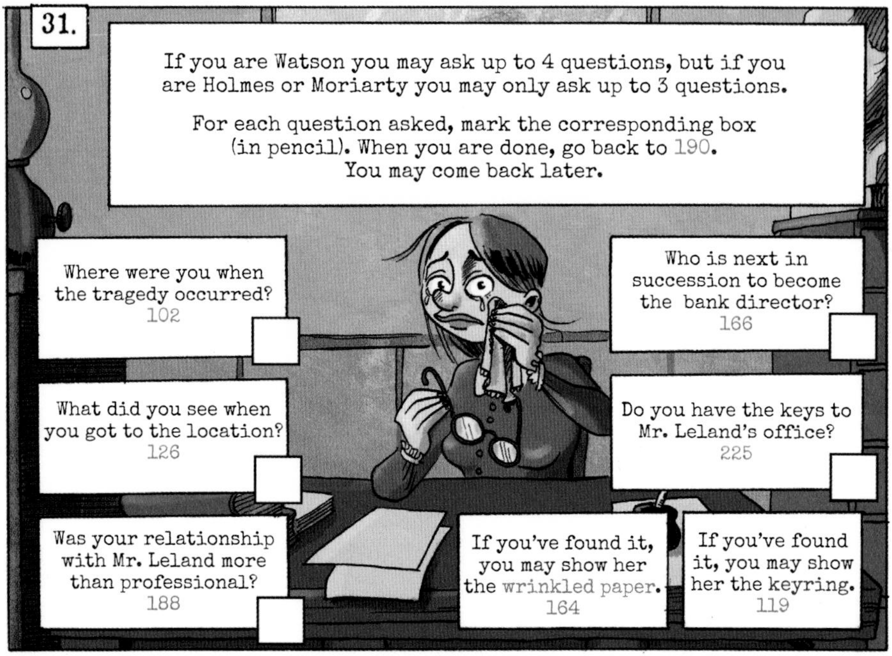
31.
If you are Watson you may ask up to 4 questions, but if you are Holmes or Moriarty you may only ask up to 3 questions.
For each question asked, mark the corresponding box (in pencil). When you are done, go back to 190. You may come back later.
Where were you when the tragedy occurred? 102
Who is next in succession to become the bank director? 166
What did you see when you got to the location? 126
Do you have the keys to Mr. Leland's office? 225
Was your relationship with Mr. Leland more than professional? 188
If you've found it, you may show her the wrinkled paper. 164
If you've found it, you may show her the keyring. 119

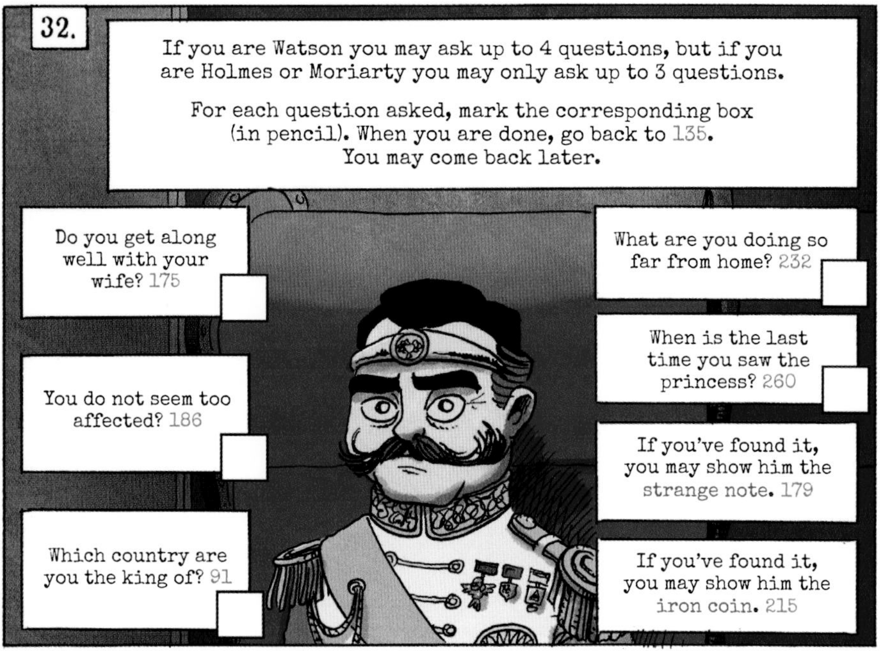
32.
If you are Watson you may ask up to 4 questions, but if you are Holmes or Moriarty you may only ask up to 3 questions.
For each question asked, mark the corresponding box (in pencil). When you are done, go back to 135. You may come back later.
Do you get along well with your wife? 175
What are you doing so far from home? 232
When is the last time you saw the princess? 260
You do not seem too affected? 186
If you've found it, you may show him the strange note. 179
Which country are you the king of? 91
If you've found it, you may show him the iron coin. 215

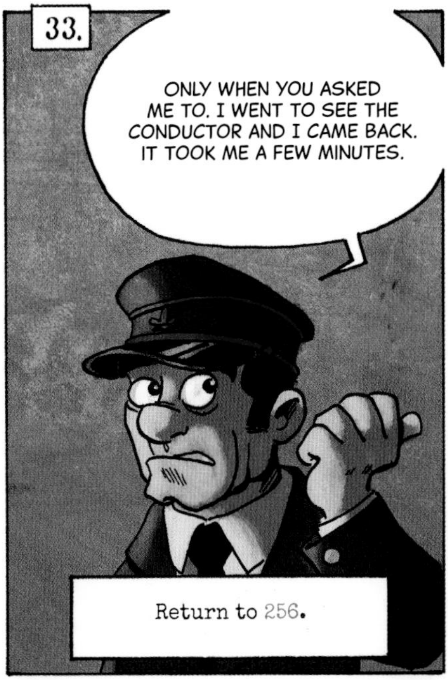
33.
ONLY WHEN YOU ASKED ME TO. I WENT TO SEE THE CONDUCTOR AND I CAME BACK. IT TOOK ME A FEW MINUTES.
Return to 256.

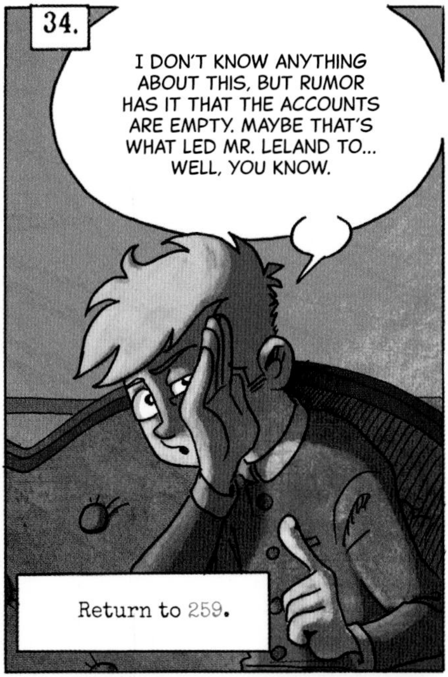
34.
I DON'T KNOW ANYTHING ABOUT THIS, BUT RUMOR HAS IT THAT THE ACCOUNTS ARE EMPTY. MAYBE THAT'S WHAT LED MR. LELAND TO... WELL, YOU KNOW.
Return to 259.

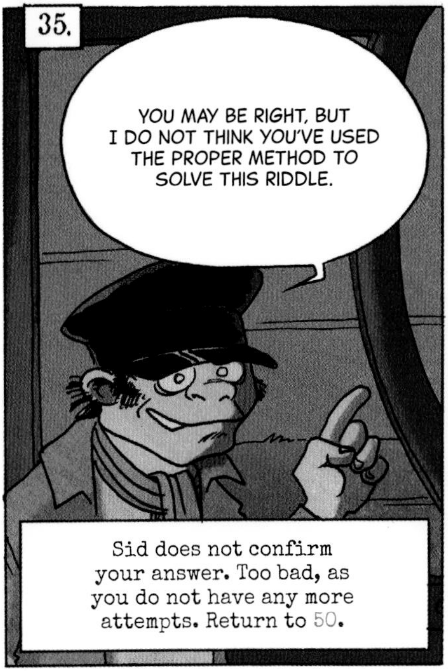
35.
YOU MAY BE RIGHT, BUT I DO NOT THINK YOU'VE USED THE PROPER METHOD TO SOLVE THIS RIDDLE.
Sid does not confirm your answer. Too bad, as you do not have any more attempts. Return to 50.

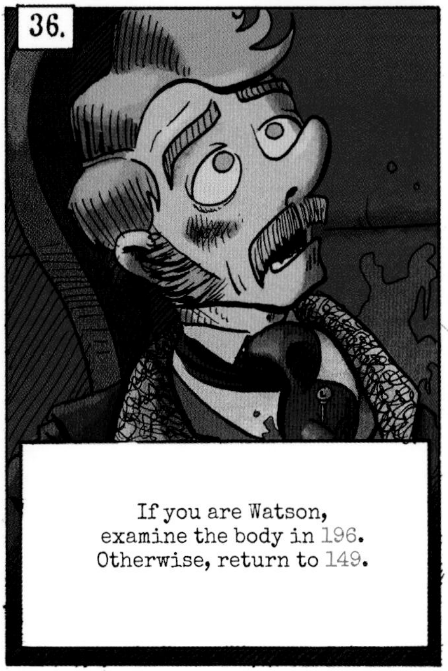
36.
If you are Watson, examine the body in 196. Otherwise, return to 149.

37.

Here is the list of suspects and a plan of the train.
Begin your investigation with the death of the Count in 2.
Once complete, write the number of the presumed guilty on your Investigation Sheet (note that these numbers do not refer to panels). Then, head to 40.

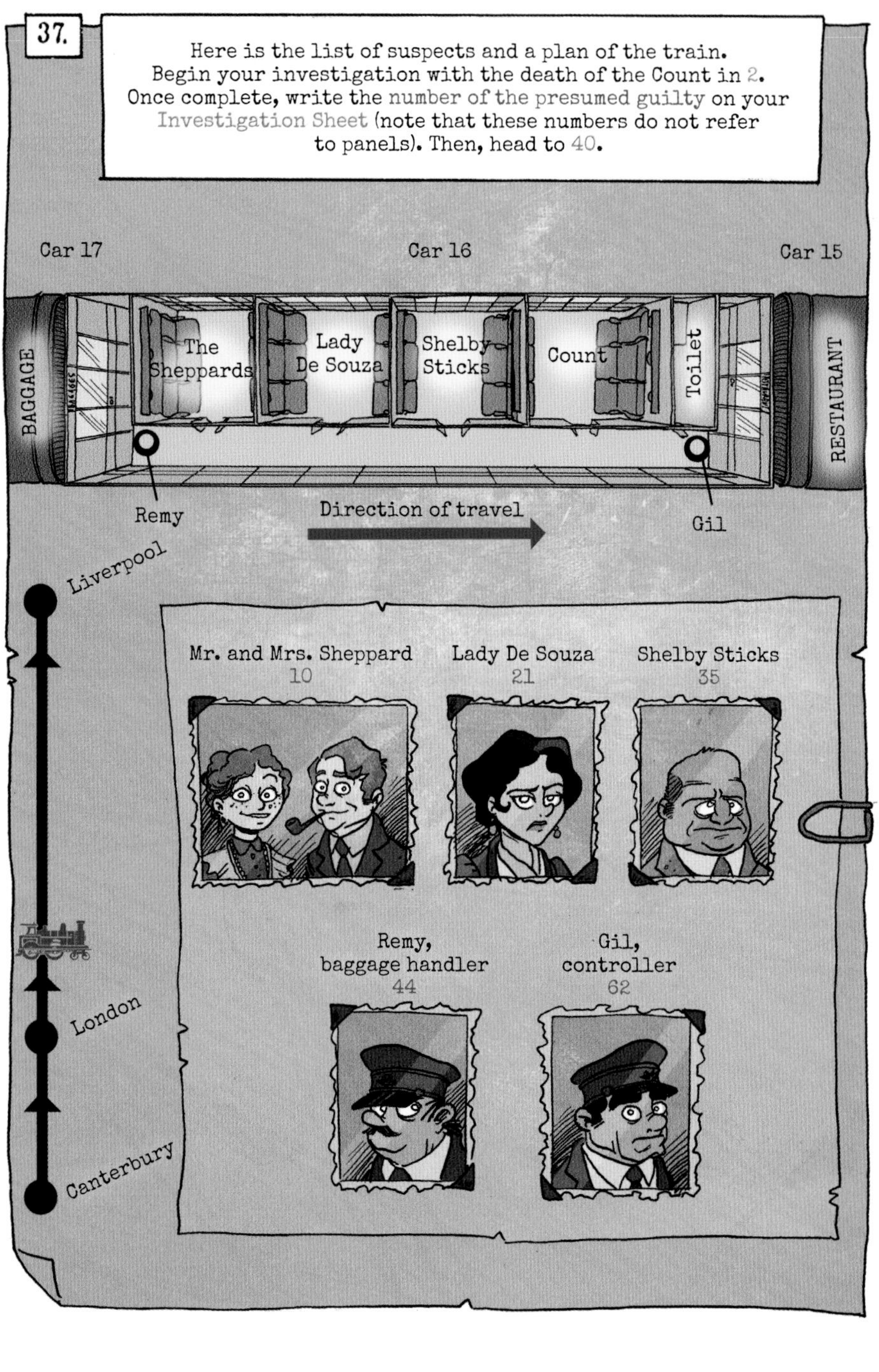

Car 17
Car 16
Car 15
BAGGAGE
The Sheppards
Lady De Souza
Shelby Sticks
Count
Toilet
RESTAURANT
Remy
Direction of travel
Gil
Liverpool
London
Canterbury
Mr. and Mrs. Sheppard
10
Lady De Souza
21
Shelby Sticks
35
Remy, baggage handler
44
Gil, controller
62

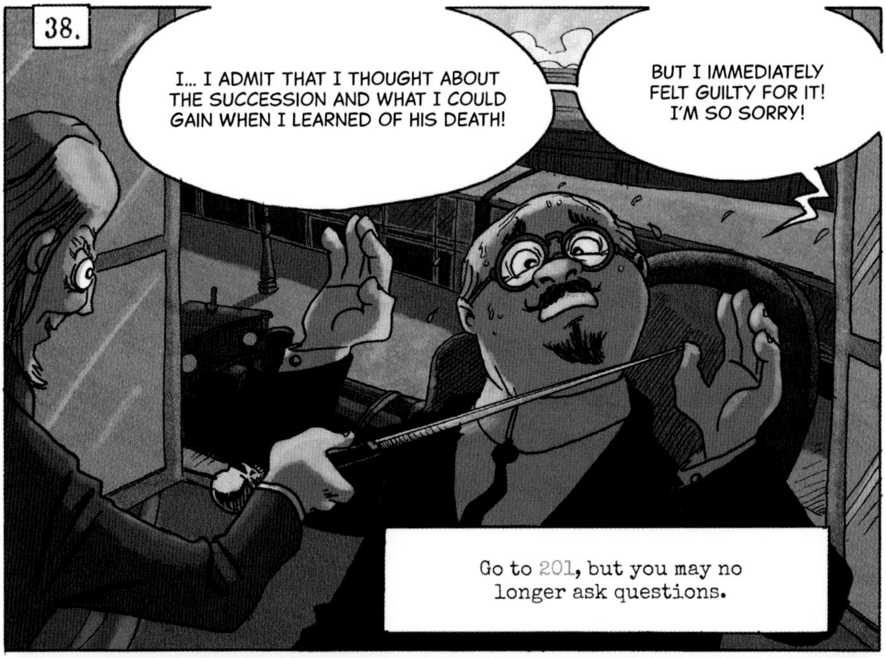
38.
I… I ADMIT THAT I THOUGHT ABOUT THE SUCCESSION AND WHAT I COULD GAIN WHEN I LEARNED OF HIS DEATH!
BUT I IMMEDIATELY FELT GUILTY FOR IT! I'M SO SORRY!
Go to 201, but you may no longer ask questions.

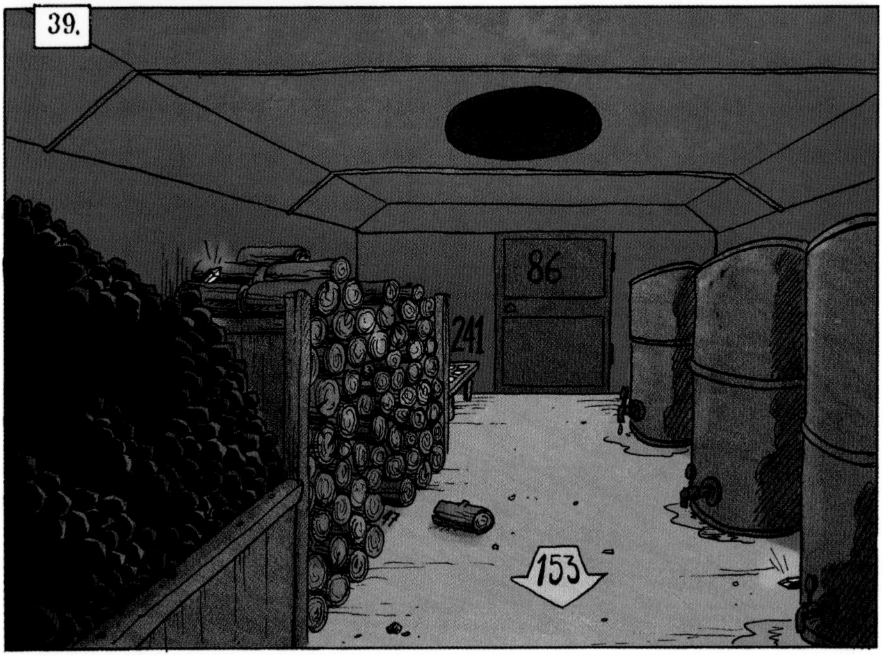
39.
86
241
153

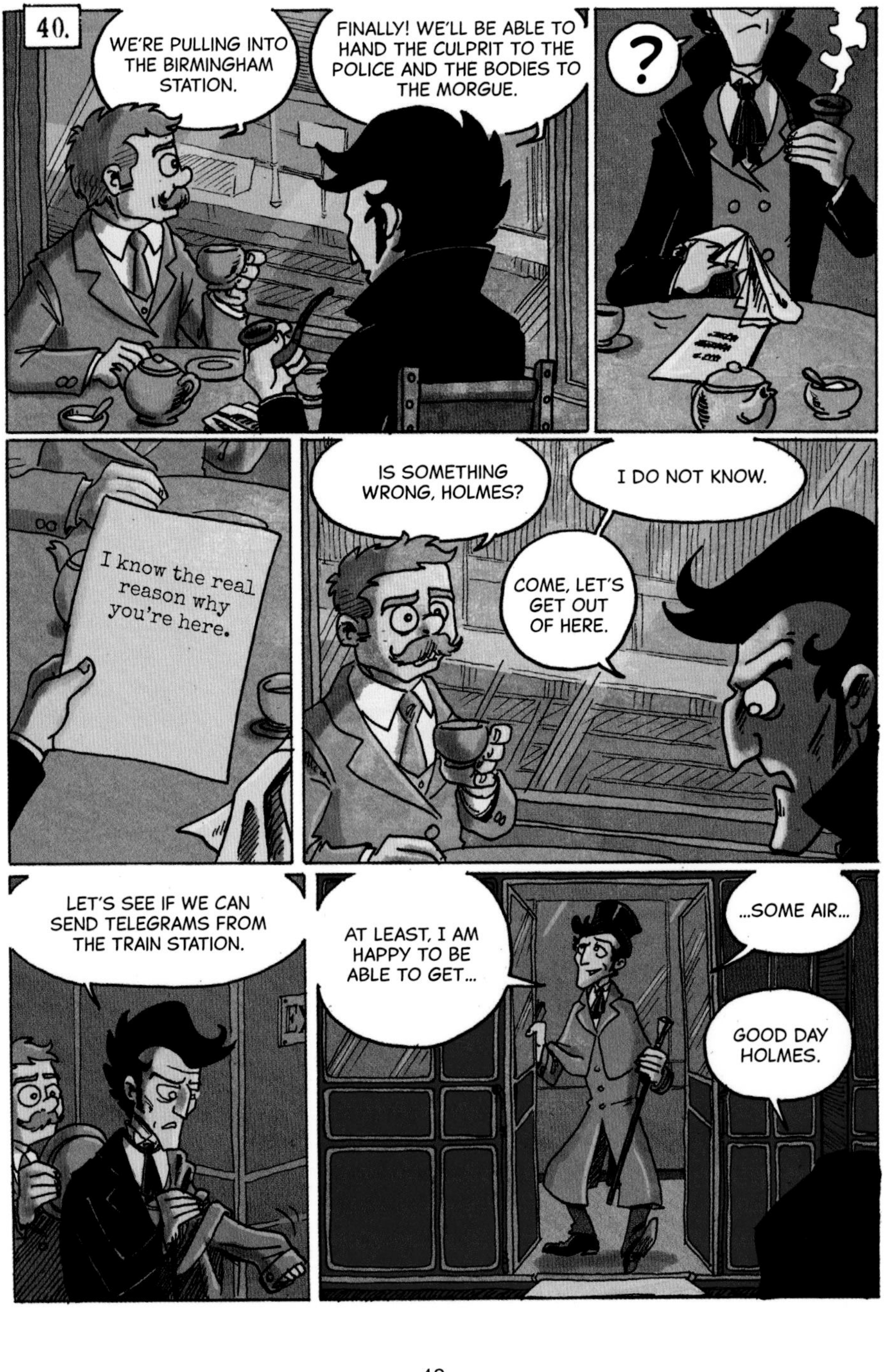
40.
WE'RE PULLING INTO THE BIRMINGHAM STATION.
FINALLY! WE'LL BE ABLE TO HAND THE CULPRIT TO THE POLICE AND THE BODIES TO THE MORGUE.
?
I know the real reason why you're here.
IS SOMETHING WRONG, HOLMES?
I DO NOT KNOW.
COME, LET'S GET OUT OF HERE.
LET'S SEE IF WE CAN SEND TELEGRAMS FROM THE TRAIN STATION.
AT LEAST, I AM HAPPY TO BE ABLE TO GET...
...SOME AIR...
GOOD DAY HOLMES.

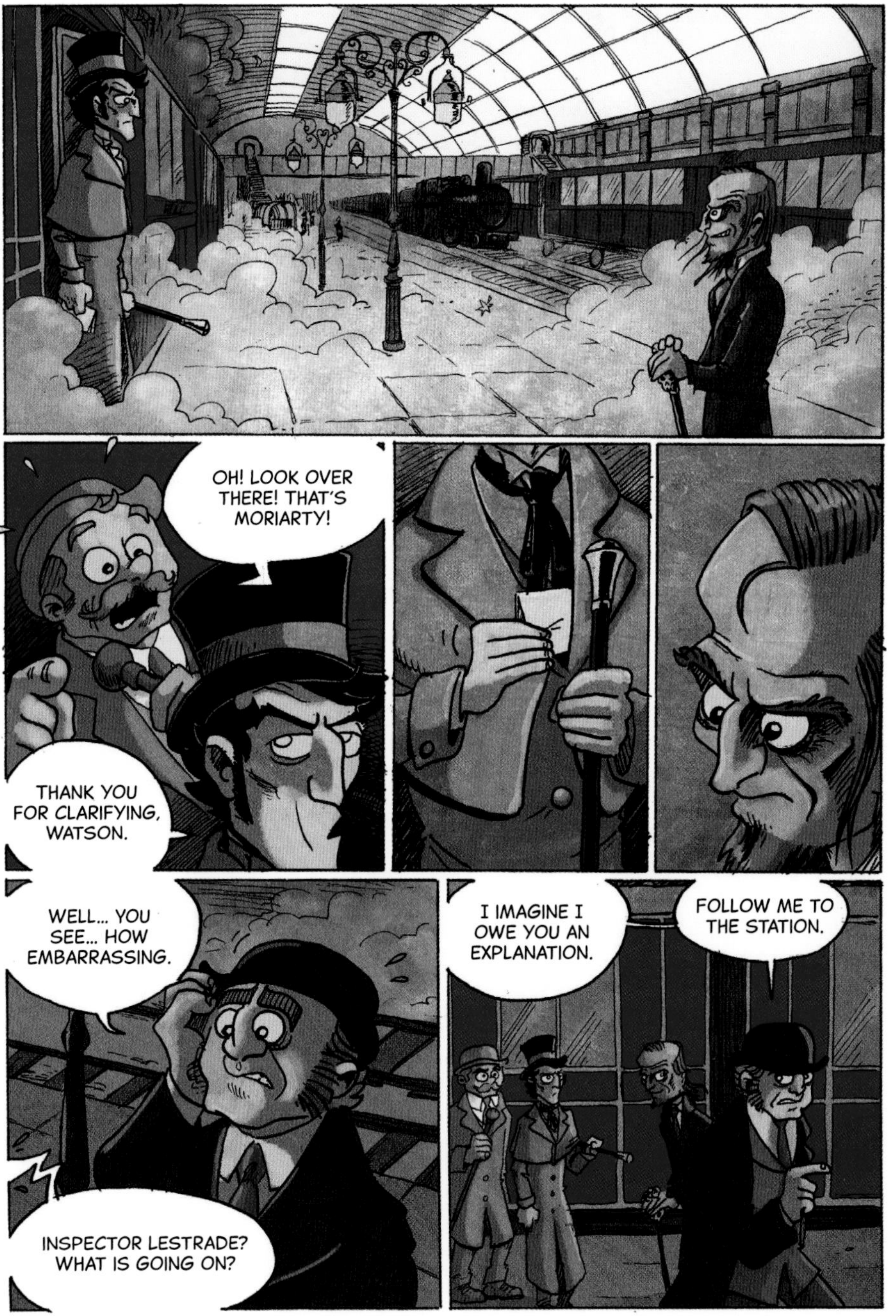
OH! LOOK OVER THERE! THAT'S MORIARTY!
THANK YOU FOR CLARIFYING, WATSON.
WELL... YOU SEE... HOW EMBARRASSING.
INSPECTOR LESTRADE? WHAT IS GOING ON?
I IMAGINE I OWE YOU AN EXPLANATION.
FOLLOW ME TO THE STATION.

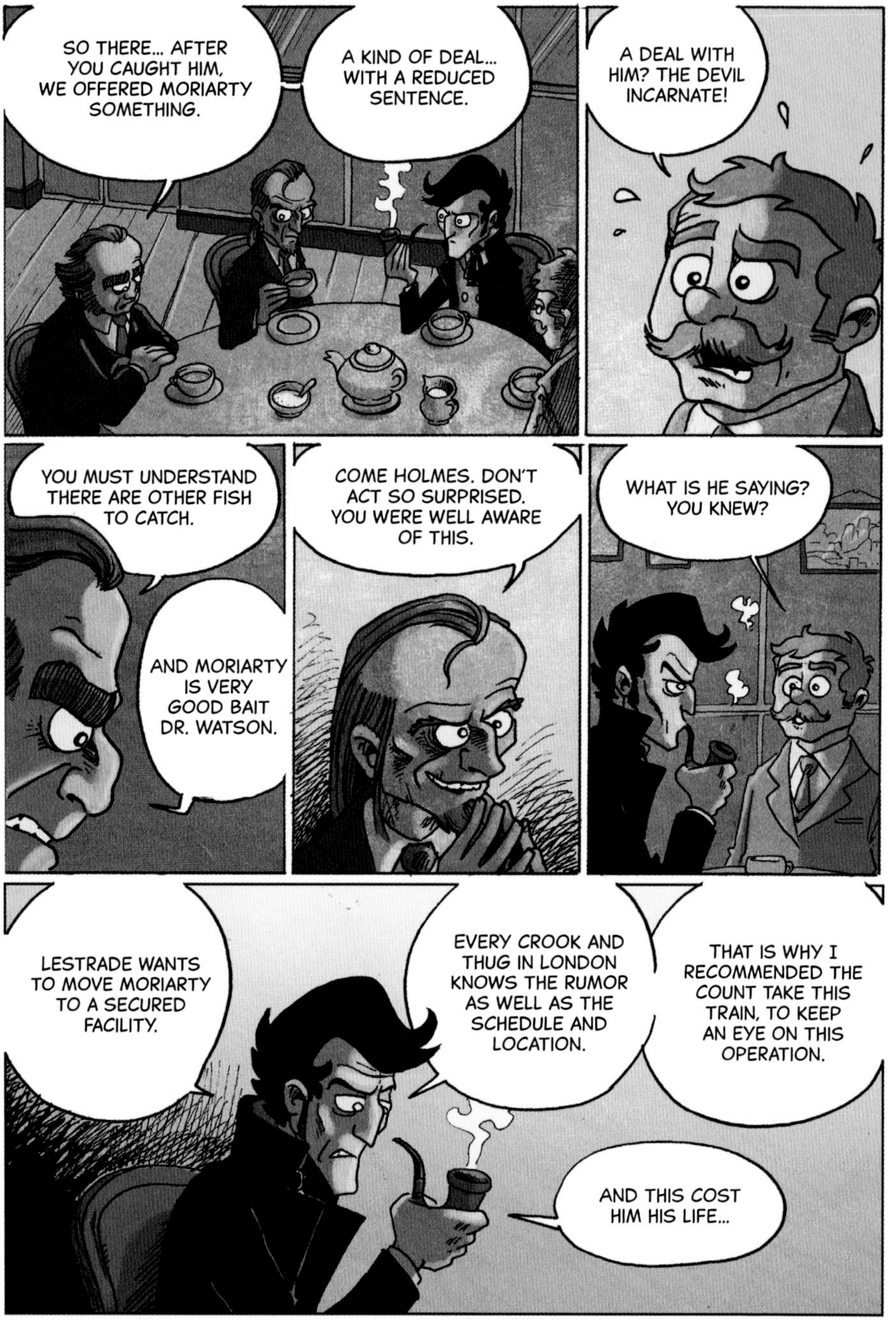
SO THERE... AFTER YOU CAUGHT HIM, WE OFFERED MORIARTY SOMETHING.
A KIND OF DEAL... WITH A REDUCED SENTENCE.
A DEAL WITH HIM? THE DEVIL INCARNATE!
YOU MUST UNDERSTAND THERE ARE OTHER FISH TO CATCH.
AND MORIARTY IS VERY GOOD BAIT DR. WATSON.
COME HOLMES. DON'T ACT SO SURPRISED. YOU WERE WELL AWARE OF THIS.
WHAT IS HE SAYING? YOU KNEW?
LESTRADE WANTS TO MOVE MORIARTY TO A SECURED FACILITY.
EVERY CROOK AND THUG IN LONDON KNOWS THE RUMOR AS WELL AS THE SCHEDULE AND LOCATION.
THAT IS WHY I RECOMMENDED THE COUNT TAKE THIS TRAIN, TO KEEP AN EYE ON THIS OPERATION.
AND THIS COST HIM HIS LIFE...

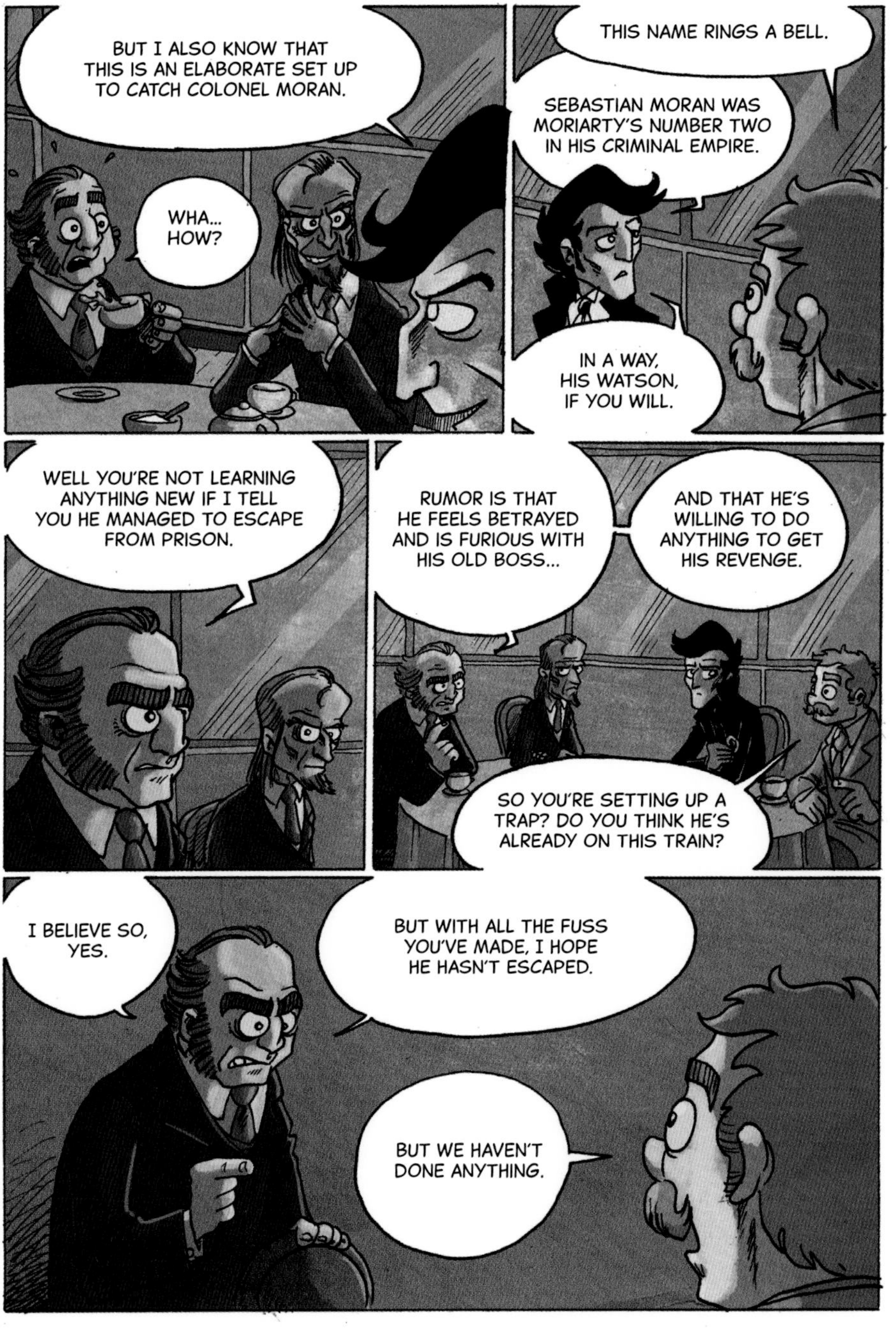
BUT I ALSO KNOW THAT THIS IS AN ELABORATE SET UP TO CATCH COLONEL MORAN.
WHA... HOW?
THIS NAME RINGS A BELL.
SEBASTIAN MORAN WAS MORIARTY'S NUMBER TWO IN HIS CRIMINAL EMPIRE.
IN A WAY, HIS WATSON, IF YOU WILL.
WELL YOU'RE NOT LEARNING ANYTHING NEW IF I TELL YOU HE MANAGED TO ESCAPE FROM PRISON.
RUMOR IS THAT HE FEELS BETRAYED AND IS FURIOUS WITH HIS OLD BOSS...
AND THAT HE'S WILLING TO DO ANYTHING TO GET HIS REVENGE.
SO YOU'RE SETTING UP A TRAP? DO YOU THINK HE'S ALREADY ON THIS TRAIN?
I BELIEVE SO, YES.
BUT WITH ALL THE FUSS YOU'VE MADE, I HOPE HE HASN'T ESCAPED.
BUT WE HAVEN'T DONE ANYTHING.

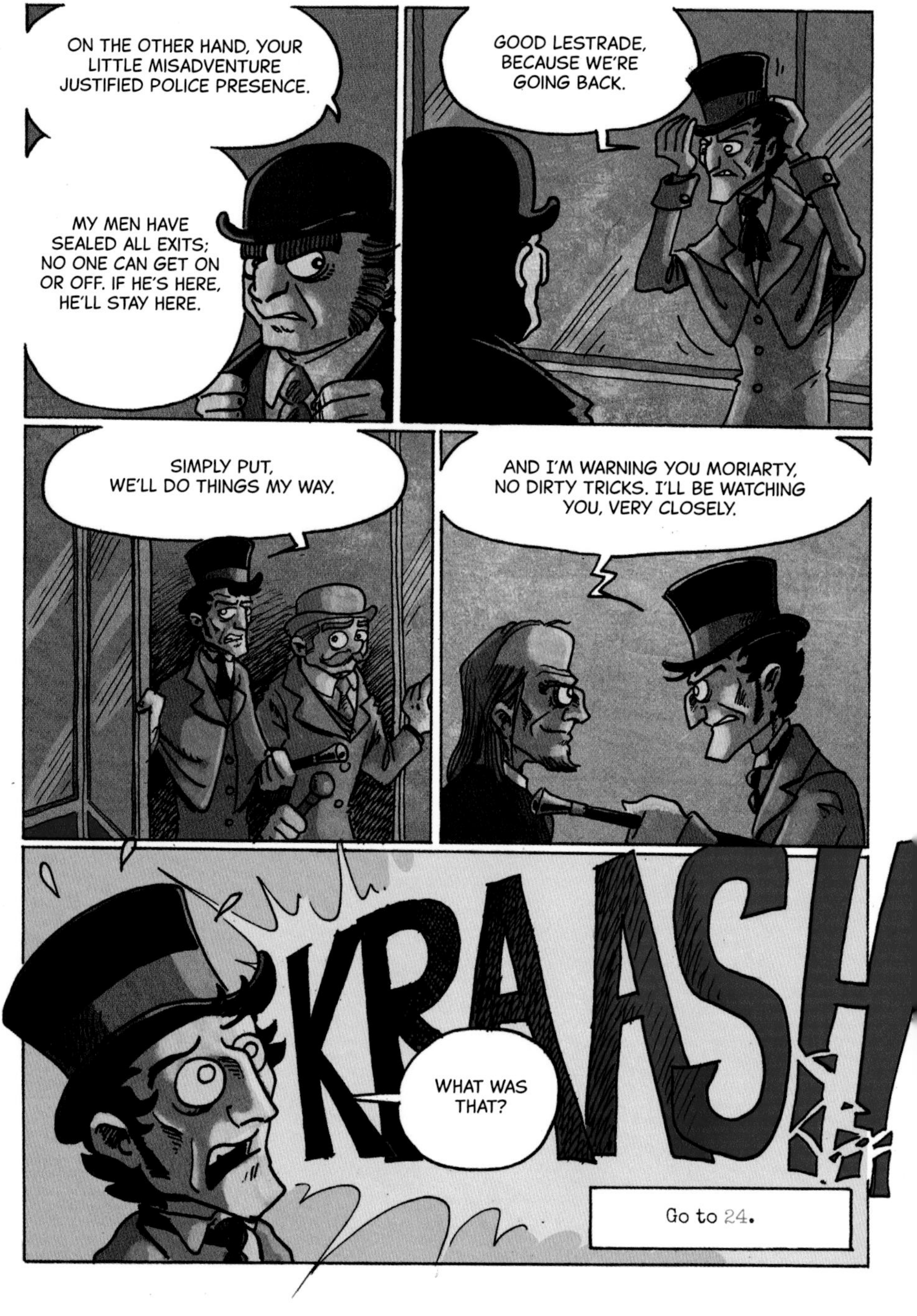
ON THE OTHER HAND, YOUR LITTLE MISADVENTURE JUSTIFIED POLICE PRESENCE.
MY MEN HAVE SEALED ALL EXITS; NO ONE CAN GET ON OR OFF. IF HE'S HERE, HE'LL STAY HERE.
GOOD LESTRADE, BECAUSE WE'RE GOING BACK.
SIMPLY PUT, WE'LL DO THINGS MY WAY.
AND I'M WARNING YOU MORIARTY, NO DIRTY TRICKS. I'LL BE WATCHING YOU, VERY CLOSELY.
KRAASH!
WHAT WAS THAT?

Go to 24.

41.

Here is the list of suspects and a plan of the train. Begin your investigation with the disappearance of the princess in 92. Once complete, write the number of the presumed guilty on your Investigation Sheet (note that these numbers do not refer to panels). Then, head to 265.

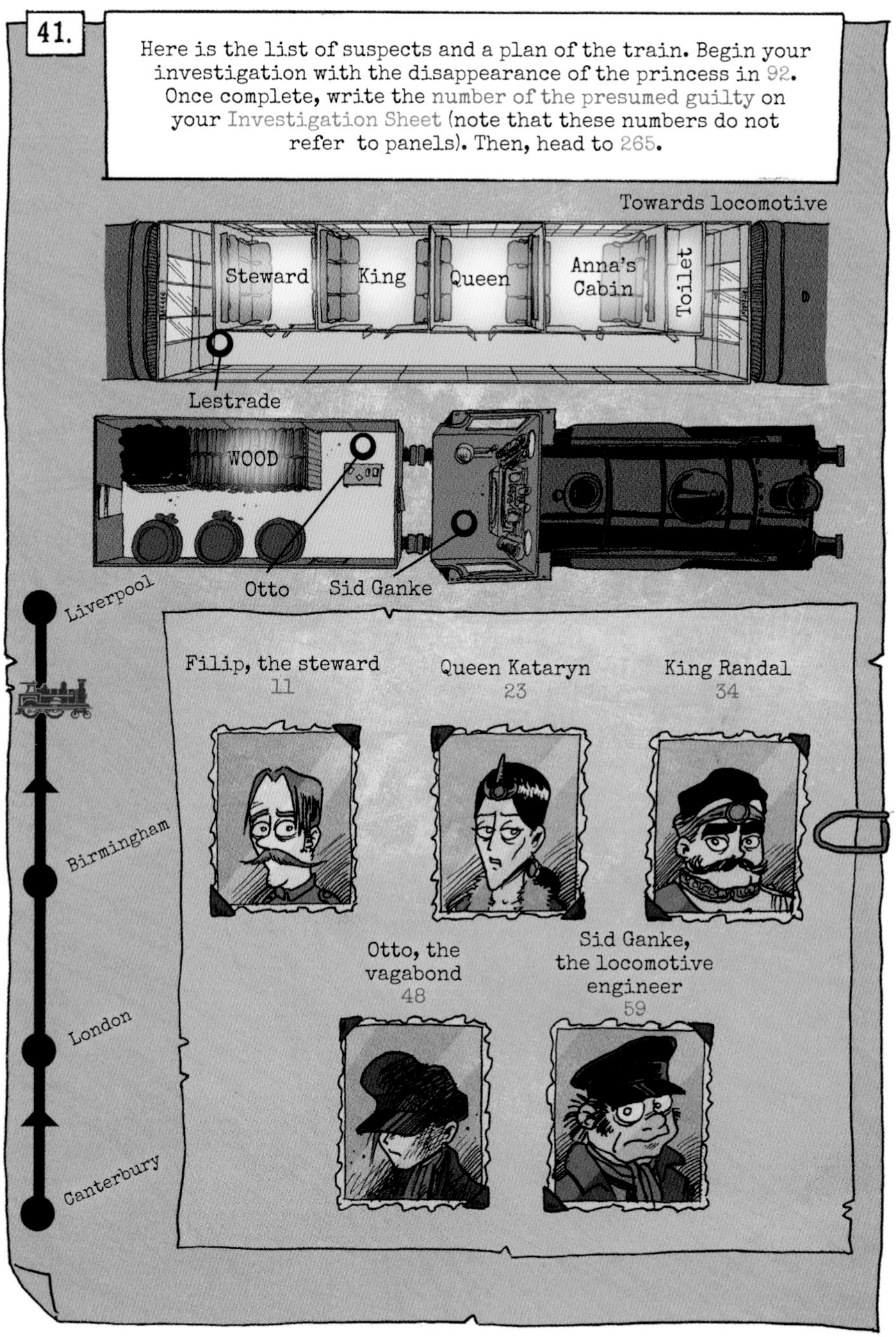

Towards locomotive
Steward
King
Queen
Anna's Cabin
Toilet
Lestrade
WOOD
Otto
Sid Ganke
Liverpool
Birmingham
London
Canterbury
Filip, the steward
11
Queen Kataryn
23
King Randal
34
Otto, the vagabond
48
Sid Ganke, the locomotive engineer
59

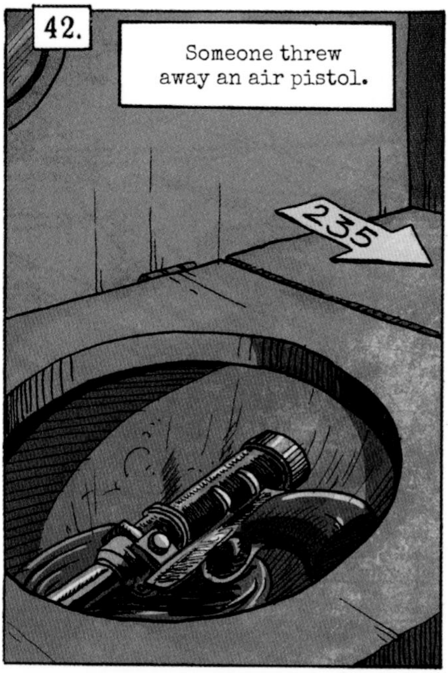
42.
Someone threw away an air pistol.
235

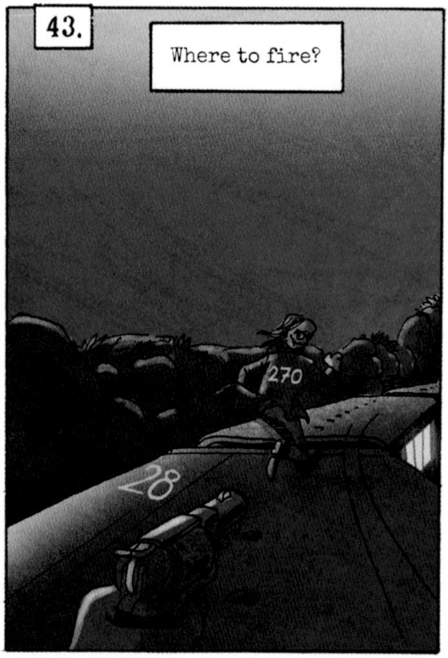
43.
Where to fire?
270
28

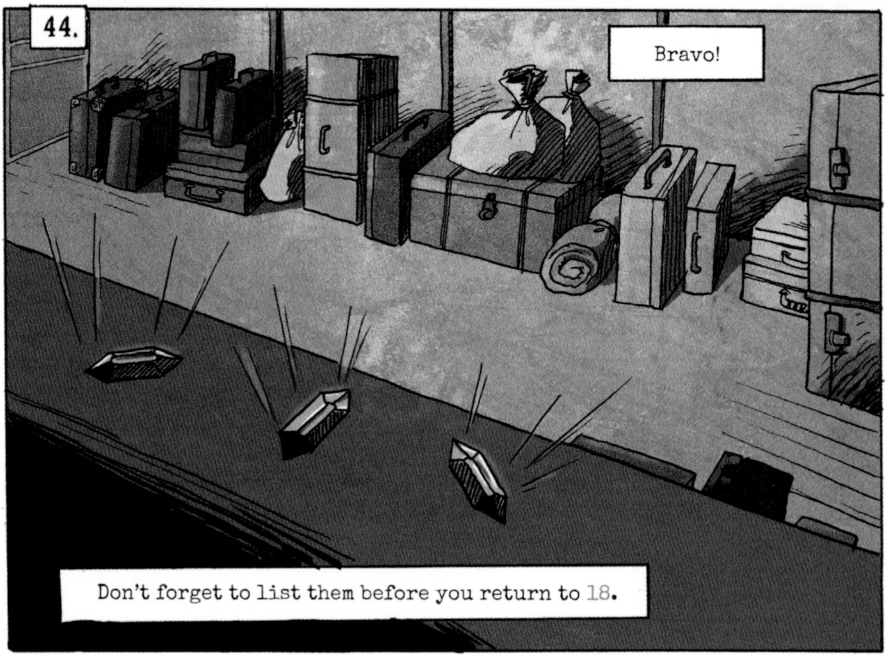
44.
Bravo!
Don't forget to list them before you return to 18.

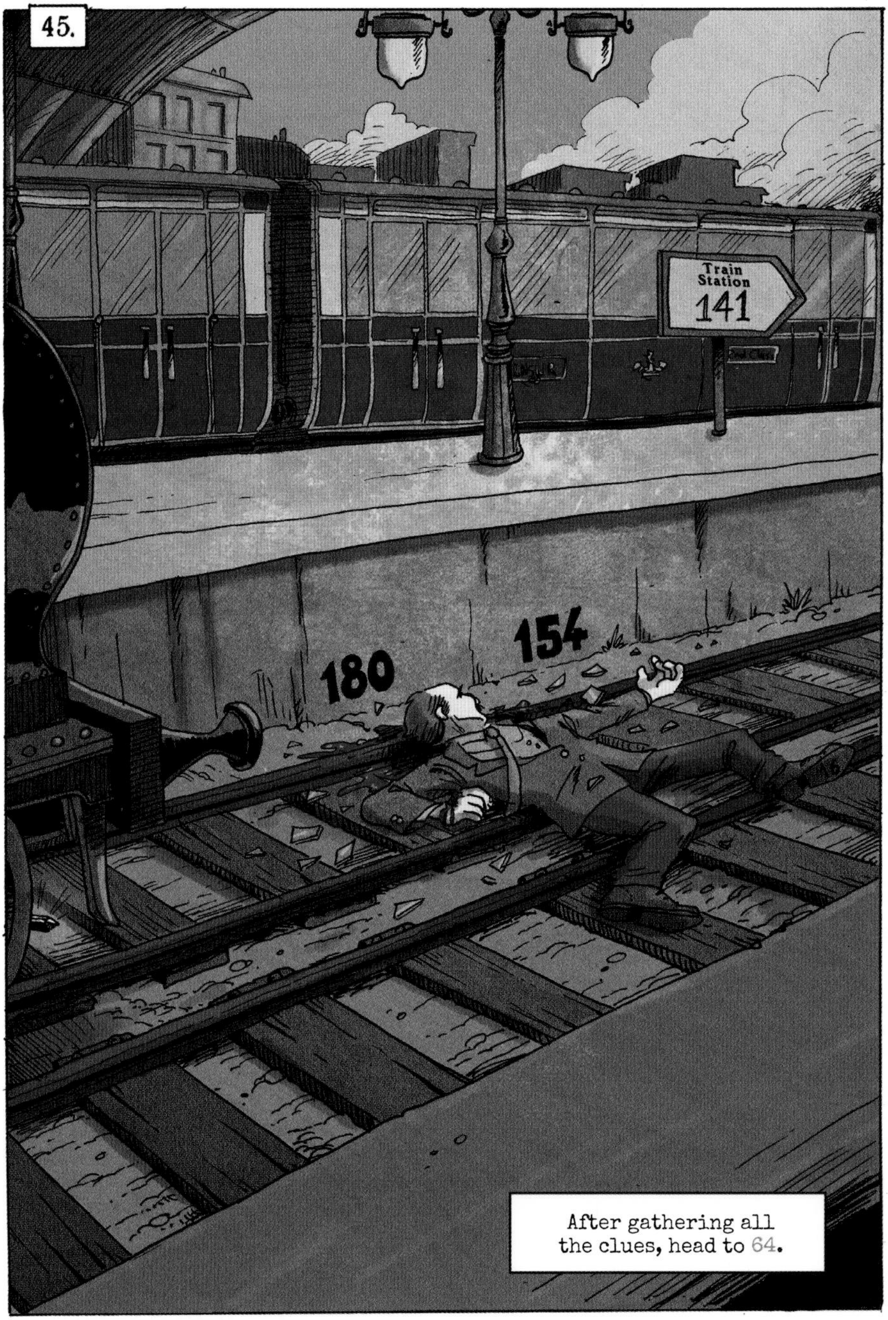
45.
Train
Station
141
154
180
After gathering all
the clues, head to 64.

46.

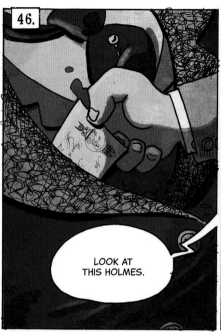

LOOK AT THIS HOLMES.

IT'S THE CHECK HE WAS GOING TO GIVE YOU.

You can consult this check in 242. Return to 2.

47.

It's impossible to sneak through this hole. If Wiggins is traveling with you, go to 182, otherwise return to 39.

48.

Sherlock Holmes's Note

Everything seems odd. Familiar footprints on the edge and glass shards that are not where they should be. What could possibly have happened here?

Return to 184.

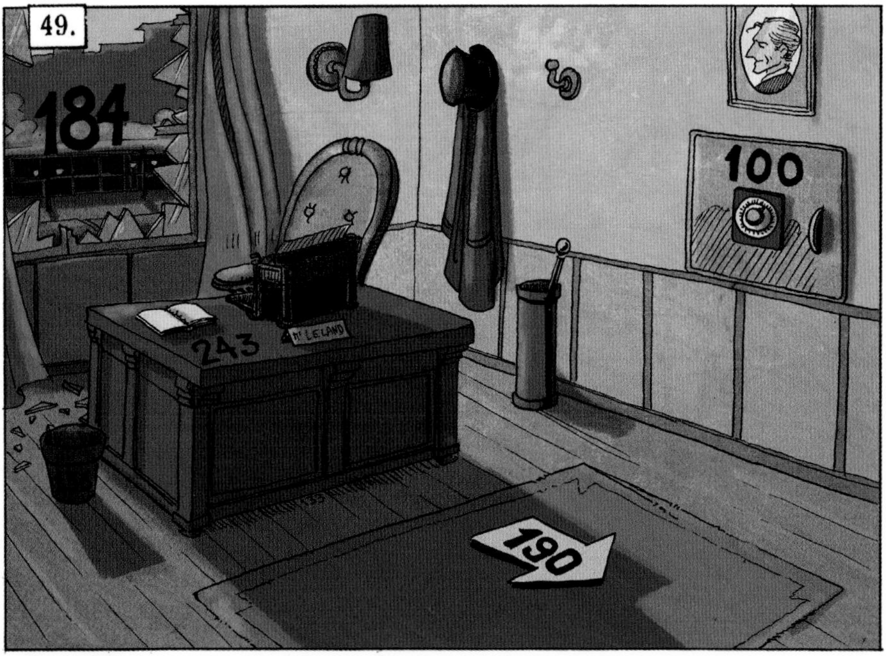
49.
184
100
243
Mr LELAND
190

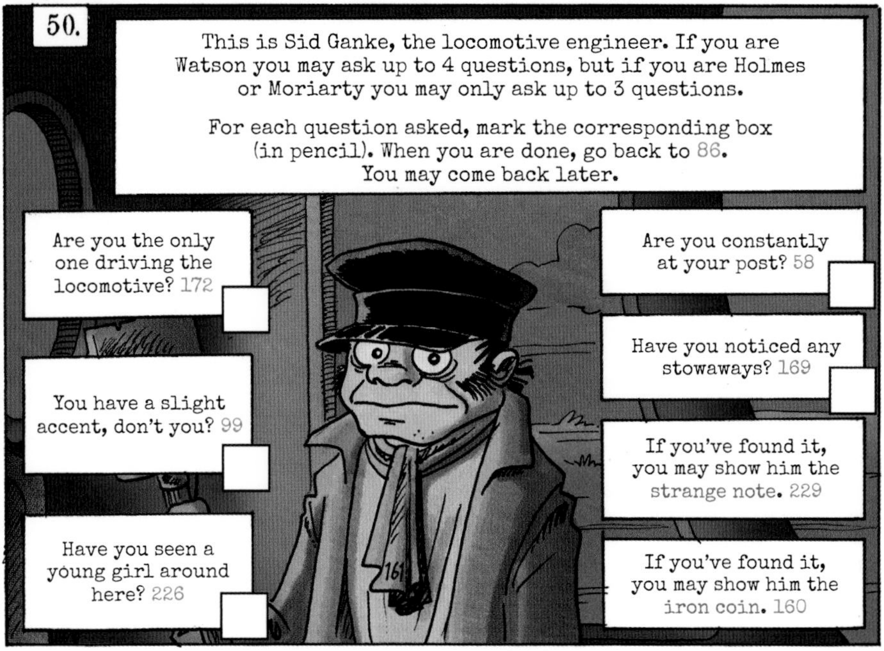
50.
This is Sid Ganke, the locomotive engineer. If you are Watson you may ask up to 4 questions, but if you are Holmes or Moriarty you may only ask up to 3 questions.
For each question asked, mark the corresponding box (in pencil). When you are done, go back to 86. You may come back later.
Are you the only one driving the locomotive? 172
You have a slight accent, don't you? 99
Have you seen a young girl around here? 226
Are you constantly at your post? 58
Have you noticed any stowaways? 169
If you've found it, you may show him the strange note. 229
If you've found it, you may show him the iron coin. 160
161

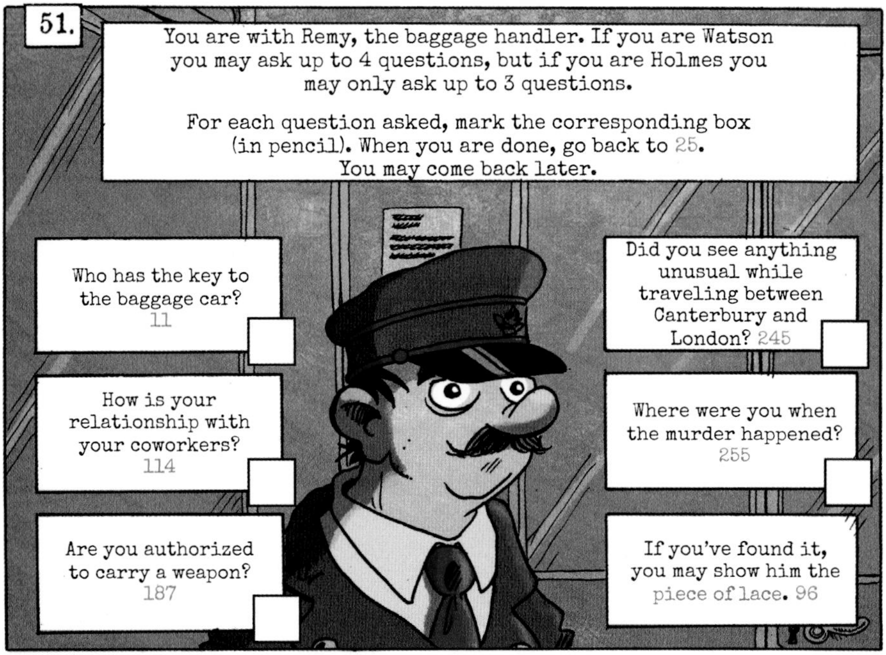
51.
You are with Remy, the baggage handler. If you are Watson you may ask up to 4 questions, but if you are Holmes you may only ask up to 3 questions.
For each question asked, mark the corresponding box (in pencil). When you are done, go back to 25. You may come back later.
Who has the key to the baggage car? 11
How is your relationship with your coworkers? 114
Are you authorized to carry a weapon? 187
Did you see anything unusual while traveling between Canterbury and London? 245
Where were you when the murder happened? 255
If you've found it, you may show him the piece of lace. 96

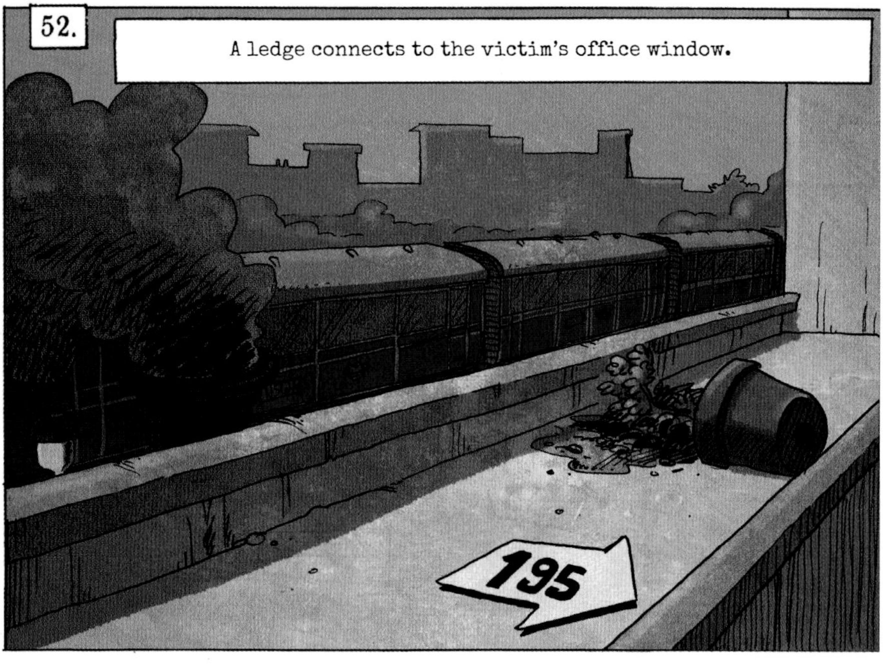
52.
A ledge connects to the victim's office window.
195

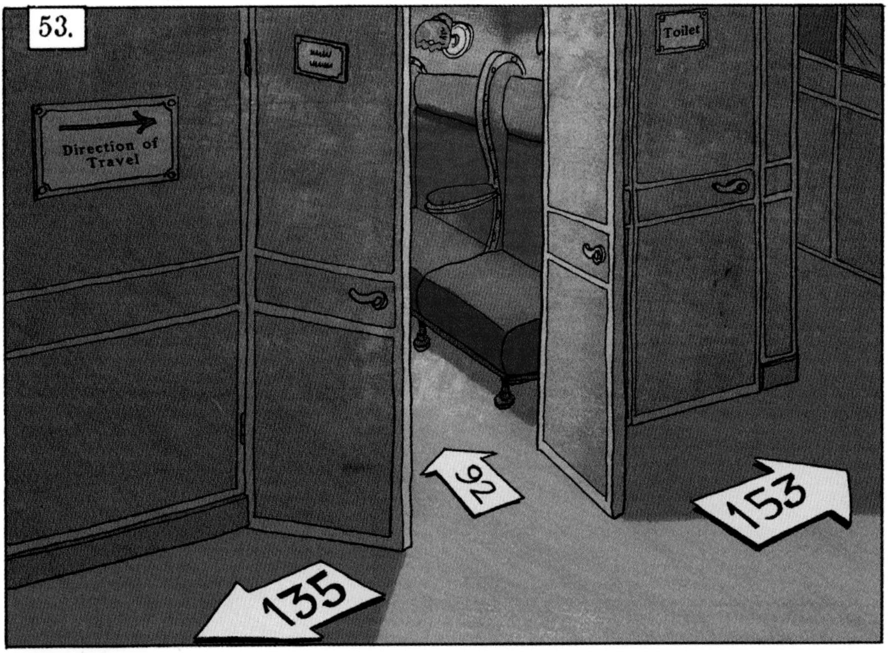
53.
Direction of Travel
Toilet
92
153
135

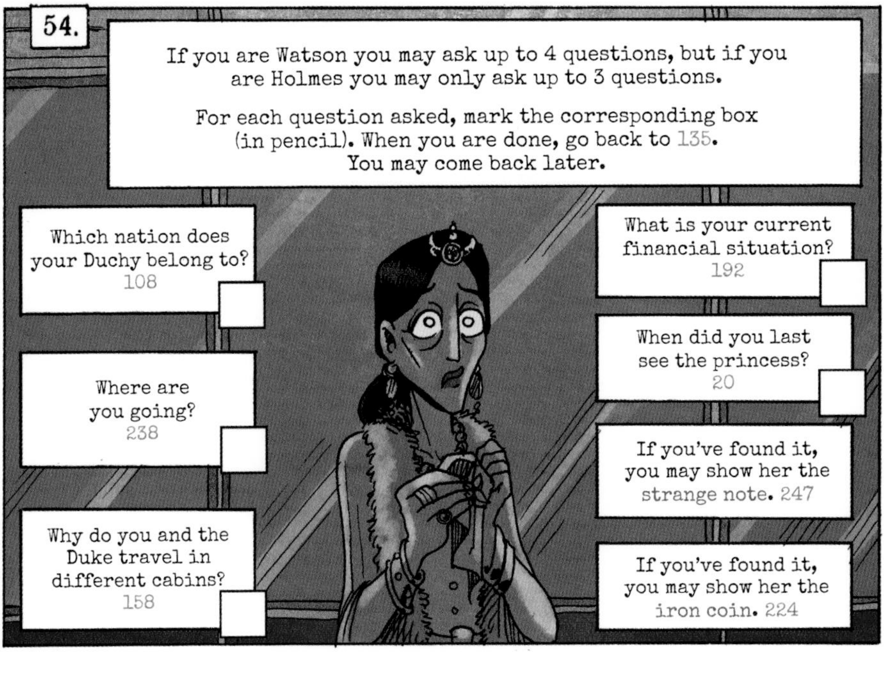
54.
If you are Watson you may ask up to 4 questions, but if you are Holmes you may only ask up to 3 questions.
For each question asked, mark the corresponding box (in pencil). When you are done, go back to 135. You may come back later.
Which nation does your Duchy belong to? 108
Where are you going? 238
Why do you and the Duke travel in different cabins? 158
What is your current financial situation? 192
When did you last see the princess? 20
If you've found it, you may show her the strange note. 247
If you've found it, you may show her the iron coin. 224

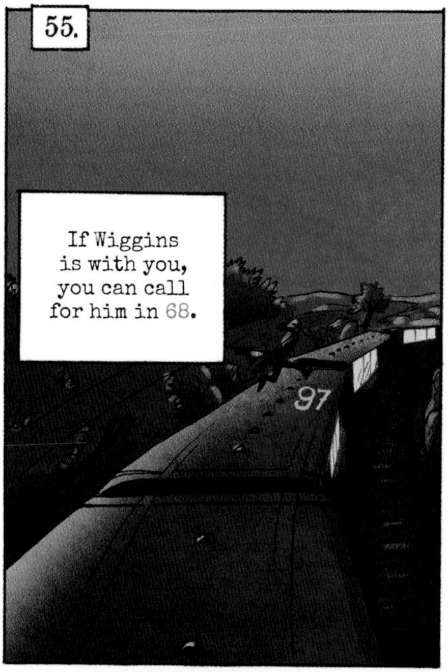
55.
If Wiggins is with you, you can call for him in 68.
97

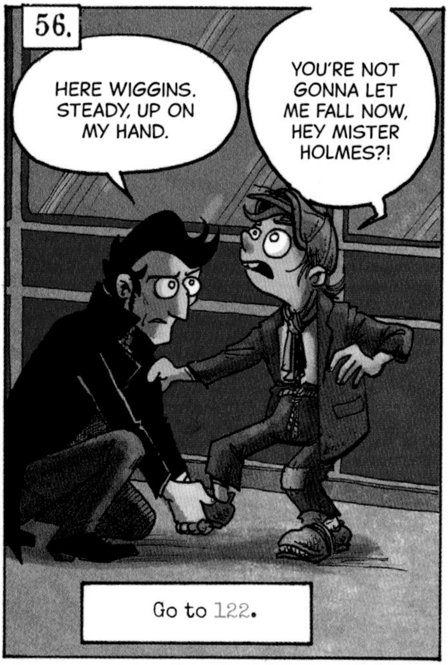
56.
HERE WIGGINS. STEADY, UP ON MY HAND.
YOU'RE NOT GONNA LET ME FALL NOW, HEY MISTER HOLMES?!
Go to 122.

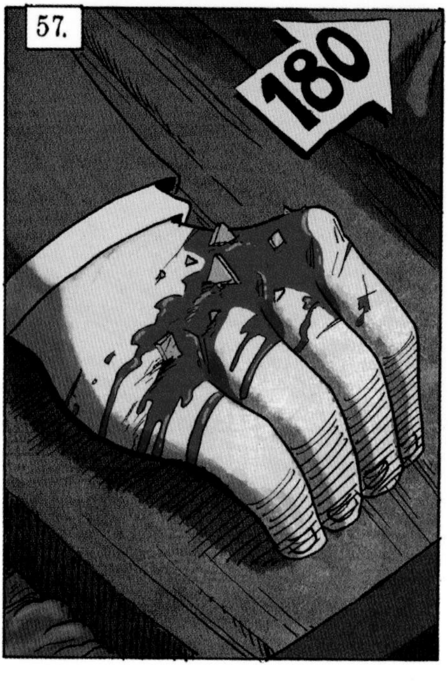
57.
180

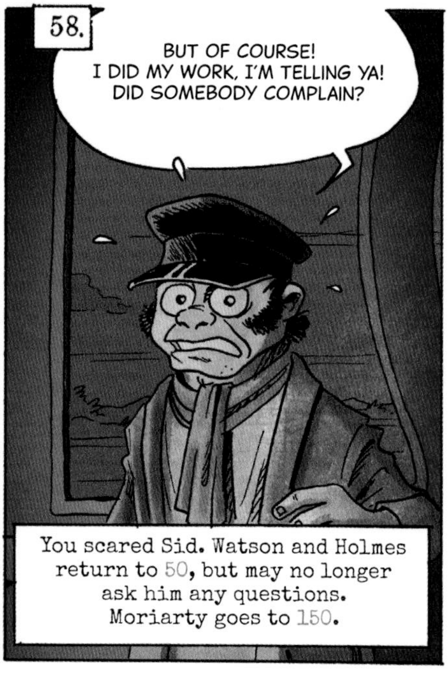
58.
BUT OF COURSE! I DID MY WORK, I'M TELLING YA! DID SOMEBODY COMPLAIN?
You scared Sid. Watson and Holmes return to 50, but may no longer ask him any questions. Moriarty goes to 150.

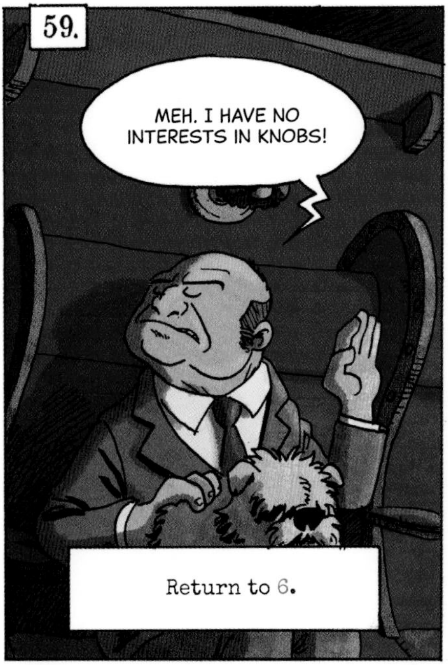
59.
MEH. I HAVE NO INTERESTS IN KNOBS!
Return to 6.

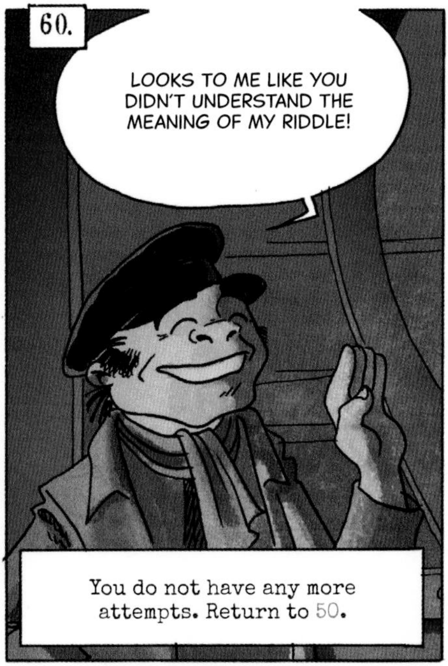
60.
LOOKS TO ME LIKE YOU DIDN'T UNDERSTAND THE MEANING OF MY RIDDLE!
You do not have any more attempts. Return to 50.

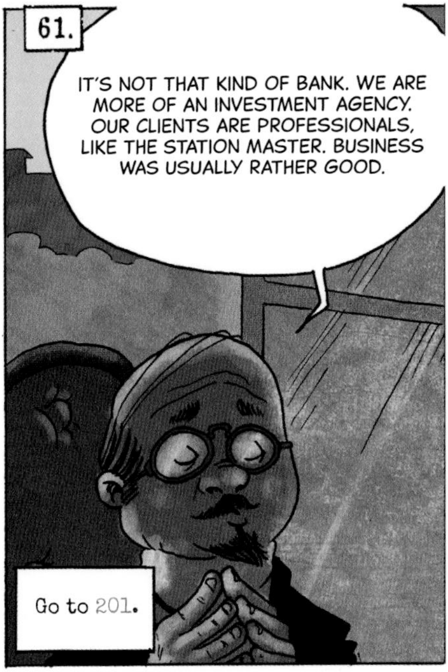
61.
IT'S NOT THAT KIND OF BANK. WE ARE MORE OF AN INVESTMENT AGENCY. OUR CLIENTS ARE PROFESSIONALS, LIKE THE STATION MASTER. BUSINESS WAS USUALLY RATHER GOOD.
Go to 201.

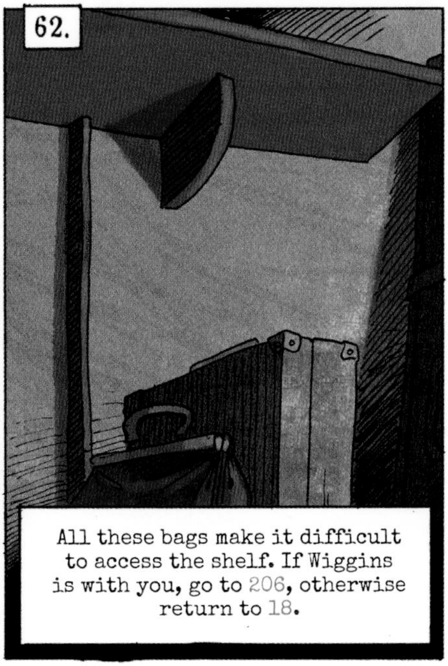
62.
All these bags make it difficult to access the shelf. If Wiggins is with you, go to 206, otherwise return to 18.

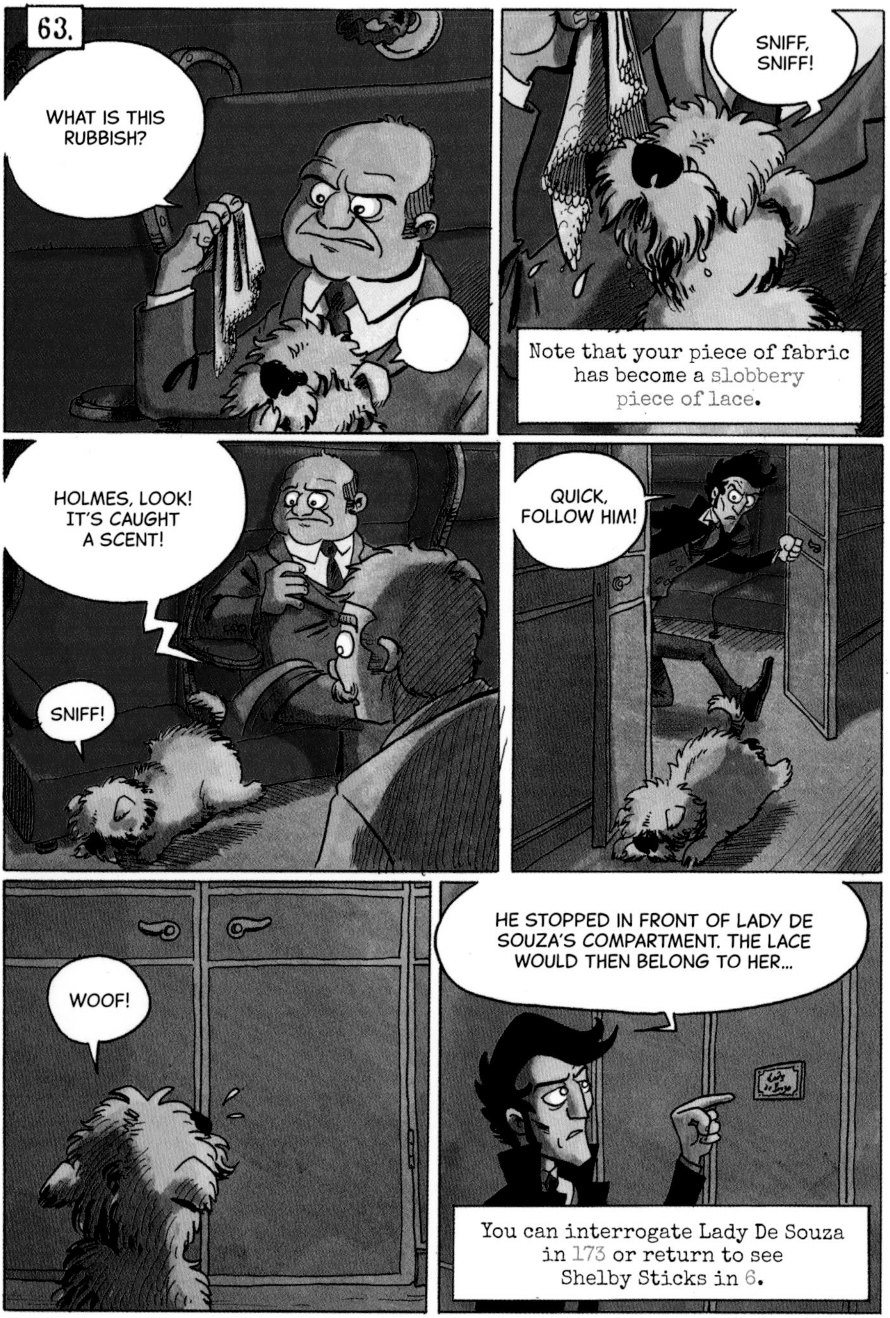
63.
WHAT IS THIS RUBBISH?
SNIFF, SNIFF!
Note that your piece of fabric has become a slobbery piece of lace.
HOLMES, LOOK! IT'S CAUGHT A SCENT!
SNIFF!
QUICK, FOLLOW HIM!
WOOF!
HE STOPPED IN FRONT OF LADY DE SOUZA'S COMPARTMENT. THE LACE WOULD THEN BELONG TO HER...
You can interrogate Lady De Souza in 173 or return to see Shelby Sticks in 6.

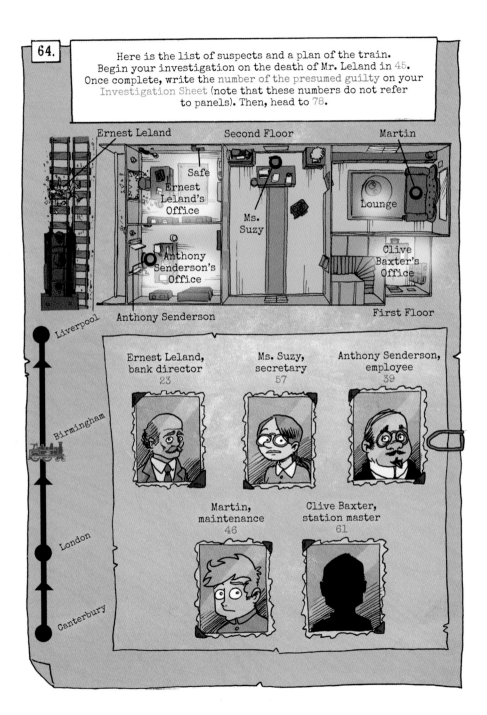

64.

Here is the list of suspects and a plan of the train.
Begin your investigation on the death of Mr. Leland in 45.
Once complete, write the number of the presumed guilty on your
Investigation Sheet (note that these numbers do not refer
to panels). Then, head to 78.

Ernest Leland   Second Floor   Martin

Safe
Ernest
Leland's
Office

Ms.
Suzy

Lounge

Clive
Baxter's
Office

Anthony
Senderson's
Office

Anthony Senderson   First Floor

Liverpool

Birmingham

London

Canterbury

Ernest Leland,
bank director
23

Ms. Suzy,
secretary
57

Anthony Senderson,
employee
39

Martin,
maintenance
46

Clive Baxter,
station master
61

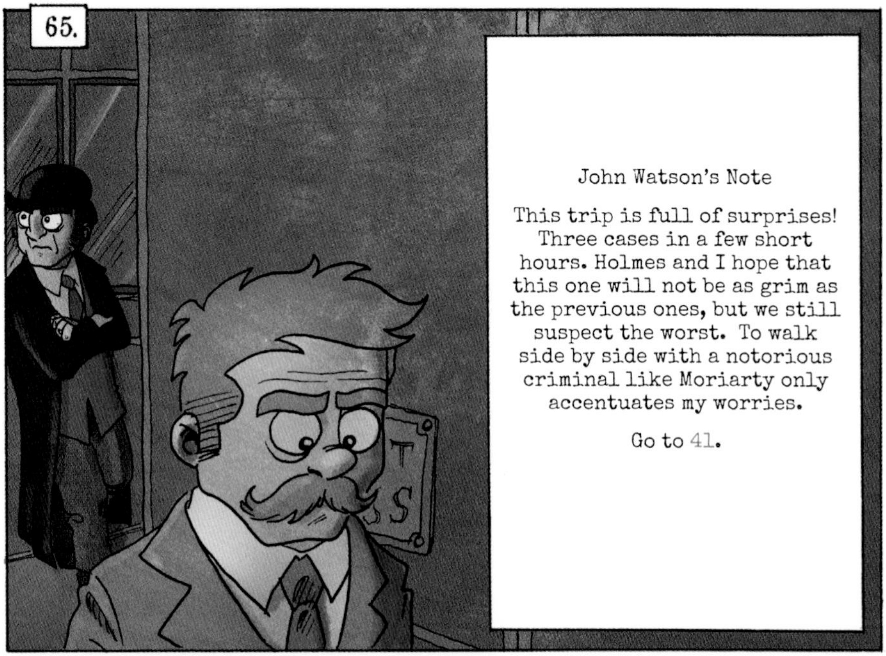
65.
John Watson’s Note
This trip is full of surprises! Three cases in a few short hours. Holmes and I hope that this one will not be as grim as the previous ones, but we still suspect the worst. To walk side by side with a notorious criminal like Moriarty only accentuates my worries.
Go to 41.

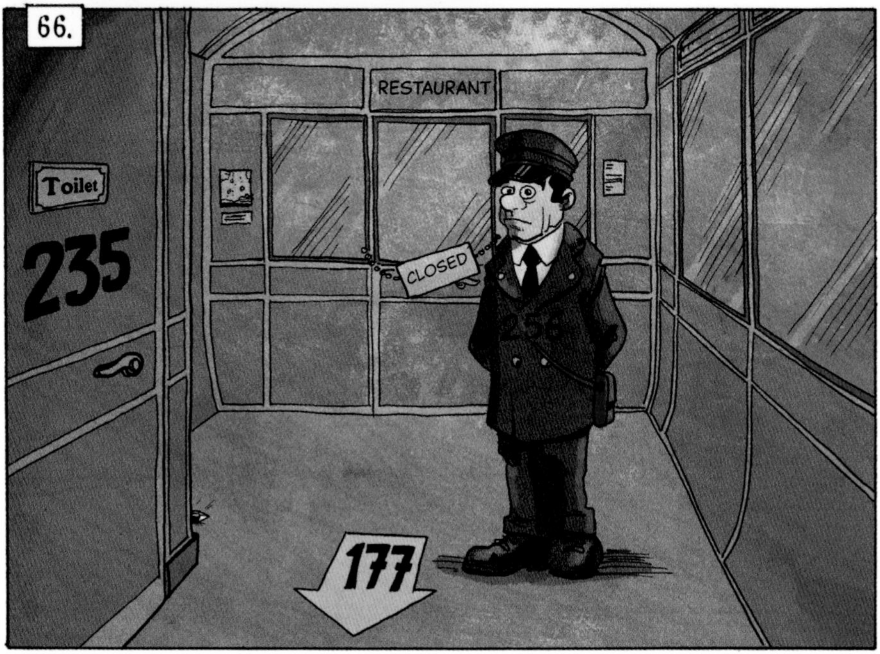
66.
RESTAURANT
Toilet
235
CLOSED
177

67.

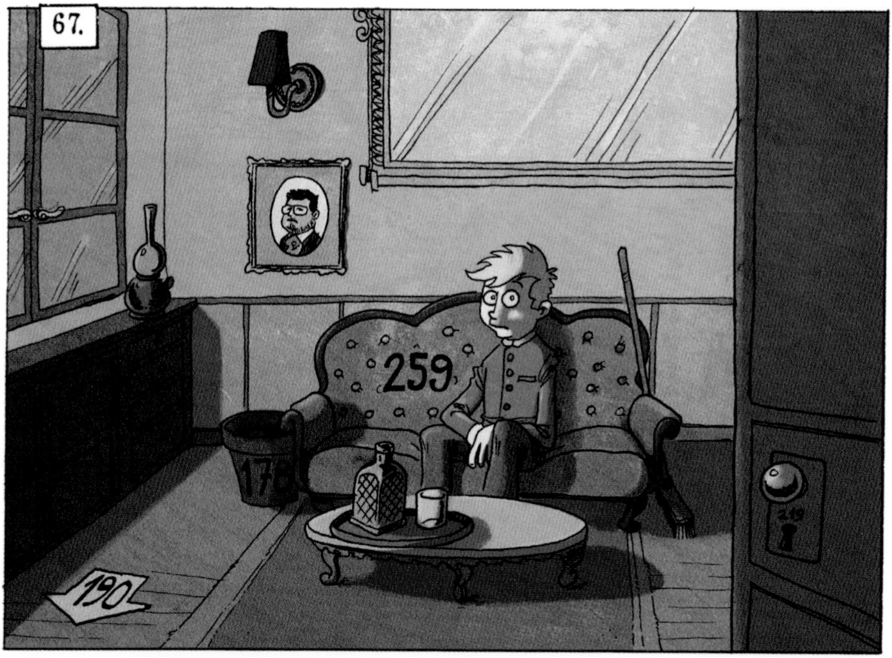
259
178
190
219

68.

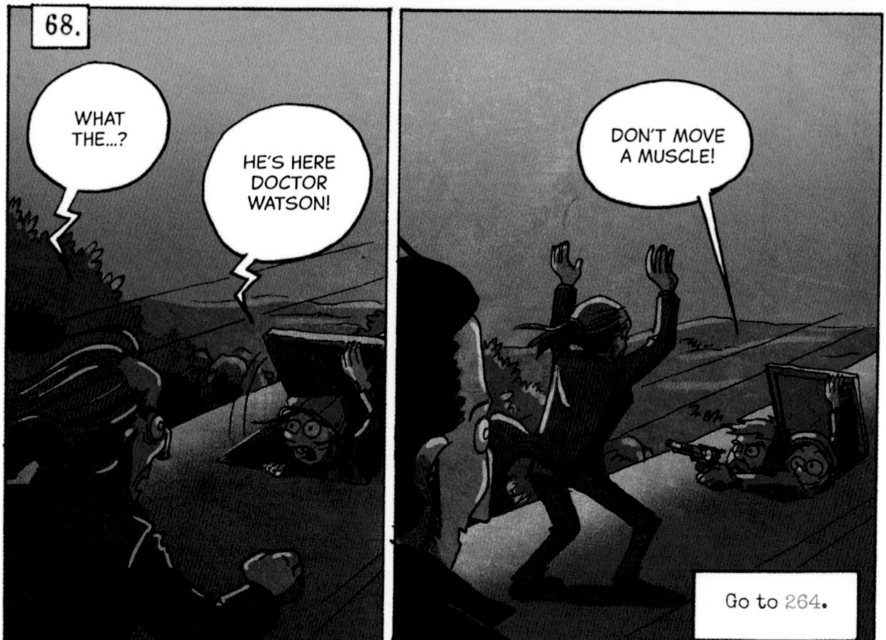
WHAT THE...?
HE'S HERE DOCTOR WATSON!
DON'T MOVE A MUSCLE!

Go to 264.

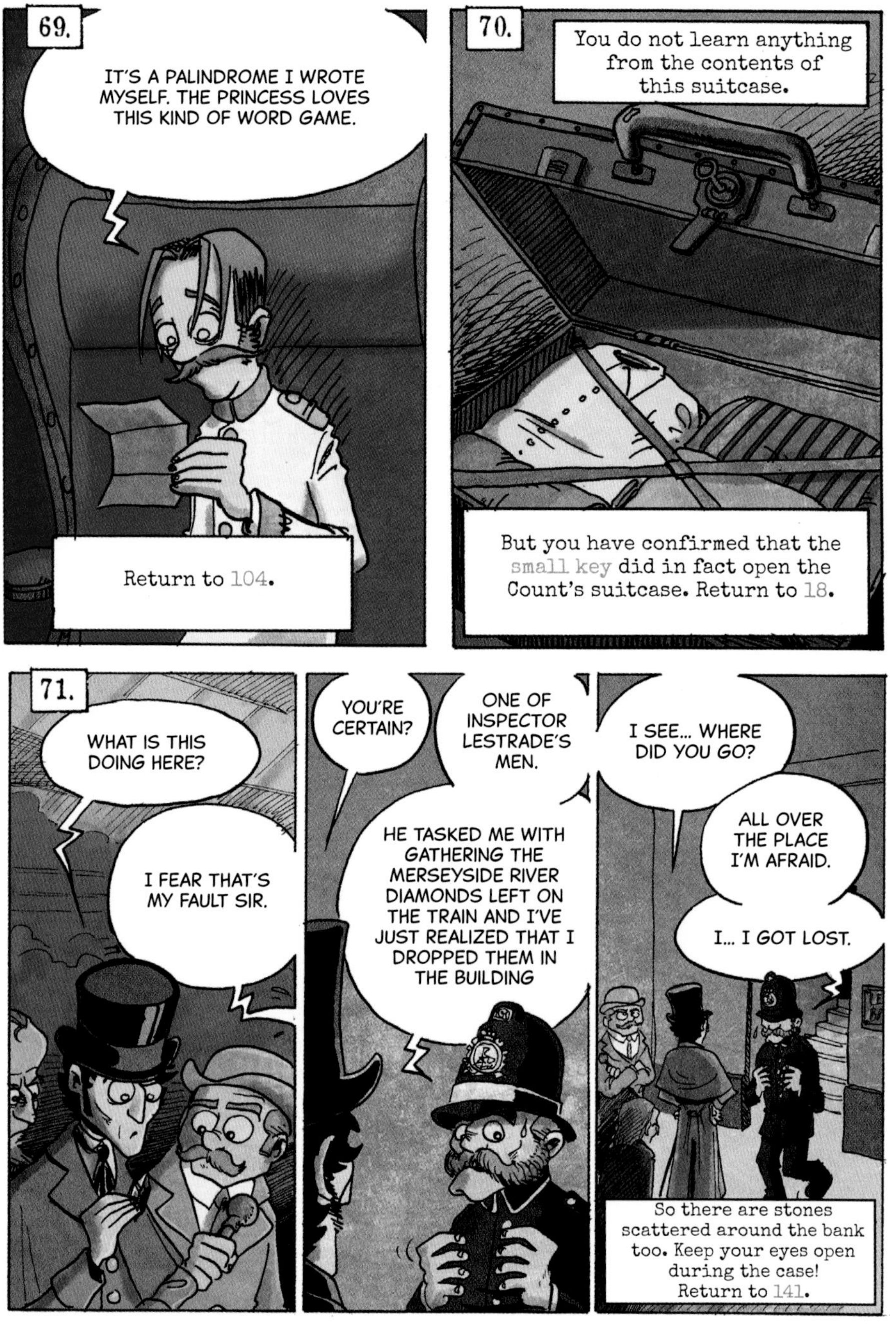
69.
IT'S A PALINDROME I WROTE MYSELF. THE PRINCESS LOVES THIS KIND OF WORD GAME.
Return to 104.
70.
You do not learn anything from the contents of this suitcase.
But you have confirmed that the small key did in fact open the Count's suitcase. Return to 18.
71.
WHAT IS THIS DOING HERE?
I FEAR THAT'S MY FAULT SIR.
YOU'RE CERTAIN?
ONE OF INSPECTOR LESTRADE'S MEN.
HE TASKED ME WITH GATHERING THE MERSEYSIDE RIVER DIAMONDS LEFT ON THE TRAIN AND I'VE JUST REALIZED THAT I DROPPED THEM IN THE BUILDING
I SEE... WHERE DID YOU GO?
ALL OVER THE PLACE I'M AFRAID.
I... I GOT LOST.
So there are stones scattered around the bank too. Keep your eyes open during the case! Return to 141.

Dear Mr. Holmes,

Allow me to introduce myself, Allan Du Barry, Count of Morcar.

While we do not know one another, you once helped my mother, the Countess of Morcar. Perhaps you remember?

As a matter of fact, I am currently traveling as per her request. I must take the train in Canterbury to get to Liverpool. With me will be one of her most precious belongings, the Merseyside River, a necklace made out of forty precious stones. It is, as I am sure you have surmised, priceless.

I have opted to follow my mother's wise advice and am asking for your assistance. Would you escort me to my destination? I am a relatively discreet man, but I fear I will not go unnoticed while traveling with such a treasure.

Needless to say, you will be well compensated for your service.

I will board the train you recommended in Canterbury, and you may join me when the train stops at the London Station.

I leave the matter to you.

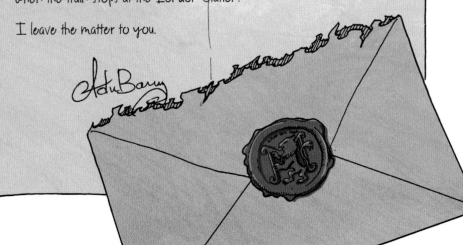

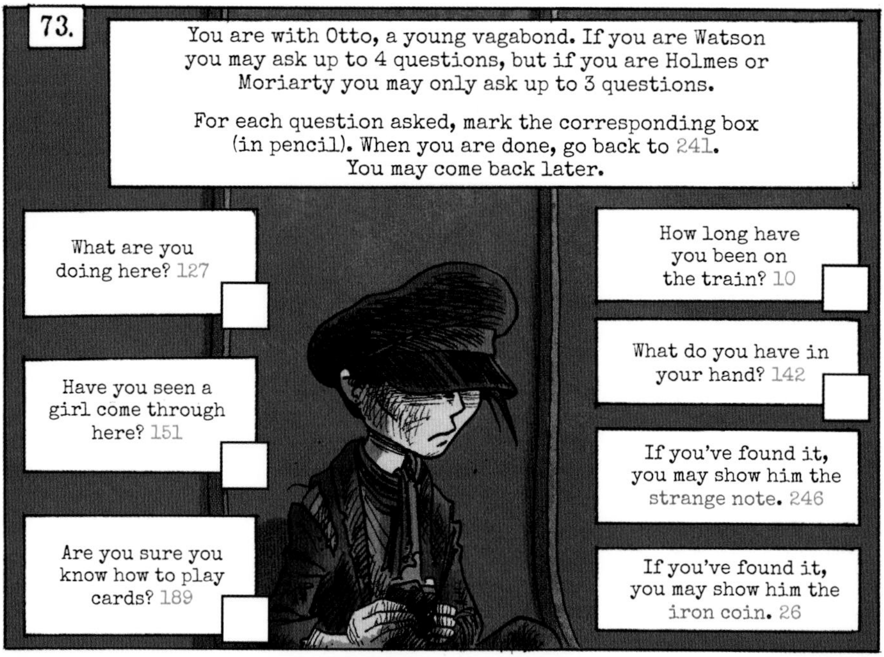
73.
You are with Otto, a young vagabond. If you are Watson you may ask up to 4 questions, but if you are Holmes or Moriarty you may only ask up to 3 questions.
For each question asked, mark the corresponding box (in pencil). When you are done, go back to 241. You may come back later.
What are you doing here? 127
Have you seen a girl come through here? 151
Are you sure you know how to play cards? 189
How long have you been on the train? 10
What do you have in your hand? 142
If you've found it, you may show him the strange note. 246
If you've found it, you may show him the iron coin. 26

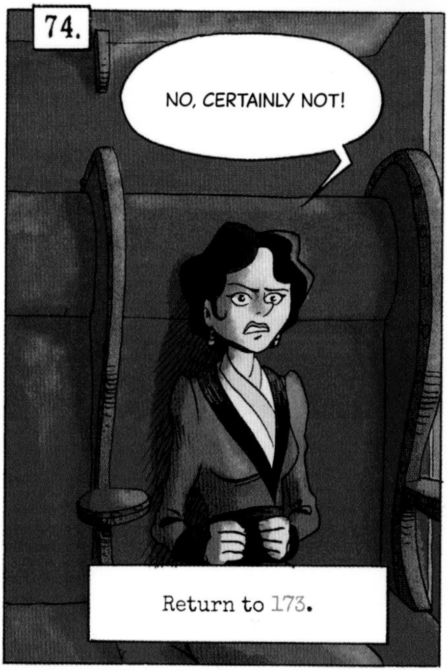
74.
NO, CERTAINLY NOT!
Return to 173.

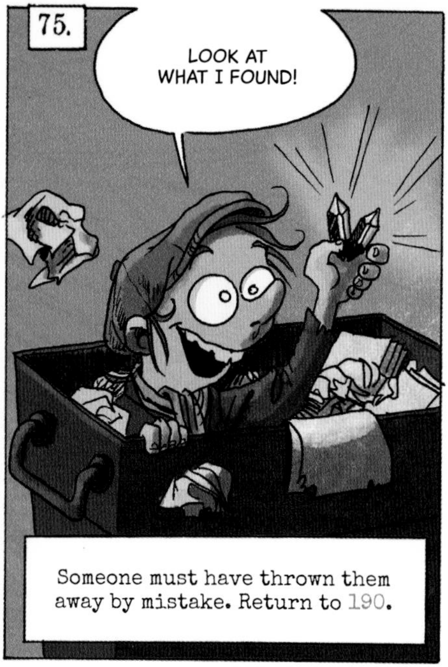
75.
LOOK AT WHAT I FOUND!
Someone must have thrown them away by mistake. Return to 190.

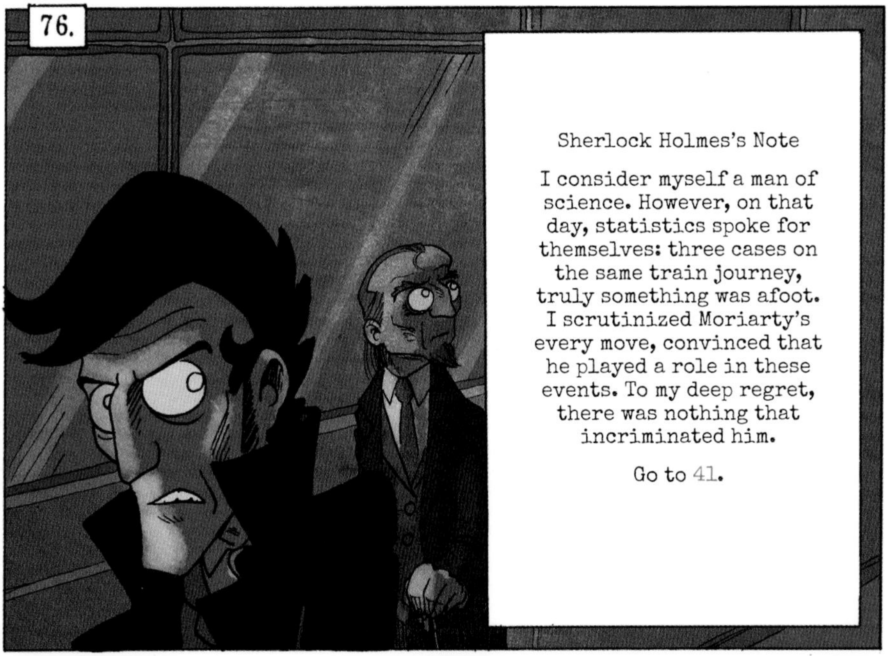
76.
Sherlock Holmes's Note
I consider myself a man of science. However, on that day, statistics spoke for themselves: three cases on the same train journey, truly something was afoot. I scrutinized Moriarty's every move, convinced that he played a role in these events. To my deep regret, there was nothing that incriminated him.
Go to 41.

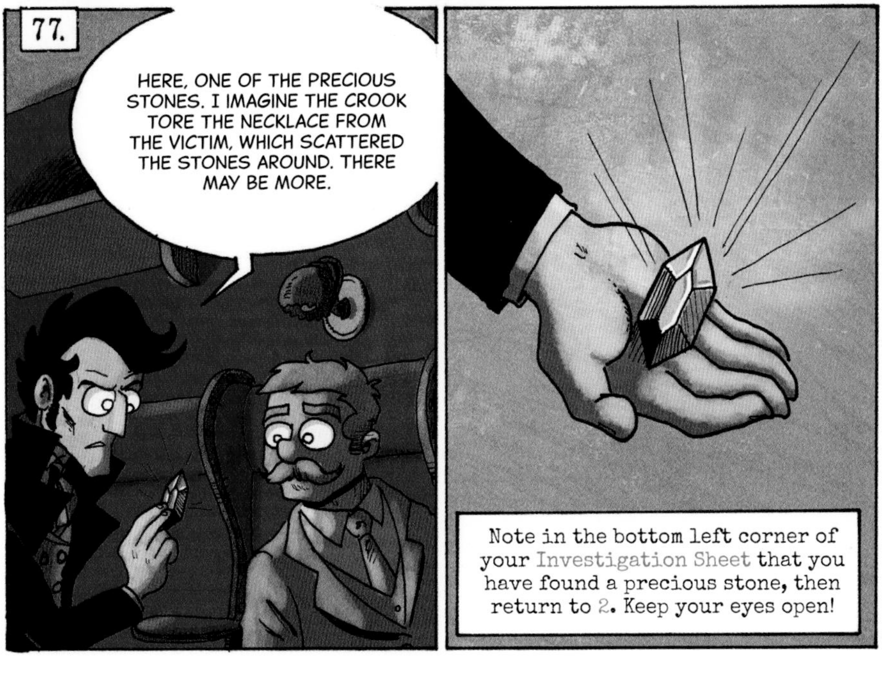
77.
HERE, ONE OF THE PRECIOUS STONES. I IMAGINE THE CROOK TORE THE NECKLACE FROM THE VICTIM, WHICH SCATTERED THE STONES AROUND. THERE MAY BE MORE.
Note in the bottom left corner of your Investigation Sheet that you have found a precious stone, then return to 2. Keep your eyes open!

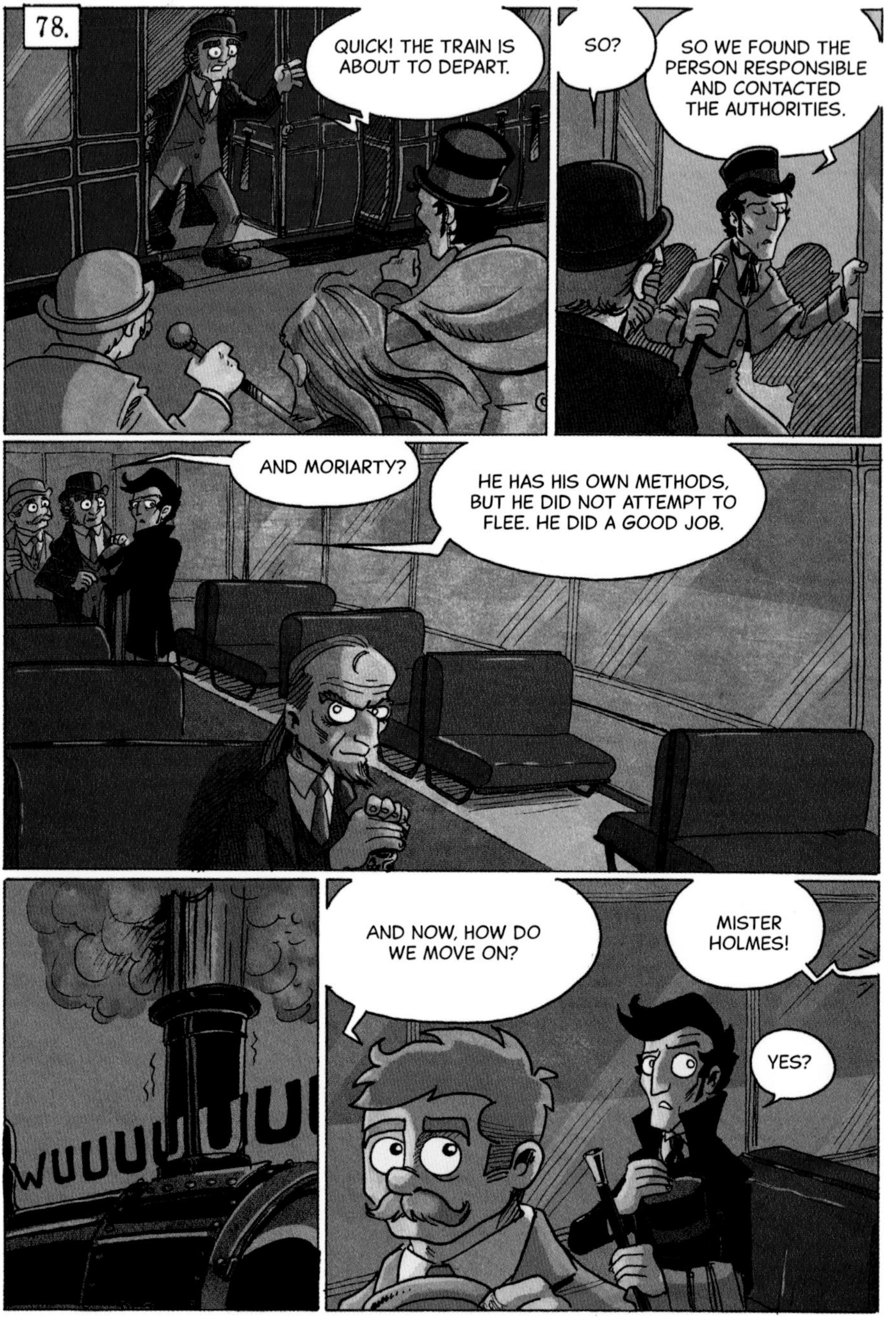
78.
QUICK! THE TRAIN IS ABOUT TO DEPART.
SO?
SO WE FOUND THE PERSON RESPONSIBLE AND CONTACTED THE AUTHORITIES.
AND MORIARTY?
HE HAS HIS OWN METHODS, BUT HE DID NOT ATTEMPT TO FLEE. HE DID A GOOD JOB.
WUUUUUUU
AND NOW, HOW DO WE MOVE ON?
MISTER HOLMES!
YES?

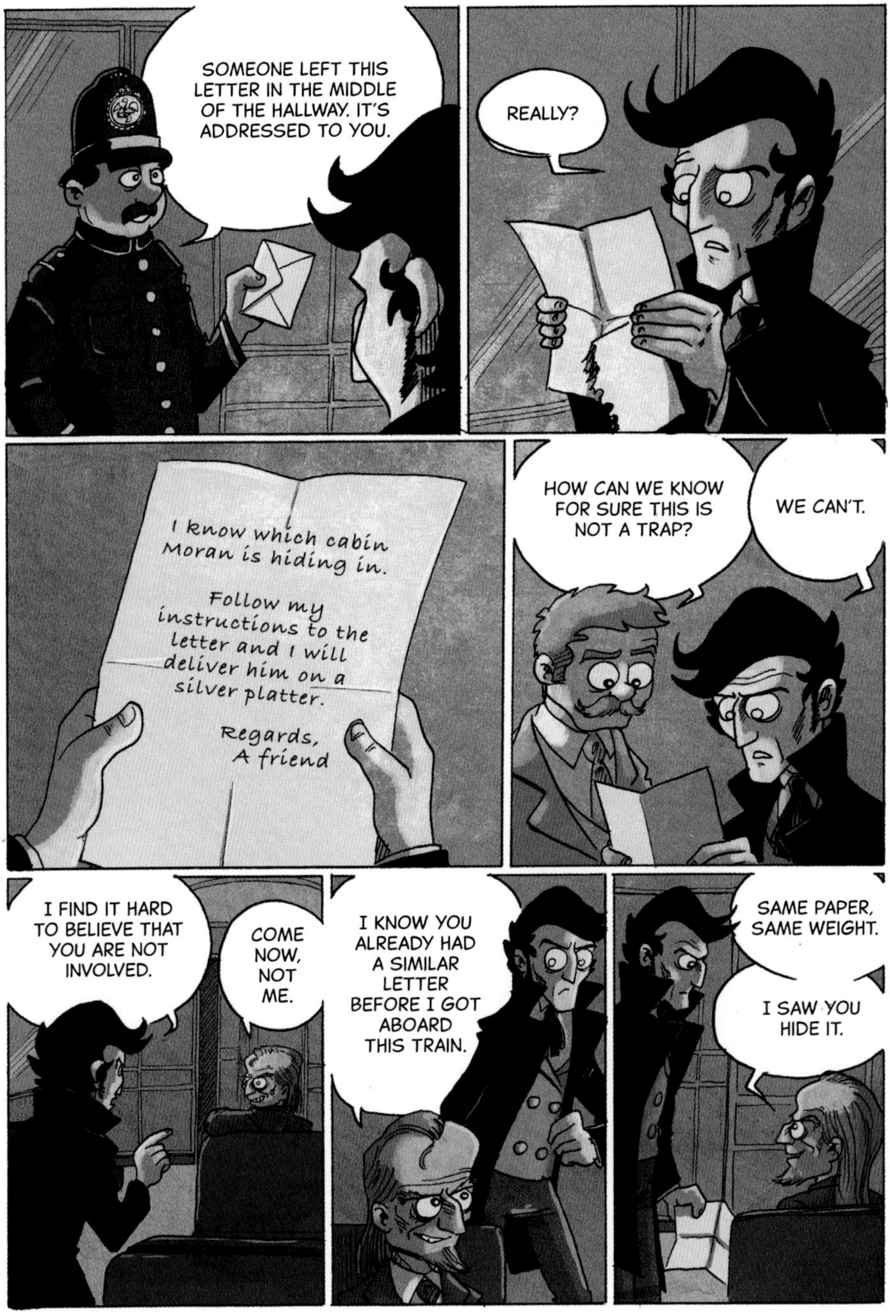
SOMEONE LEFT THIS LETTER IN THE MIDDLE OF THE HALLWAY. IT'S ADDRESSED TO YOU.
REALLY?
I know which cabin Moran is hiding in.
Follow my instructions to the letter and I will deliver him on a silver platter.
Regards,
A friend
HOW CAN WE KNOW FOR SURE THIS IS NOT A TRAP?
WE CAN'T.
I FIND IT HARD TO BELIEVE THAT YOU ARE NOT INVOLVED.
COME NOW, NOT ME.
I KNOW YOU ALREADY HAD A SIMILAR LETTER BEFORE I GOT ABOARD THIS TRAIN.
SAME PAPER, SAME WEIGHT.
I SAW YOU HIDE IT.

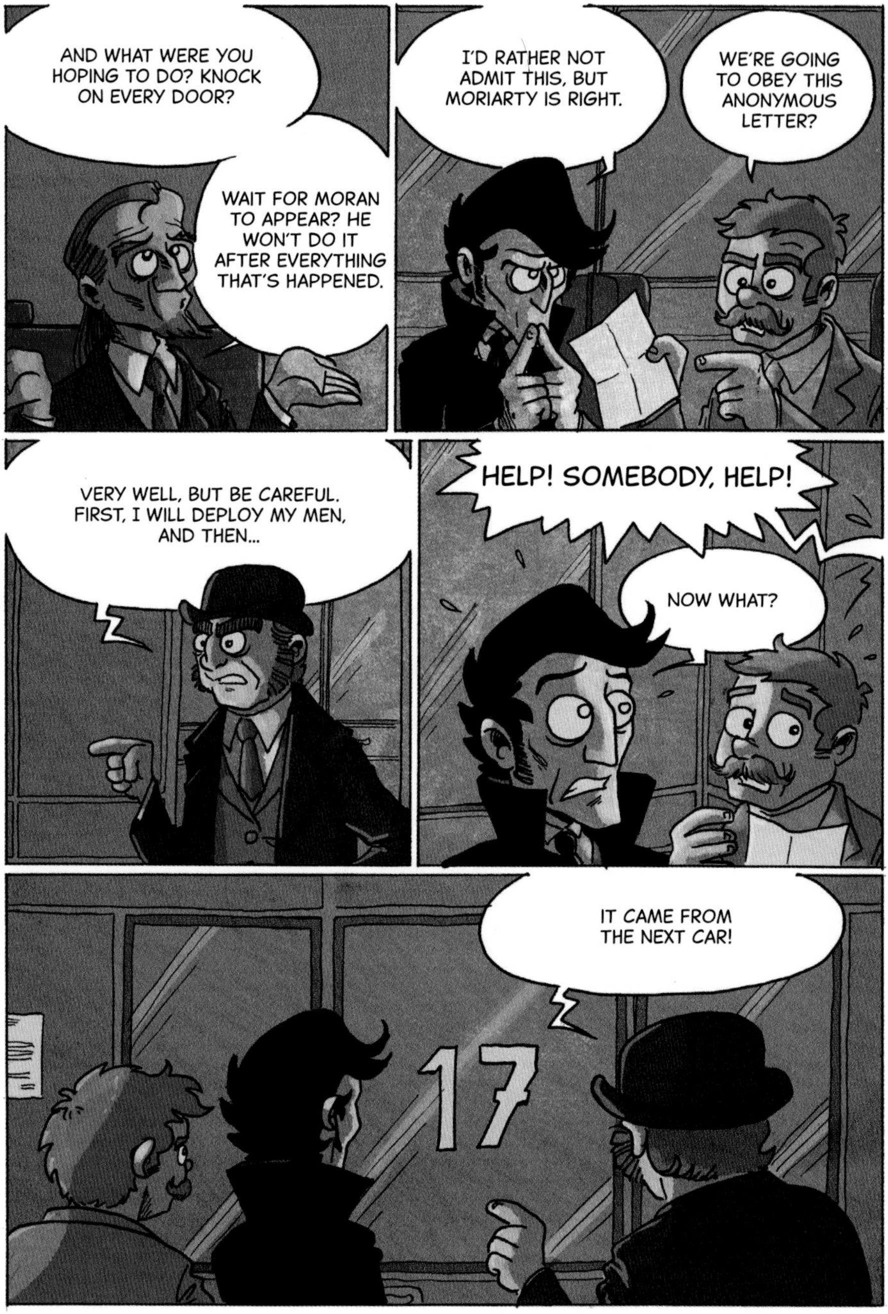
AND WHAT WERE YOU HOPING TO DO? KNOCK ON EVERY DOOR?
WAIT FOR MORAN TO APPEAR? HE WON'T DO IT AFTER EVERYTHING THAT'S HAPPENED.
I'D RATHER NOT ADMIT THIS, BUT MORIARTY IS RIGHT.
WE'RE GOING TO OBEY THIS ANONYMOUS LETTER?
VERY WELL, BUT BE CAREFUL. FIRST, I WILL DEPLOY MY MEN, AND THEN...
HELP! SOMEBODY, HELP!
NOW WHAT?
IT CAME FROM THE NEXT CAR!
17

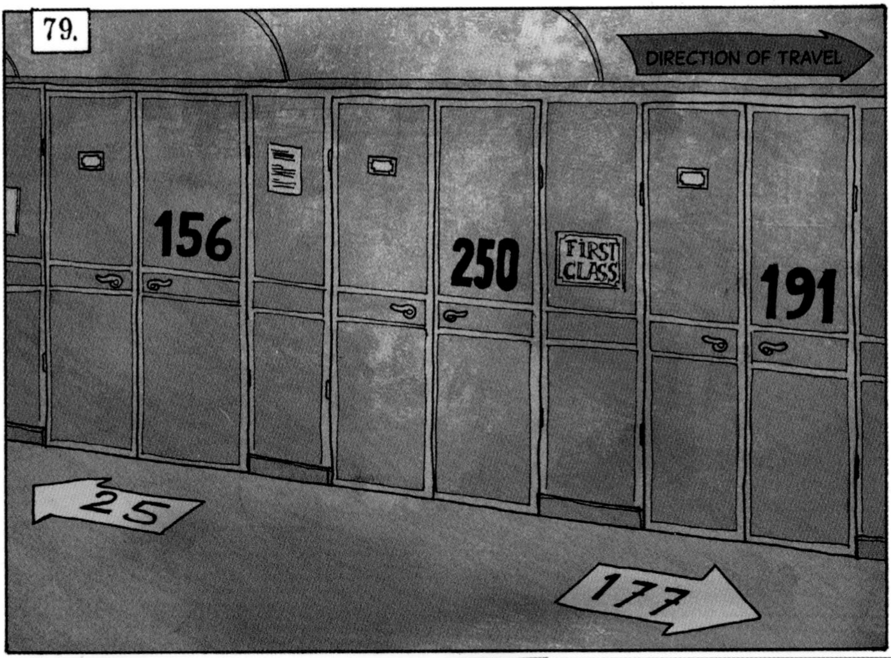
79.
DIRECTION OF TRAVEL
156
250
FIRST CLASS
191
25
177

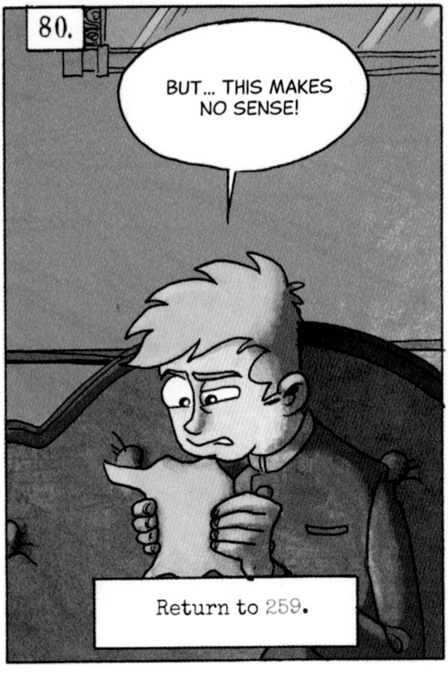
80.
BUT... THIS MAKES NO SENSE!
Return to 259.

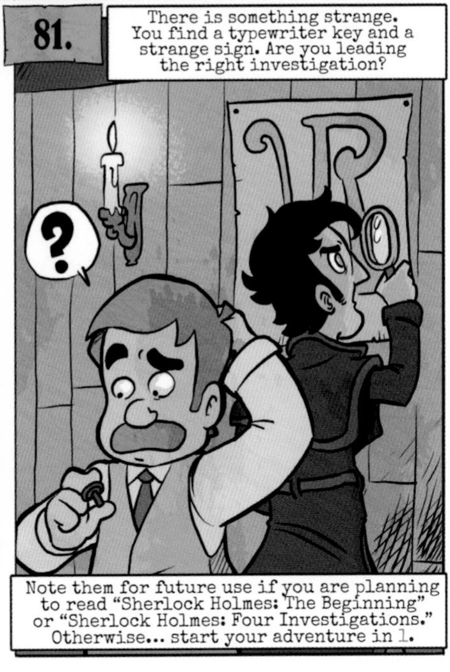
81.
There is something strange. You find a typewriter key and a strange sign. Are you leading the right investigation?
?
Note them for future use if you are planning to read "Sherlock Holmes: The Beginning" or "Sherlock Holmes: Four Investigations." Otherwise... start your adventure in 1.

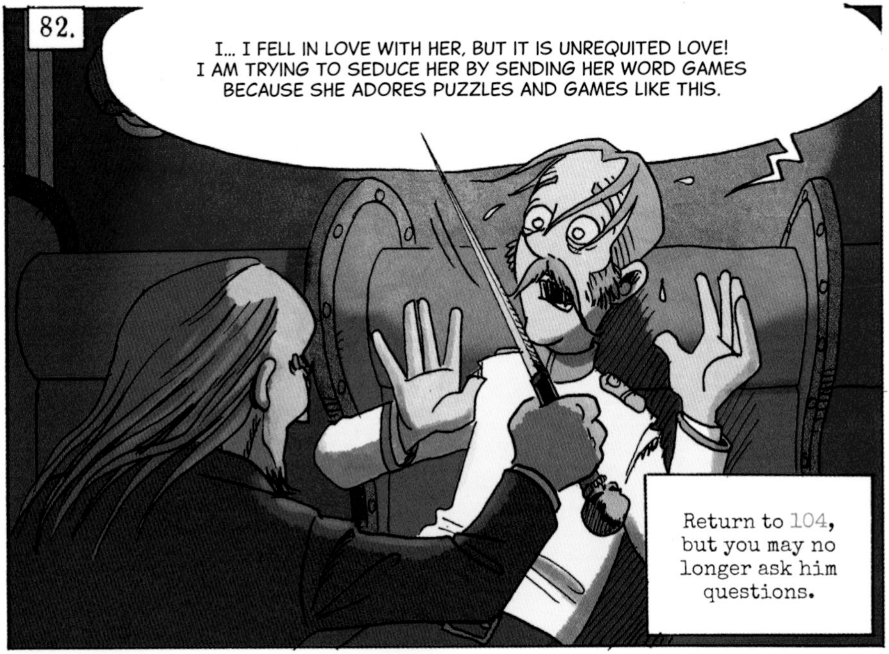
82.
I... I FELL IN LOVE WITH HER, BUT IT IS UNREQUITED LOVE! I AM TRYING TO SEDUCE HER BY SENDING HER WORD GAMES BECAUSE SHE ADORES PUZZLES AND GAMES LIKE THIS.
Return to 104, but you may no longer ask him questions.

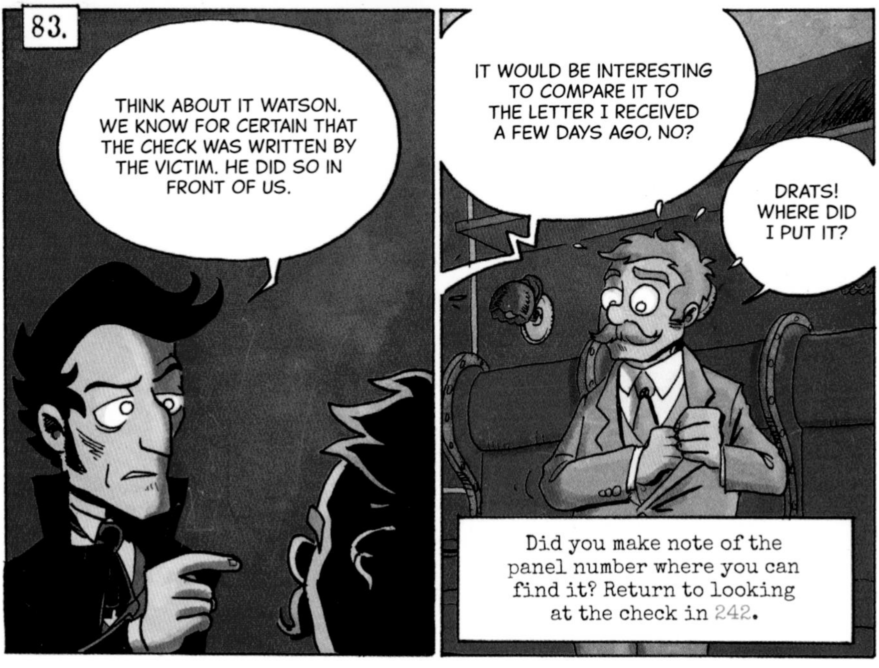
83.
THINK ABOUT IT WATSON. WE KNOW FOR CERTAIN THAT THE CHECK WAS WRITTEN BY THE VICTIM. HE DID SO IN FRONT OF US.
IT WOULD BE INTERESTING TO COMPARE IT TO THE LETTER I RECEIVED A FEW DAYS AGO, NO?
DRATS! WHERE DID I PUT IT?
Did you make note of the panel number where you can find it? Return to looking at the check in 242.

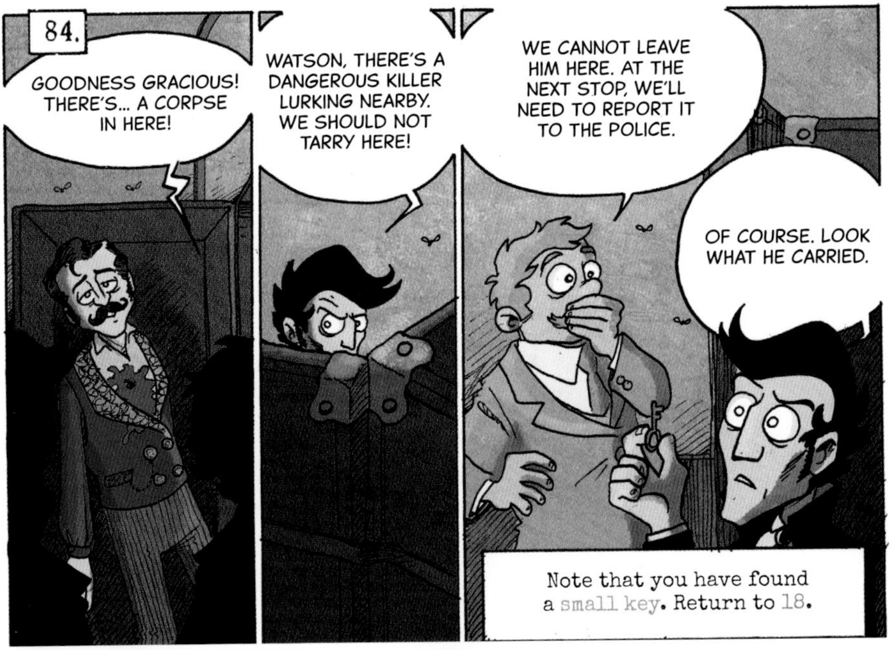
84.
GOODNESS GRACIOUS! THERE'S... A CORPSE IN HERE!
WATSON, THERE'S A DANGEROUS KILLER LURKING NEARBY. WE SHOULD NOT TARRY HERE!
WE CANNOT LEAVE HIM HERE. AT THE NEXT STOP, WE'LL NEED TO REPORT IT TO THE POLICE.
OF COURSE. LOOK WHAT HE CARRIED.
Note that you have found a small key. Return to 18.

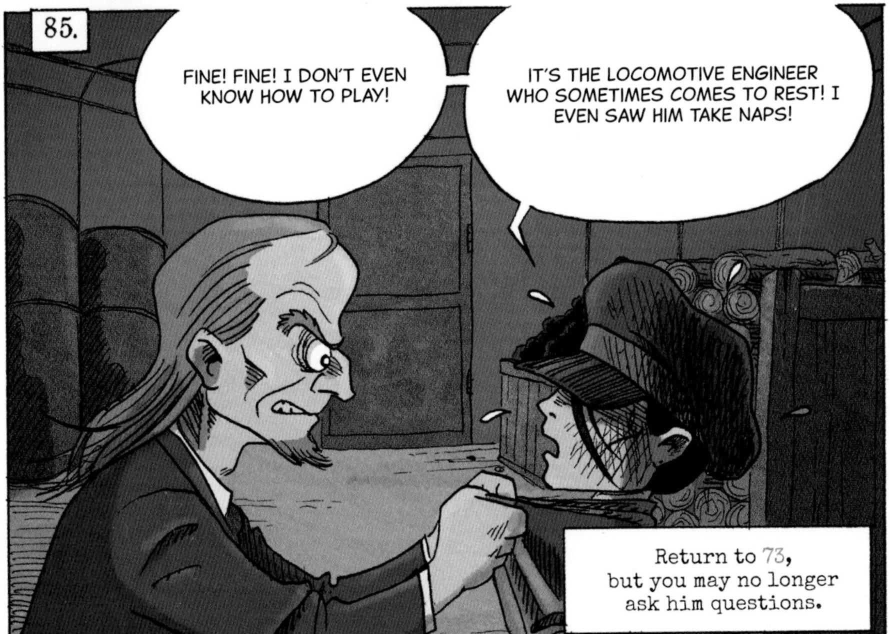
85.
FINE! FINE! I DON'T EVEN KNOW HOW TO PLAY!
IT'S THE LOCOMOTIVE ENGINEER WHO SOMETIMES COMES TO REST! I EVEN SAW HIM TAKE NAPS!
Return to 73, but you may no longer ask him questions.

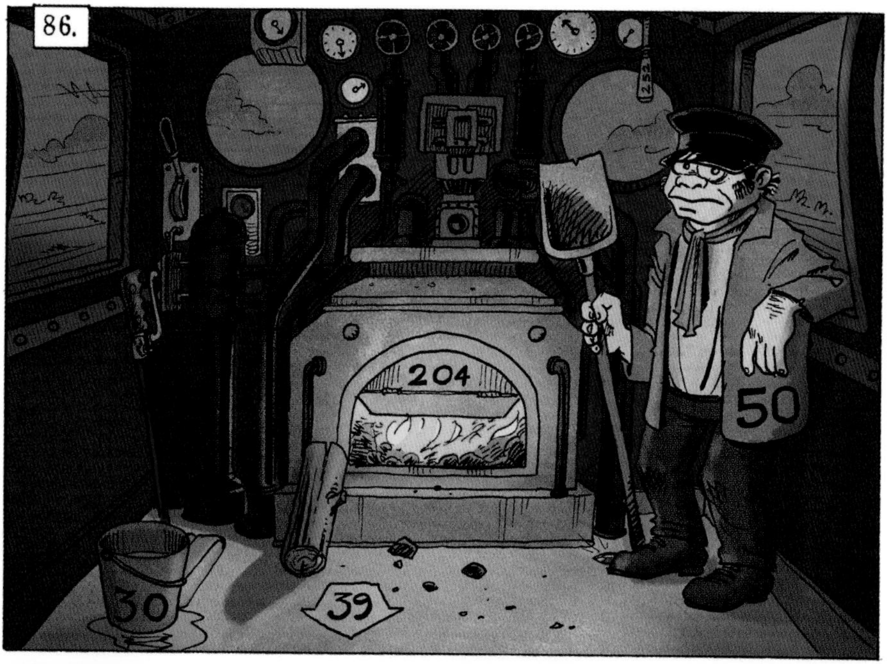
86.
204
50
30
39
252

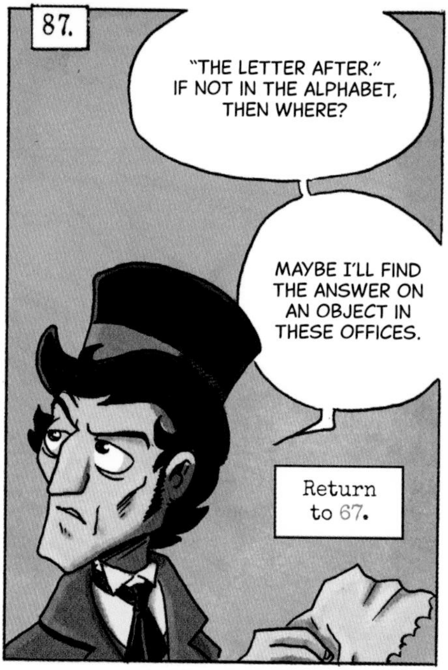
87.
"THE LETTER AFTER." IF NOT IN THE ALPHABET, THEN WHERE?
MAYBE I'LL FIND THE ANSWER ON AN OBJECT IN THESE OFFICES.
Return to 67.

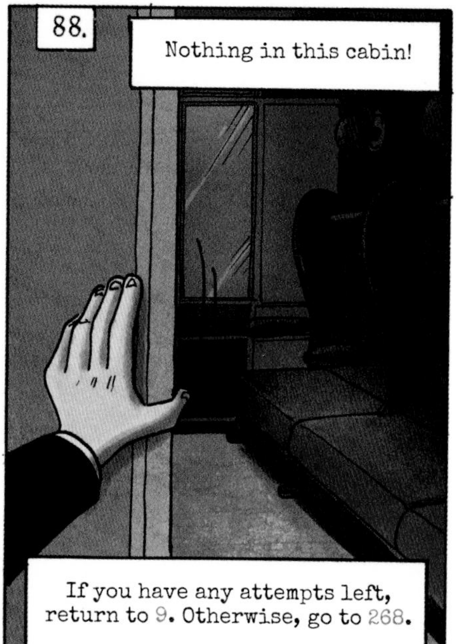
88.
Nothing in this cabin!
If you have any attempts left, return to 9. Otherwise, go to 268.

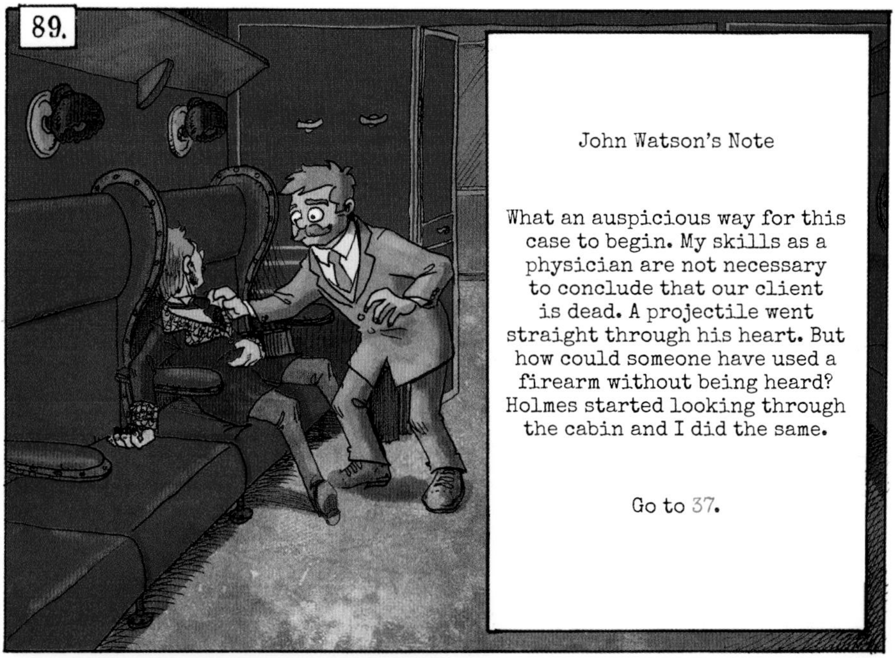
89.
John Watson's Note
What an auspicious way for this case to begin. My skills as a physician are not necessary to conclude that our client is dead. A projectile went straight through his heart. But how could someone have used a firearm without being heard? Holmes started looking through the cabin and I did the same.
Go to 37.

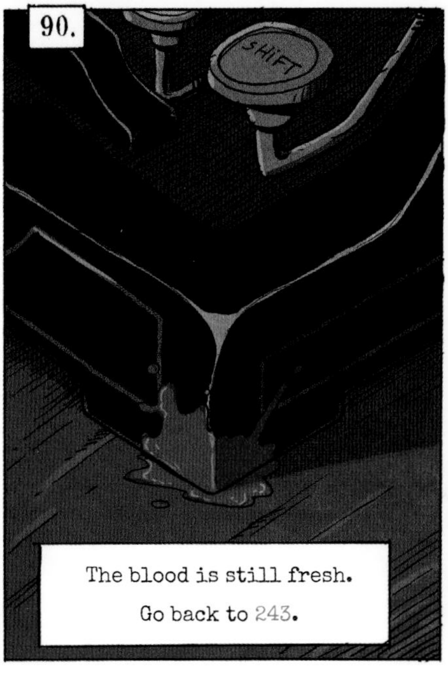
90.
SHIFT
The blood is still fresh.
Go back to 243.

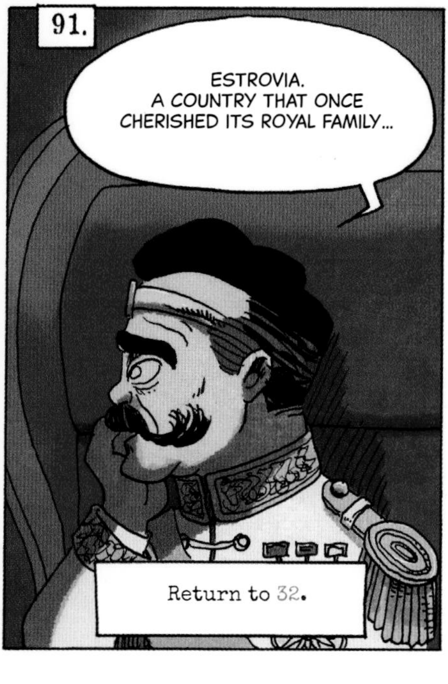
91.
ESTROVIA. A COUNTRY THAT ONCE CHERISHED ITS ROYAL FAMILY...
Return to 32.

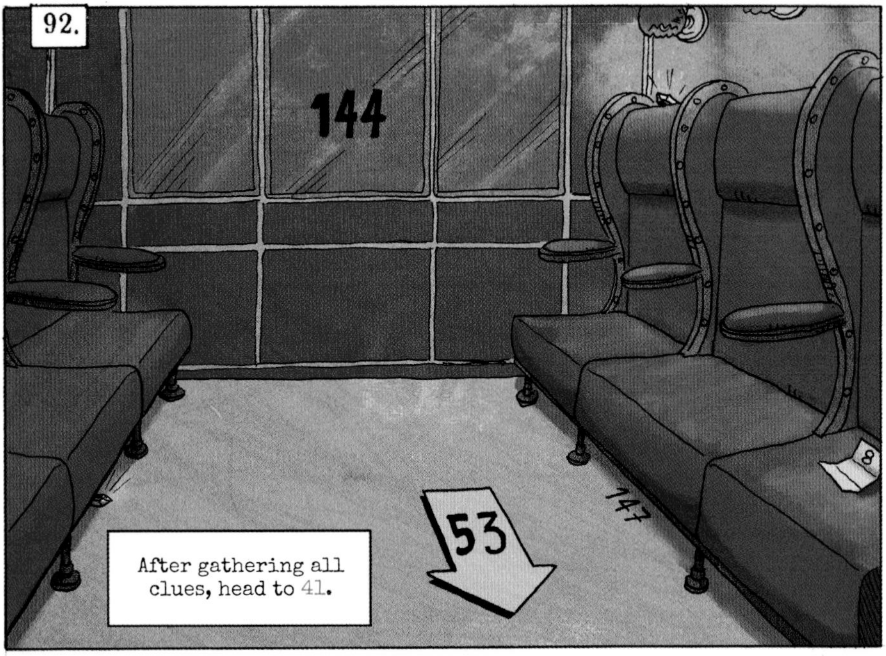
92.
144
53
147
8
After gathering all clues, head to 41.

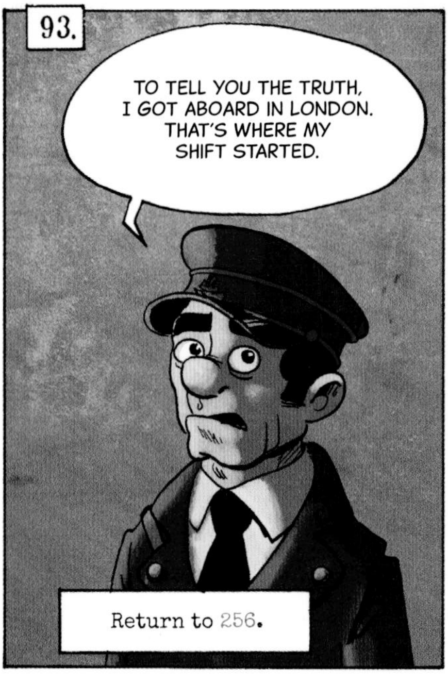
93.
TO TELL YOU THE TRUTH, I GOT ABOARD IN LONDON. THAT'S WHERE MY SHIFT STARTED.
Return to 256.

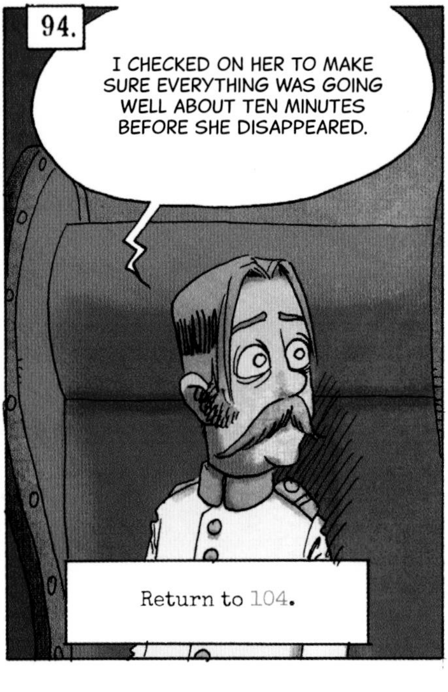
94.
I CHECKED ON HER TO MAKE SURE EVERYTHING WAS GOING WELL ABOUT TEN MINUTES BEFORE SHE DISAPPEARED.
Return to 104.

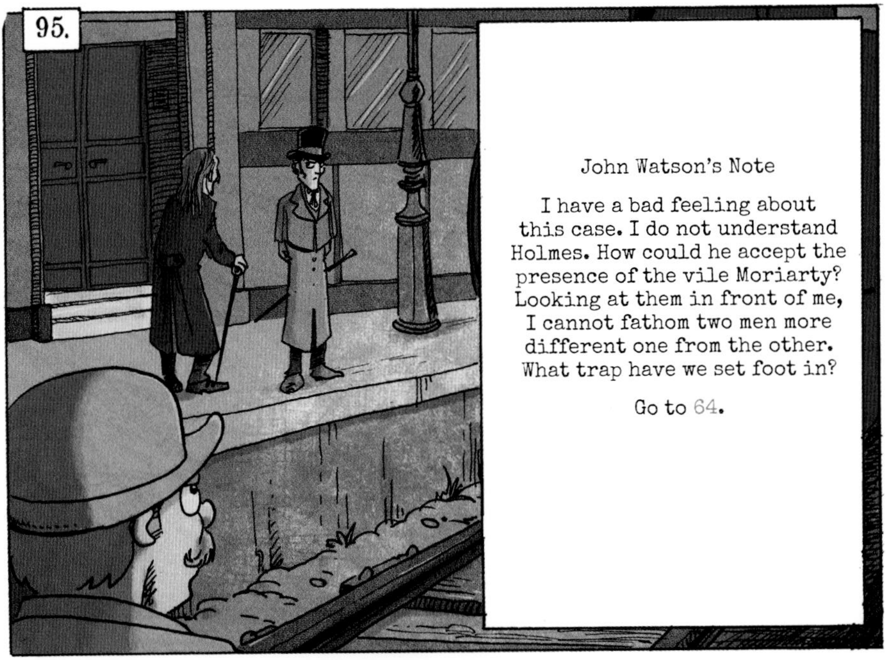
95.
John Watson's Note
I have a bad feeling about this case. I do not understand Holmes. How could he accept the presence of the vile Moriarty? Looking at them in front of me, I cannot fathom two men more different one from the other. What trap have we set foot in?
Go to 64.

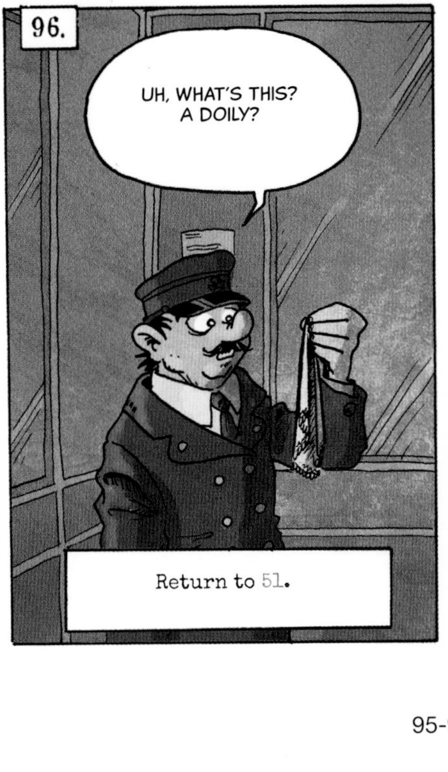
96.
UH, WHAT'S THIS? A DOILY?
Return to 51.

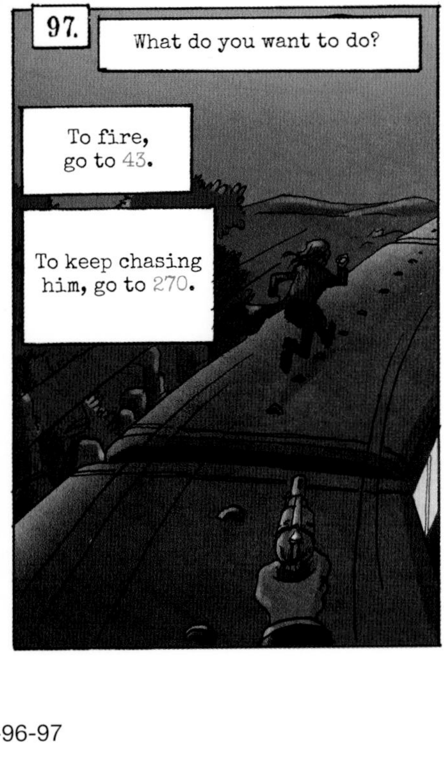
97.
What do you want to do?
To fire, go to 43.
To keep chasing him, go to 270.

98.

YOU CAN STOP ACTING NOW! WE KNOW FOR A FACT THAT IT BELONGS TO YOU!

FINE. I SIMPLY DID NOT WANT TO GET INVOLVED IN ALL OF THIS. IT IS MINE, IT WAS IN MY BAGGAGE. YOU HAVE MY AUTHORIZATION TO SEARCH IT. YOU WILL FIND IT IN THE BAGGAGE CAR.

Note that you are authorized to search Lady De Souza's baggage. Return to 173.

99.

I CAME HERE FROM EASTERN EUROPE. BUT MY COUNTRY IS SO POOR, I HAD TO COME HERE FOR WORK.

Return to 50.

100.

If you know the safe's combination, add up the numbers and head to the matching panel.

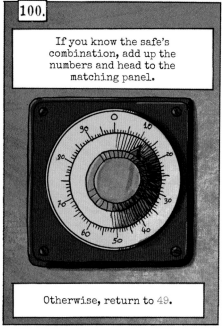

Otherwise, return to 49.

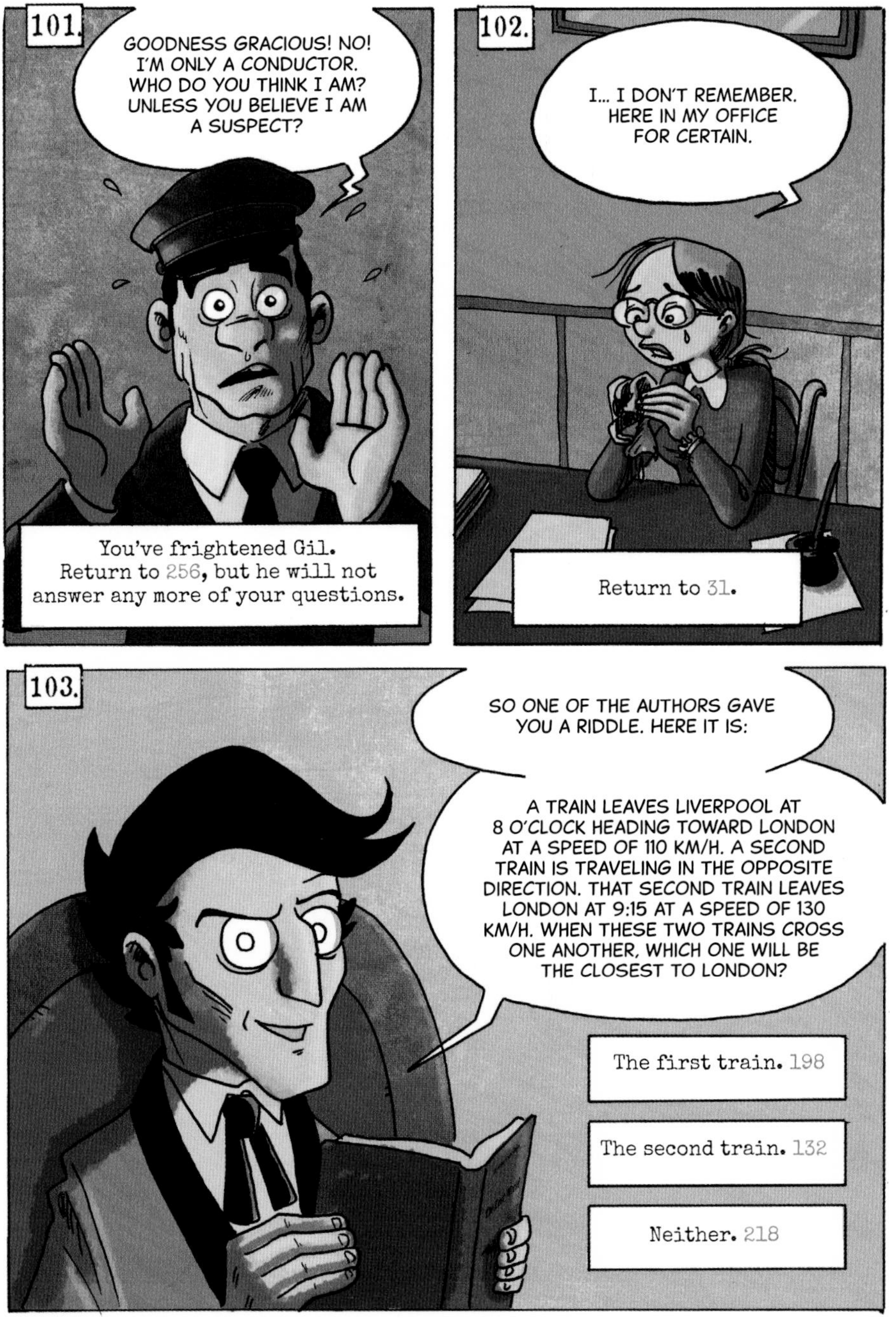
101.
GOODNESS GRACIOUS! NO! I'M ONLY A CONDUCTOR. WHO DO YOU THINK I AM? UNLESS YOU BELIEVE I AM A SUSPECT?
You've frightened Gil. Return to 256, but he will not answer any more of your questions.
102.
I... I DON'T REMEMBER. HERE IN MY OFFICE FOR CERTAIN.
Return to 31.
103.
SO ONE OF THE AUTHORS GAVE YOU A RIDDLE. HERE IT IS:
A TRAIN LEAVES LIVERPOOL AT 8 O'CLOCK HEADING TOWARD LONDON AT A SPEED OF 110 KM/H. A SECOND TRAIN IS TRAVELING IN THE OPPOSITE DIRECTION. THAT SECOND TRAIN LEAVES LONDON AT 9:15 AT A SPEED OF 130 KM/H. WHEN THESE TWO TRAINS CROSS ONE ANOTHER, WHICH ONE WILL BE THE CLOSEST TO LONDON?
The first train. 198
The second train. 132
Neither. 218

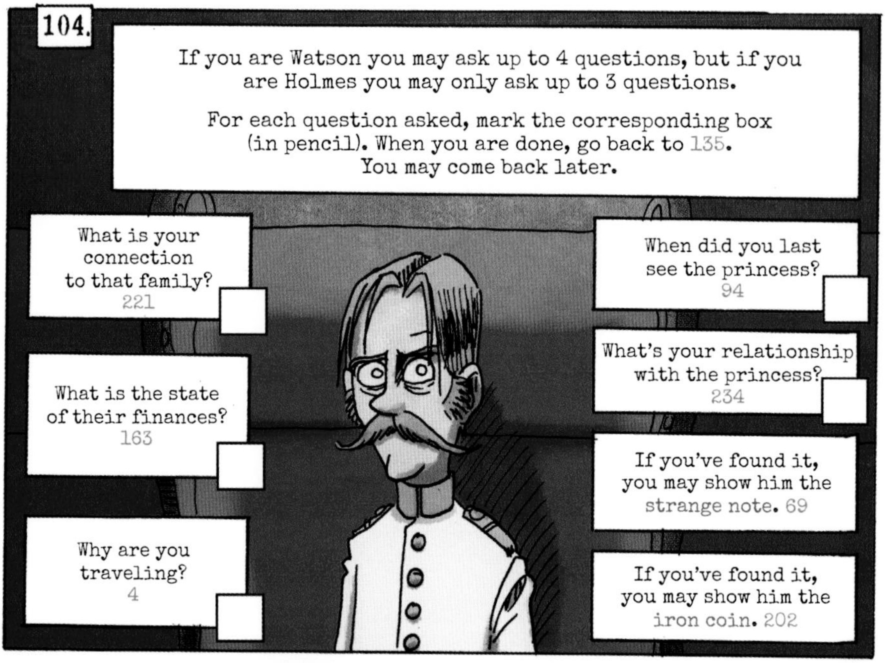
104.
If you are Watson you may ask up to 4 questions, but if you are Holmes you may only ask up to 3 questions.
For each question asked, mark the corresponding box (in pencil). When you are done, go back to 135. You may come back later.
What is your connection to that family? 221
What is the state of their finances? 163
Why are you traveling? 4
When did you last see the princess? 94
What's your relationship with the princess? 234
If you've found it, you may show him the strange note. 69
If you've found it, you may show him the iron coin. 202

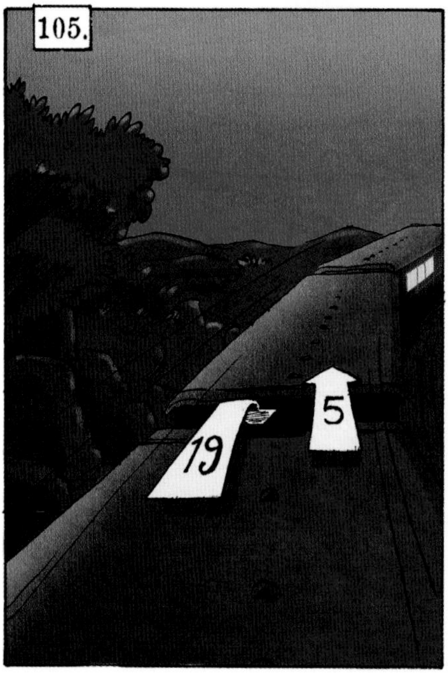
105.
19
5

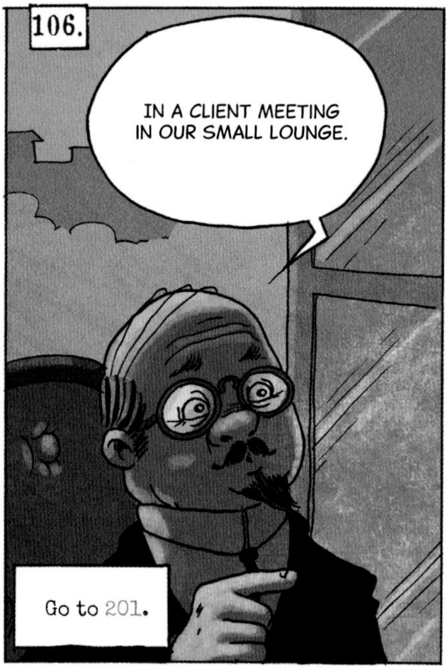
106.
IN A CLIENT MEETING IN OUR SMALL LOUNGE.
Go to 201.

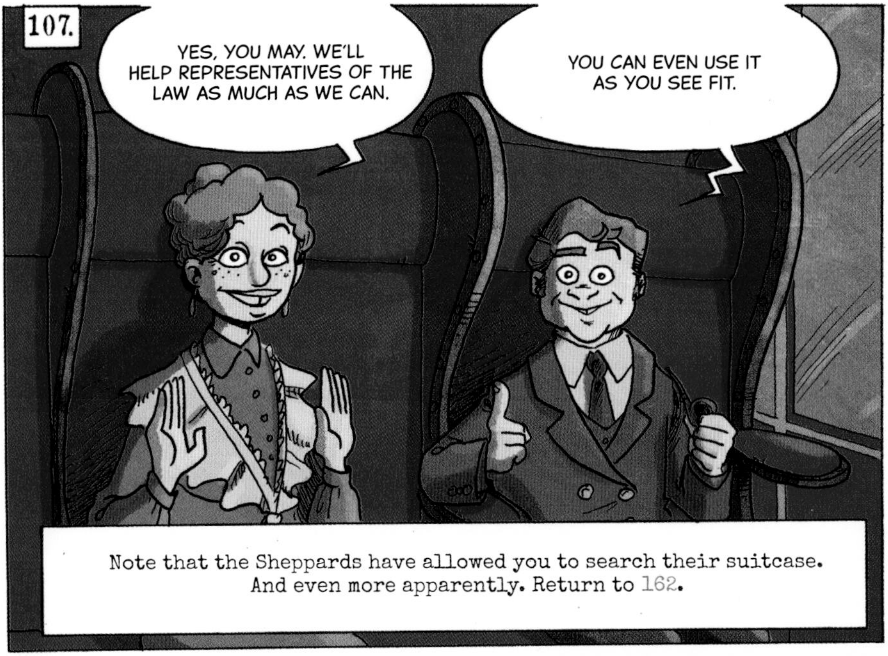
107.
YES, YOU MAY. WE'LL HELP REPRESENTATIVES OF THE LAW AS MUCH AS WE CAN.
YOU CAN EVEN USE IT AS YOU SEE FIT.
Note that the Sheppards have allowed you to search their suitcase. And even more apparently. Return to 162.

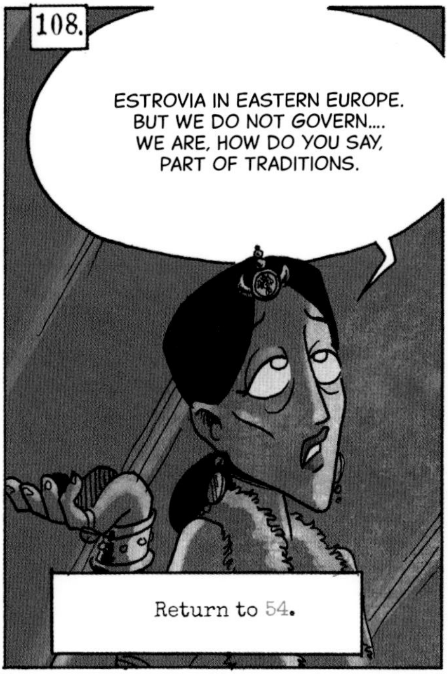
108.
ESTROVIA IN EASTERN EUROPE. BUT WE DO NOT GOVERN.... WE ARE, HOW DO YOU SAY, PART OF TRADITIONS.
Return to 54.

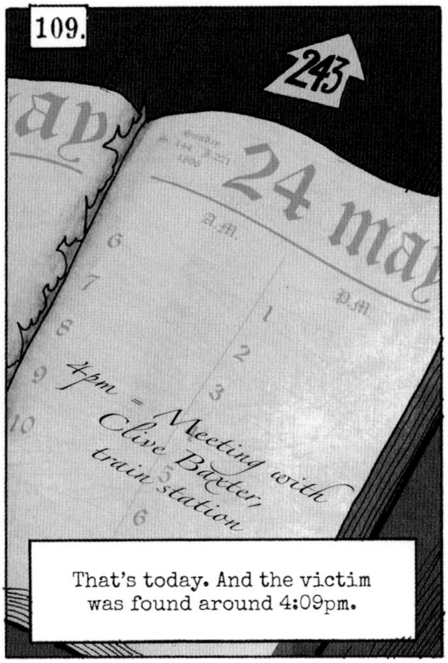
109.
243
24 may
4pm = Meeting with Clive Baxter, train station
That's today. And the victim was found around 4:09pm.

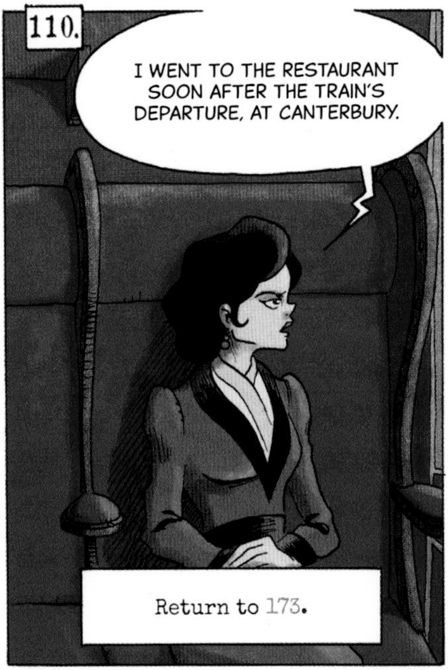
110.
I WENT TO THE RESTAURANT SOON AFTER THE TRAIN'S DEPARTURE, AT CANTERBURY.
Return to 173.

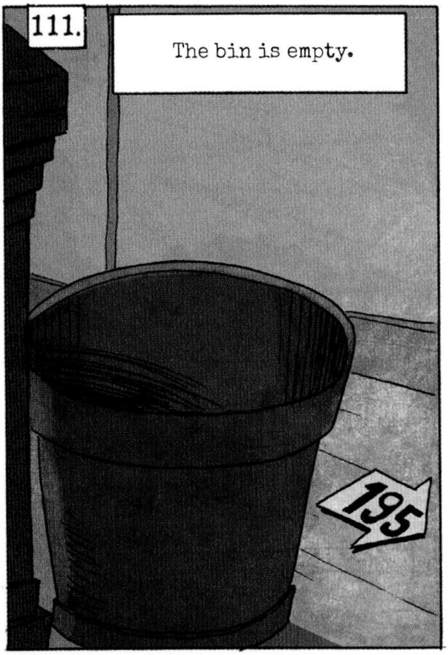
111.
The bin is empty.
195

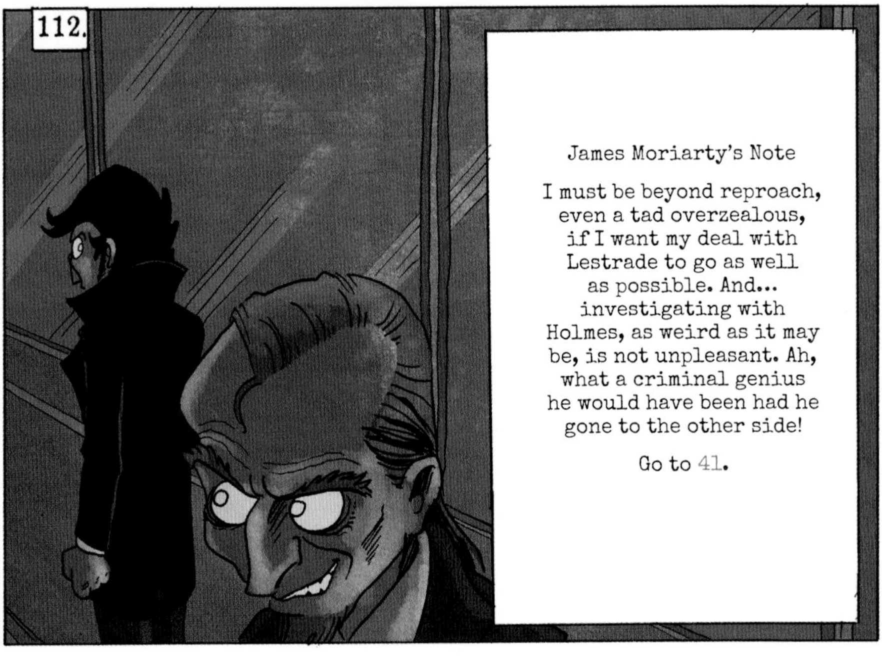
112.
James Moriarty's Note
I must be beyond reproach, even a tad overzealous, if I want my deal with Lestrade to go as well as possible. And... investigating with Holmes, as weird as it may be, is not unpleasant. Ah, what a criminal genius he would have been had he gone to the other side!
Go to 41.

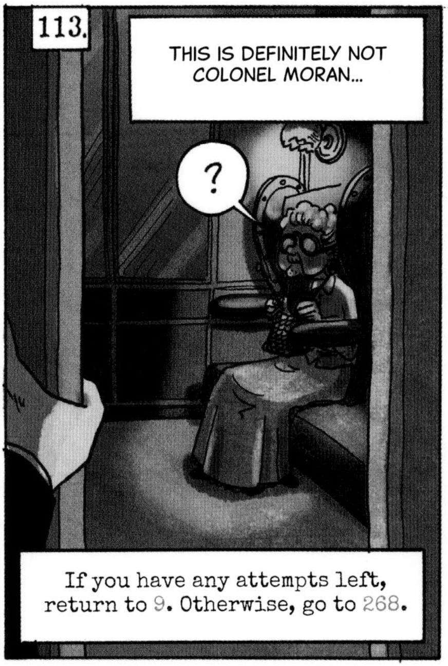
113.
THIS IS DEFINITELY NOT COLONEL MORAN...
?
If you have any attempts left, return to 9. Otherwise, go to 268.

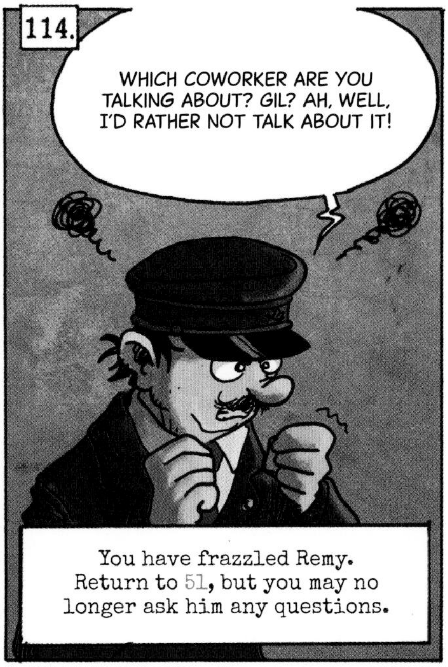
114.
WHICH COWORKER ARE YOU TALKING ABOUT? GIL? AH, WELL, I'D RATHER NOT TALK ABOUT IT!
You have frazzled Remy. Return to 51, but you may no longer ask him any questions.

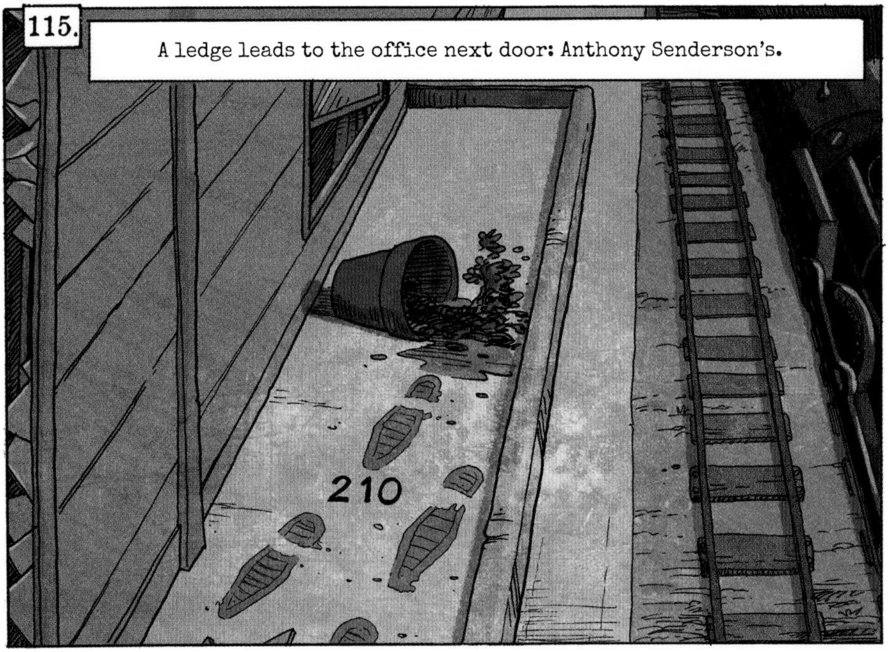
115.
A ledge leads to the office next door: Anthony Senderson's.
210

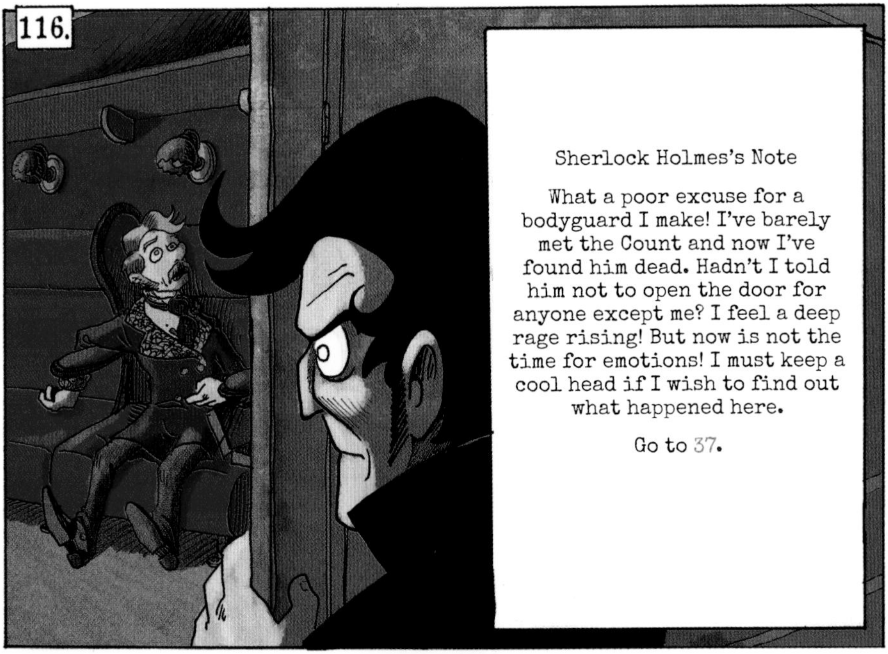
116.
Sherlock Holmes's Note
What a poor excuse for a bodyguard I make! I've barely met the Count and now I've found him dead. Hadn't I told him not to open the door for anyone except me? I feel a deep rage rising! But now is not the time for emotions! I must keep a cool head if I wish to find out what happened here.
Go to 37.

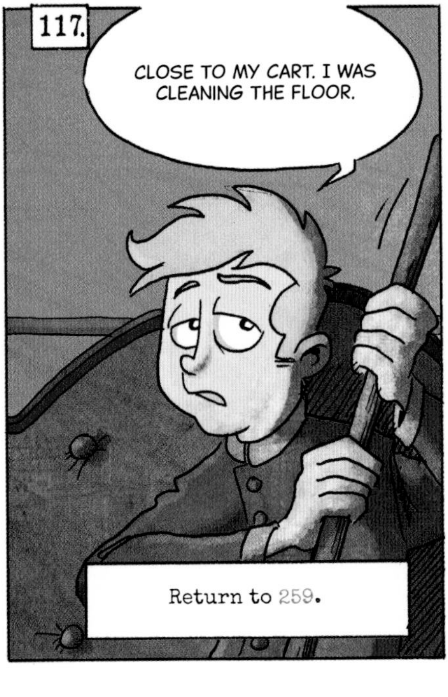
117.
CLOSE TO MY CART. I WAS CLEANING THE FLOOR.
Return to 259.

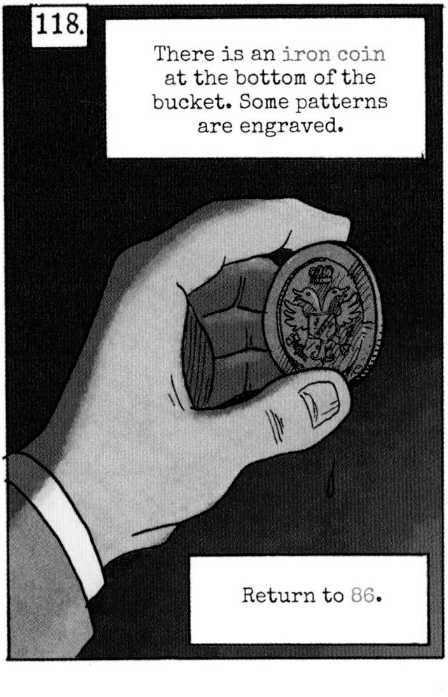
118.
There is an iron coin at the bottom of the bucket. Some patterns are engraved.
Return to 86.

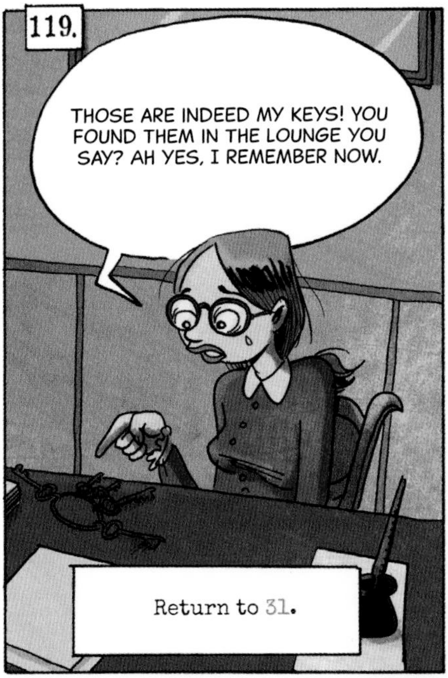
119.
THOSE ARE INDEED MY KEYS! YOU FOUND THEM IN THE LOUNGE YOU SAY? AH YES, I REMEMBER NOW.
Return to 31.

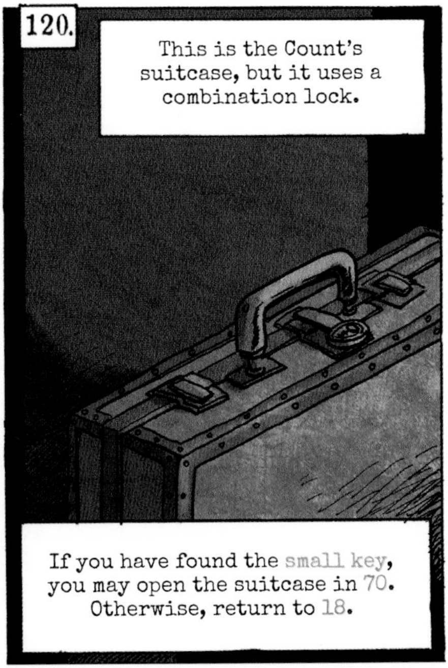
120.
This is the Count's suitcase, but it uses a combination lock.
If you have found the small key, you may open the suitcase in 70. Otherwise, return to 18.

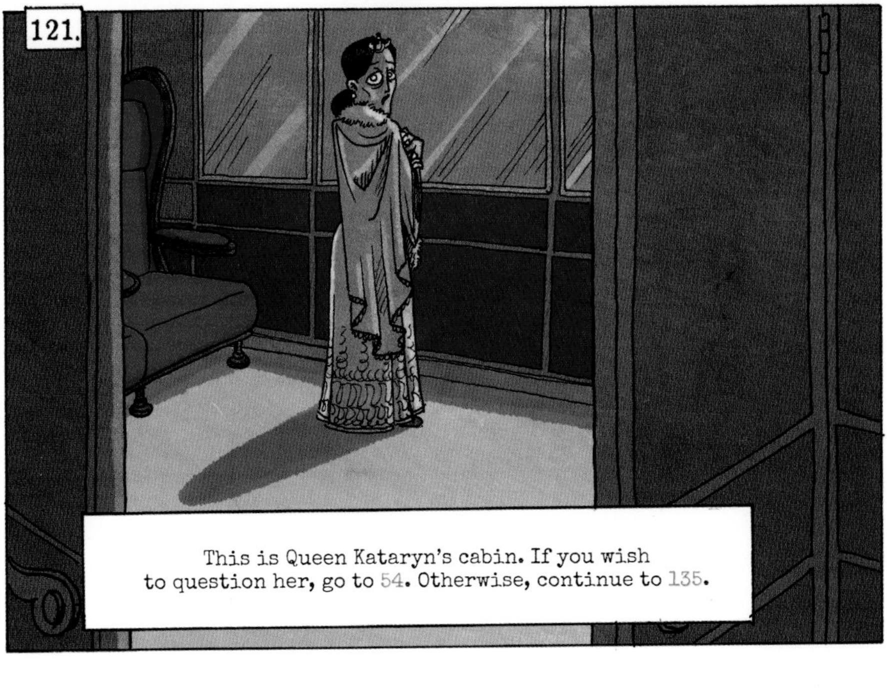
121.
This is Queen Kataryn's cabin. If you wish to question her, go to 54. Otherwise, continue to 135.

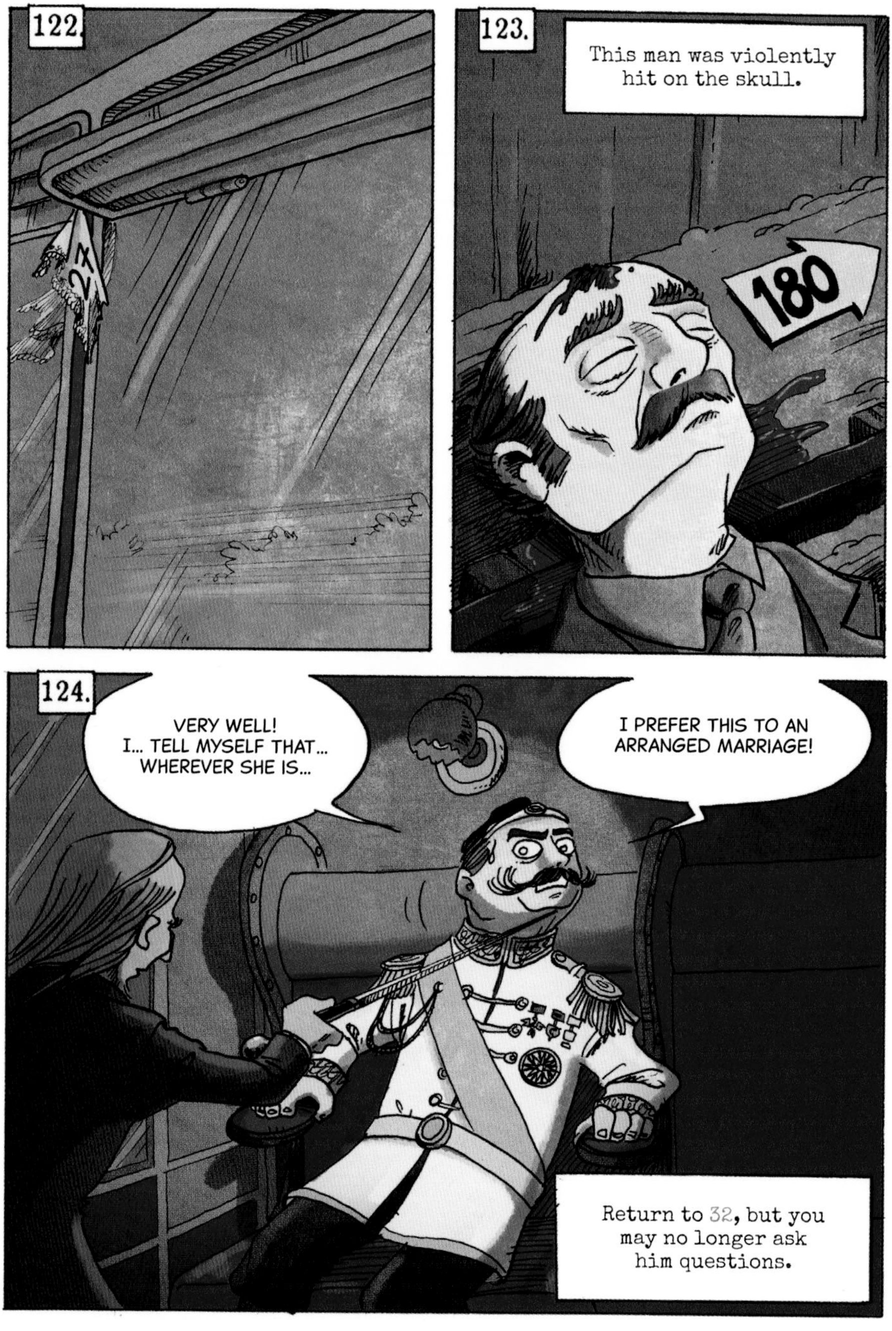
122.
123.
This man was violently hit on the skull.
180
124.
VERY WELL! I... TELL MYSELF THAT... WHEREVER SHE IS...
I PREFER THIS TO AN ARRANGED MARRIAGE!
Return to 32, but you may no longer ask him questions.

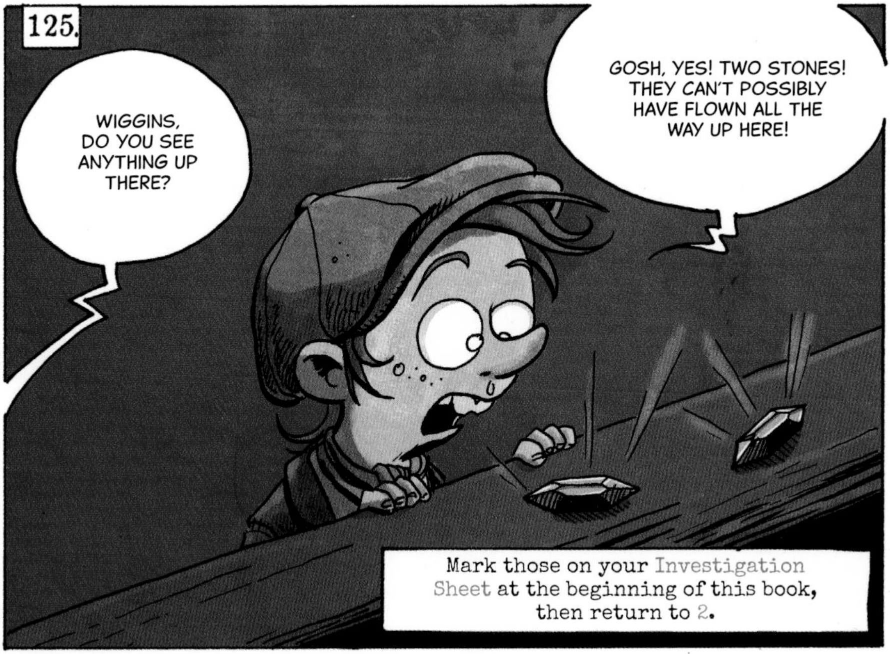
125.
WIGGINS, DO YOU SEE ANYTHING UP THERE?
GOSH, YES! TWO STONES! THEY CAN'T POSSIBLY HAVE FLOWN ALL THE WAY UP HERE!
Mark those on your Investigation Sheet at the beginning of this book, then return to 2.

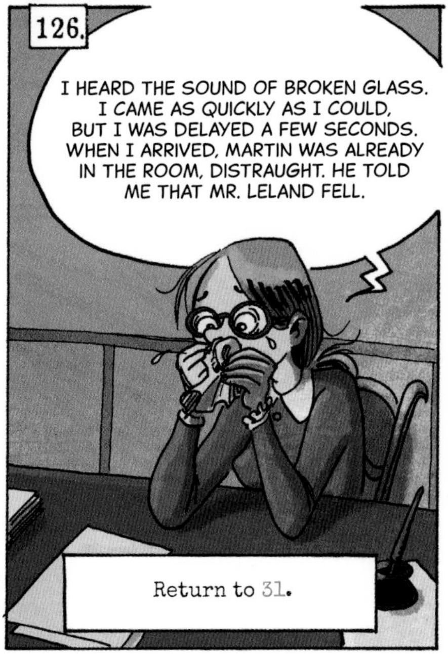
126.
I HEARD THE SOUND OF BROKEN GLASS. I CAME AS QUICKLY AS I COULD, BUT I WAS DELAYED A FEW SECONDS. WHEN I ARRIVED, MARTIN WAS ALREADY IN THE ROOM, DISTRAUGHT. HE TOLD ME THAT MR. LELAND FELL.
Return to 31.

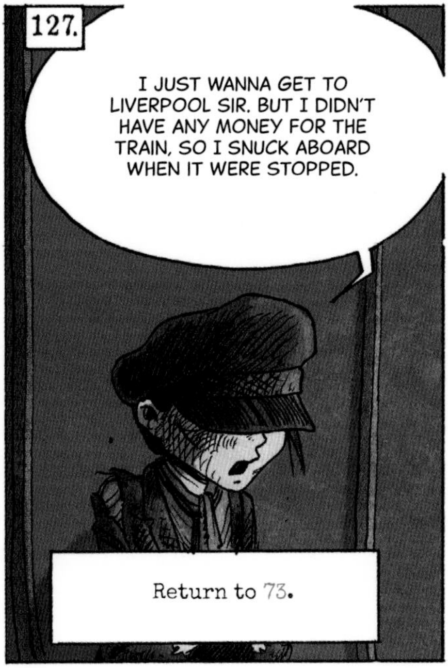
127.
I JUST WANNA GET TO LIVERPOOL SIR. BUT I DIDN'T HAVE ANY MONEY FOR THE TRAIN, SO I SNUCK ABOARD WHEN IT WERE STOPPED.
Return to 73.

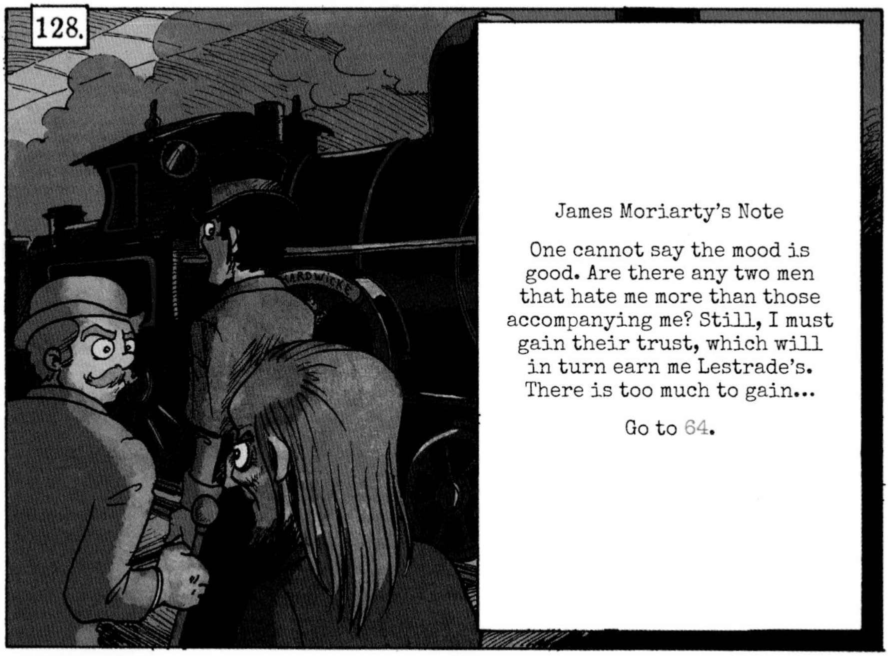
128.
James Moriarty's Note
One cannot say the mood is good. Are there any two men that hate me more than those accompanying me? Still, I must gain their trust, which will in turn earn me Lestrade's. There is too much to gain...
Go to 64.

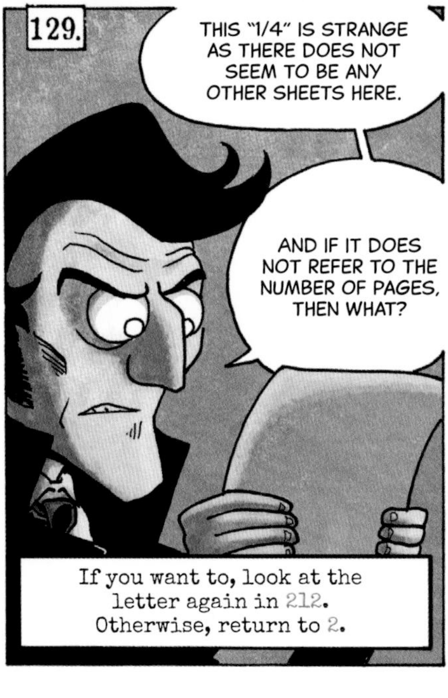
129.
THIS "1/4" IS STRANGE AS THERE DOES NOT SEEM TO BE ANY OTHER SHEETS HERE.
AND IF IT DOES NOT REFER TO THE NUMBER OF PAGES, THEN WHAT?
If you want to, look at the letter again in 212. Otherwise, return to 2.

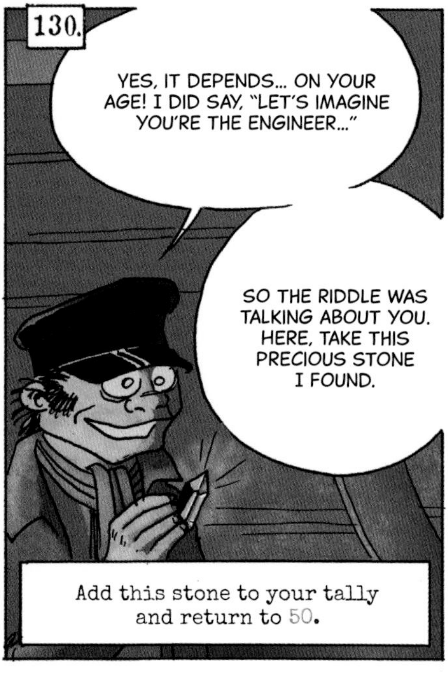
130.
YES, IT DEPENDS... ON YOUR AGE! I DID SAY, "LET'S IMAGINE YOU'RE THE ENGINEER..."
SO THE RIDDLE WAS TALKING ABOUT YOU. HERE, TAKE THIS PRECIOUS STONE I FOUND.
Add this stone to your tally and return to 50.

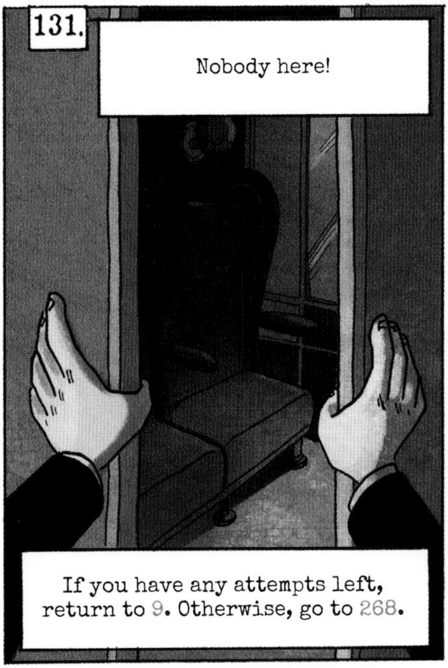
131.
Nobody here!
If you have any attempts left, return to 9. Otherwise, go to 268.

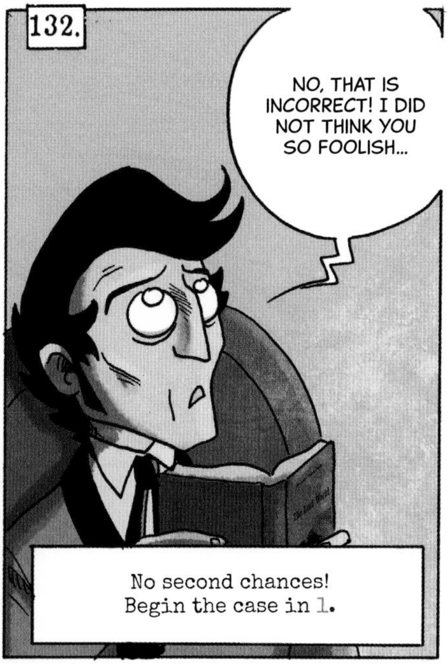
132.
NO, THAT IS INCORRECT! I DID NOT THINK YOU SO FOOLISH...
No second chances! Begin the case in 1.

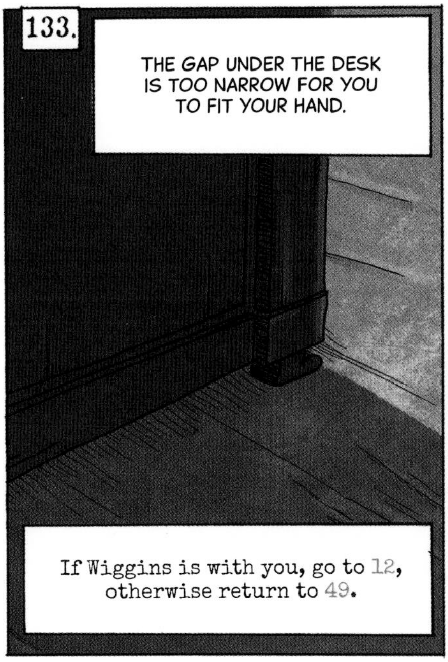
133.
THE GAP UNDER THE DESK IS TOO NARROW FOR YOU TO FIT YOUR HAND.
If Wiggins is with you, go to 12, otherwise return to 49.

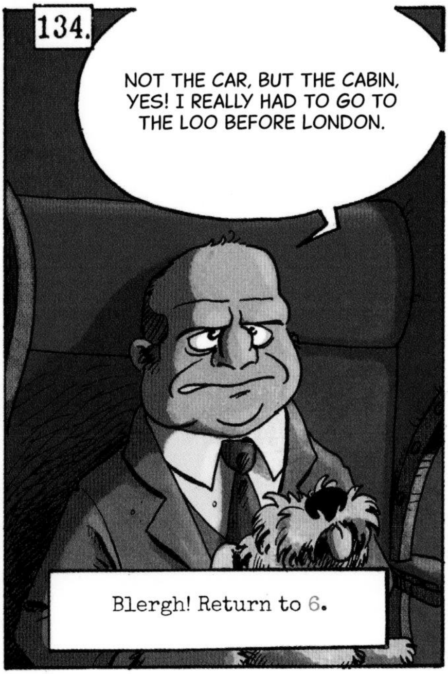
134.
NOT THE CAR, BUT THE CABIN, YES! I REALLY HAD TO GO TO THE LOO BEFORE LONDON.
Blergh! Return to 6.

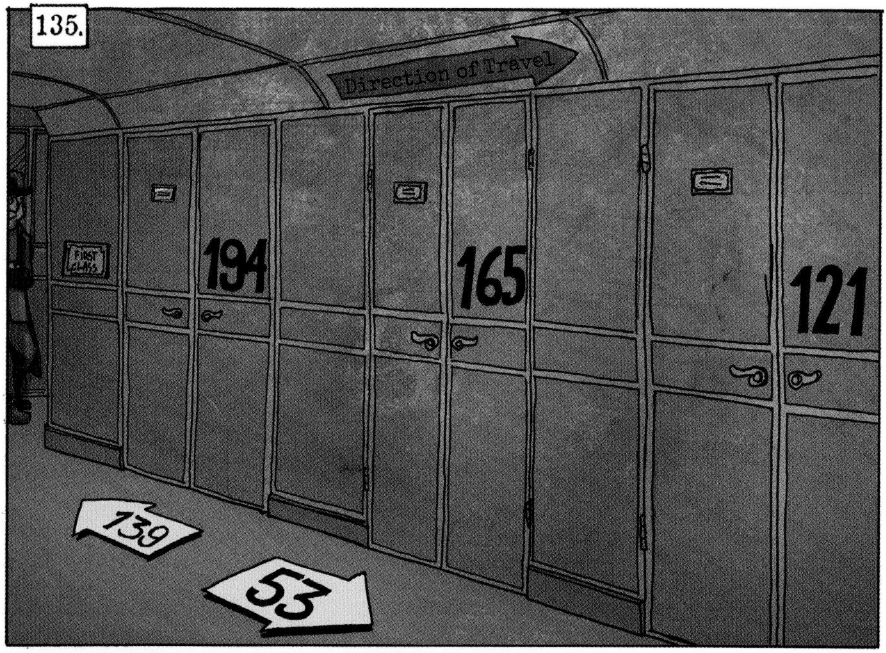
135.
Direction of Travel
194
165
121
FIRST CLASS
139
53

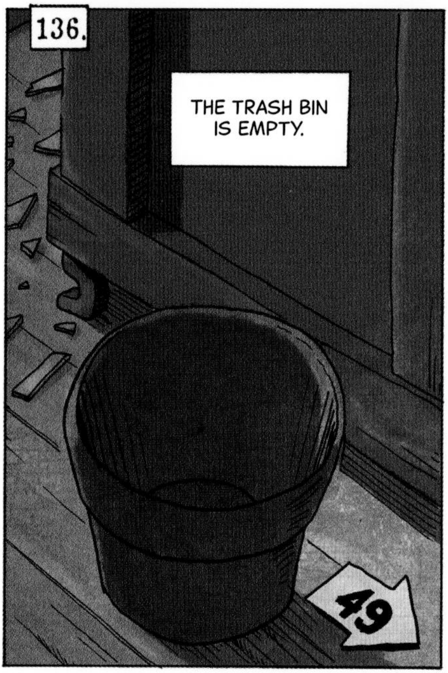
136.
THE TRASH BIN IS EMPTY.
49

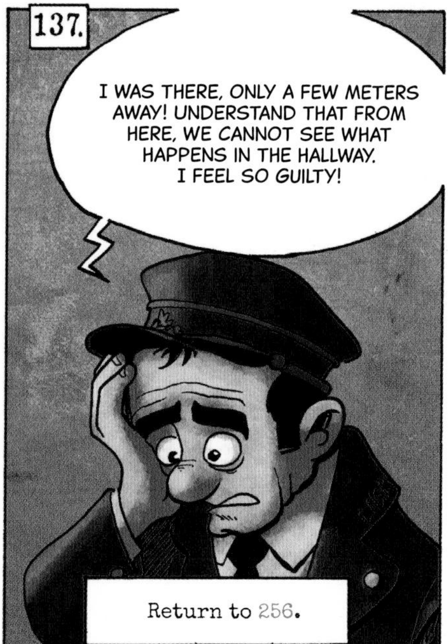
137.
I WAS THERE, ONLY A FEW METERS AWAY! UNDERSTAND THAT FROM HERE, WE CANNOT SEE WHAT HAPPENS IN THE HALLWAY. I FEEL SO GUILTY!
Return to 256.

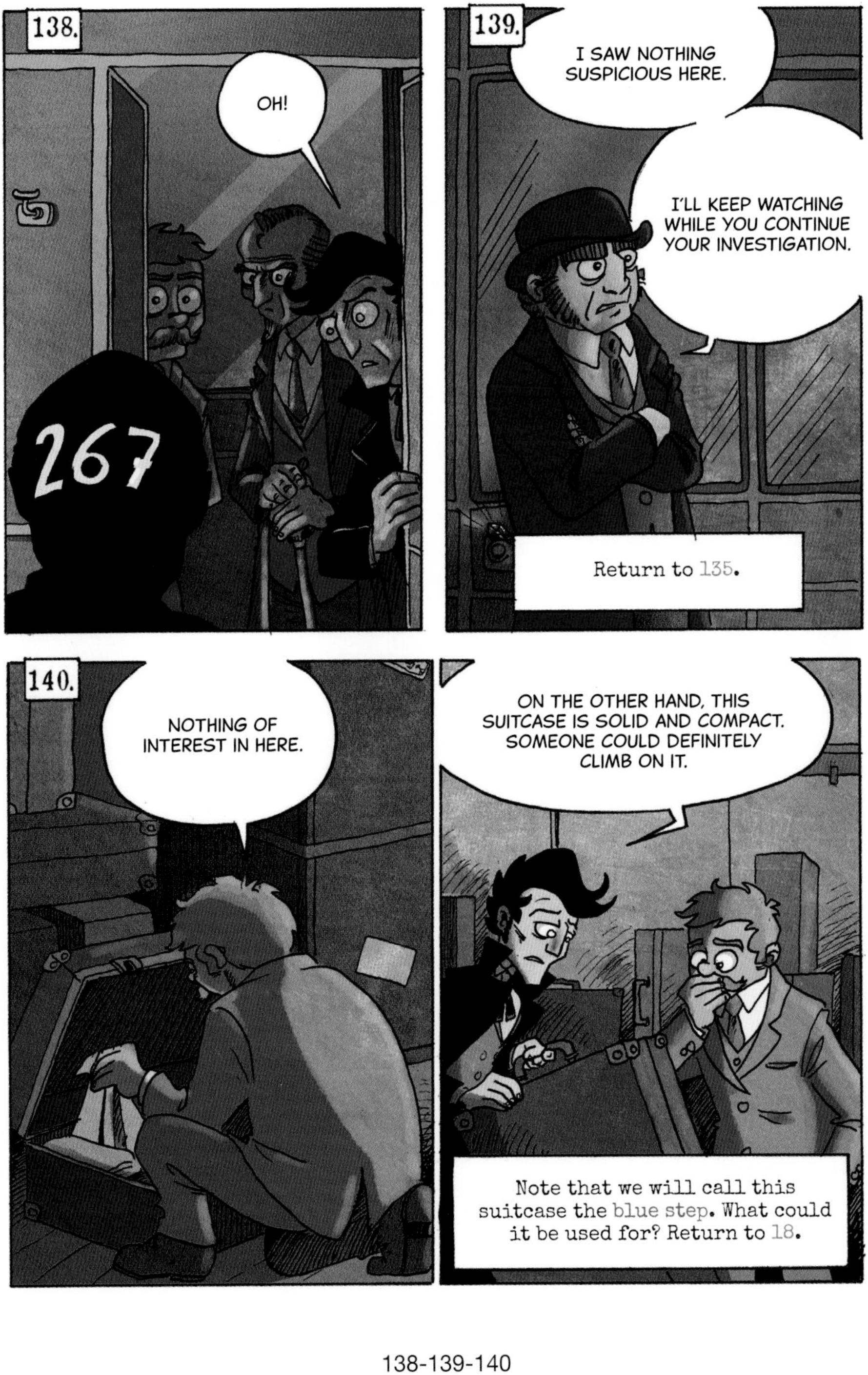
138.
OH!
267
139.
I SAW NOTHING SUSPICIOUS HERE.
I'LL KEEP WATCHING WHILE YOU CONTINUE YOUR INVESTIGATION.
Return to 135.
140.
NOTHING OF INTEREST IN HERE.
ON THE OTHER HAND, THIS SUITCASE IS SOLID AND COMPACT. SOMEONE COULD DEFINITELY CLIMB ON IT.
Note that we will call this suitcase the blue step. What could it be used for? Return to 18.

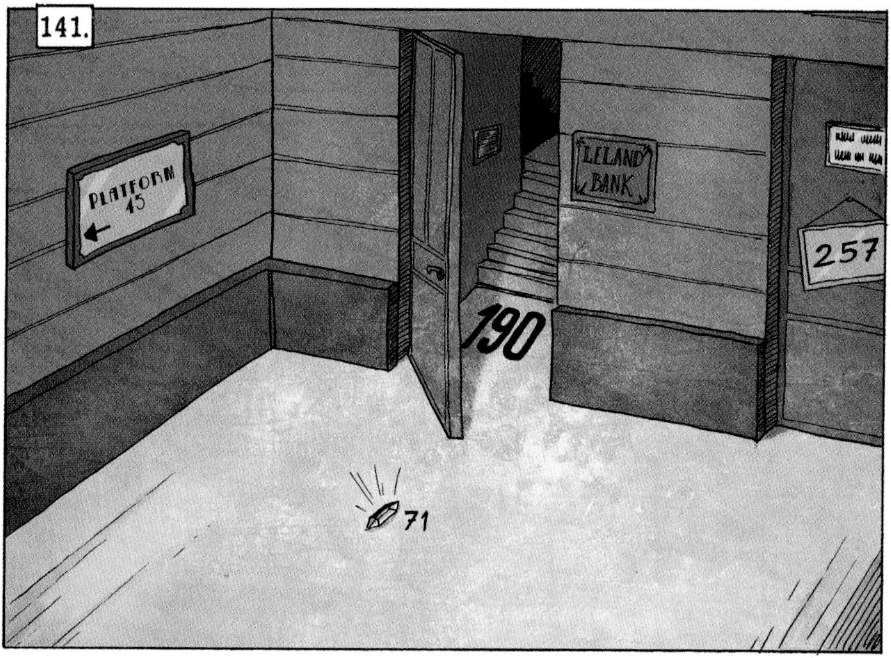
141.
PLATFORM 45
LELAND BANK
257
190
71

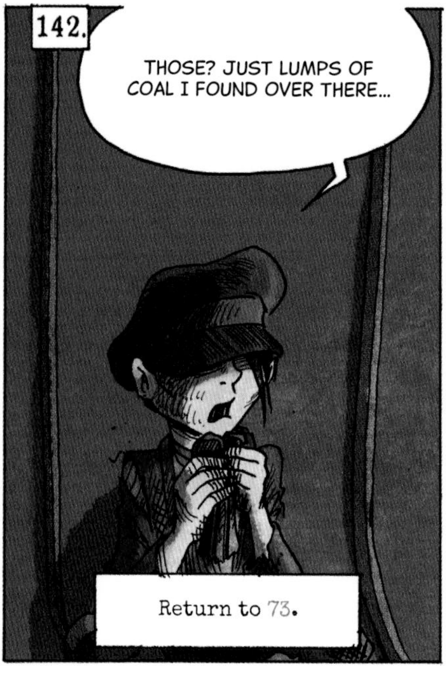
142.
THOSE? JUST LUMPS OF COAL I FOUND OVER THERE...
Return to 73.

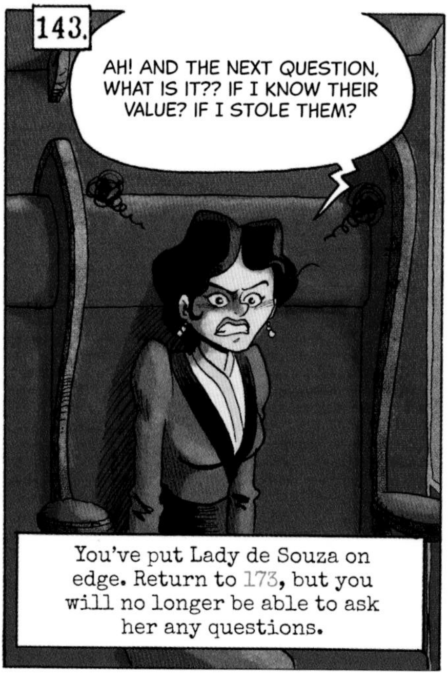
143.
AH! AND THE NEXT QUESTION, WHAT IS IT?? IF I KNOW THEIR VALUE? IF I STOLE THEM?
You've put Lady de Souza on edge. Return to 173, but you will no longer be able to ask her any questions.

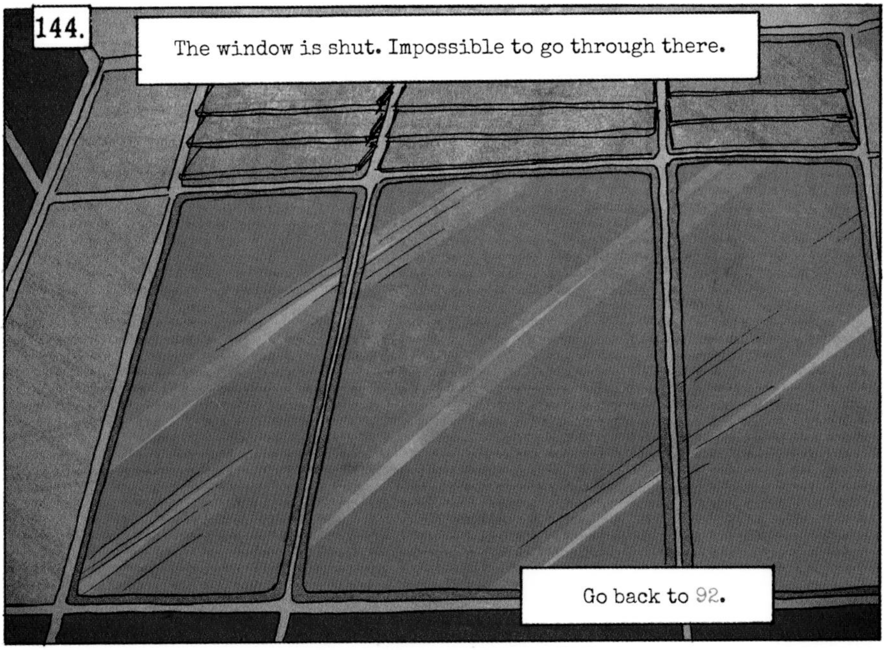
144.
The window is shut. Impossible to go through there.
Go back to 92.

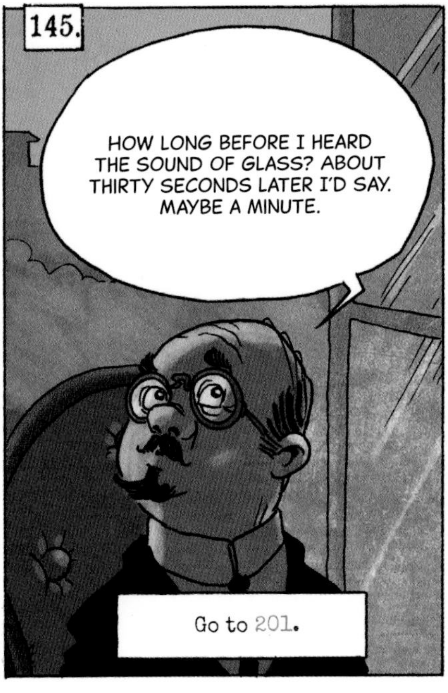
145.
HOW LONG BEFORE I HEARD THE SOUND OF GLASS? ABOUT THIRTY SECONDS LATER I'D SAY. MAYBE A MINUTE.
Go to 201.

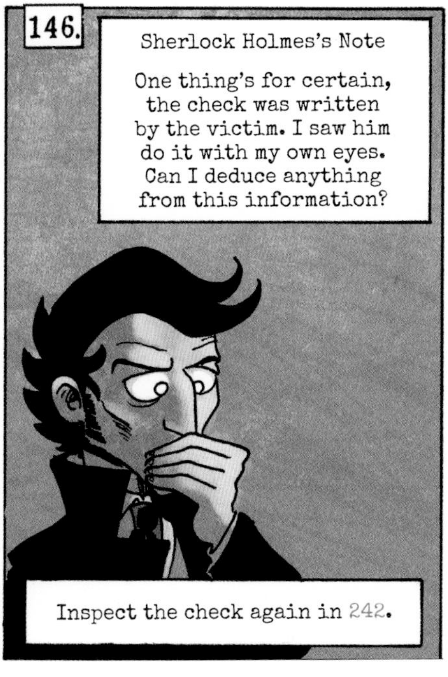
146.
Sherlock Holmes's Note
One thing's for certain, the check was written by the victim. I saw him do it with my own eyes. Can I deduce anything from this information?
Inspect the check again in 242.

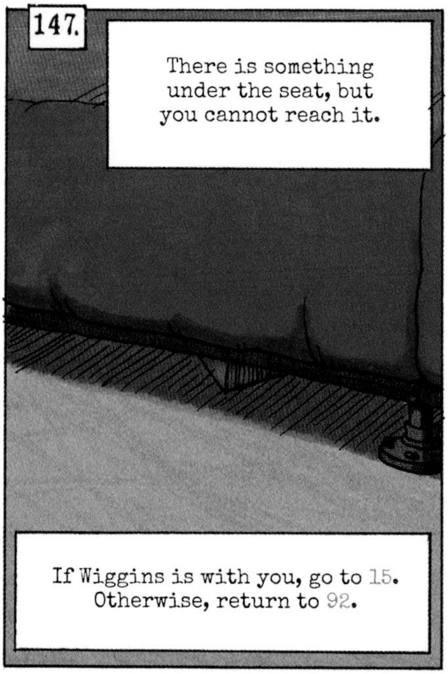
147.
There is something under the seat, but you cannot reach it.
If Wiggins is with you, go to 15. Otherwise, return to 92.

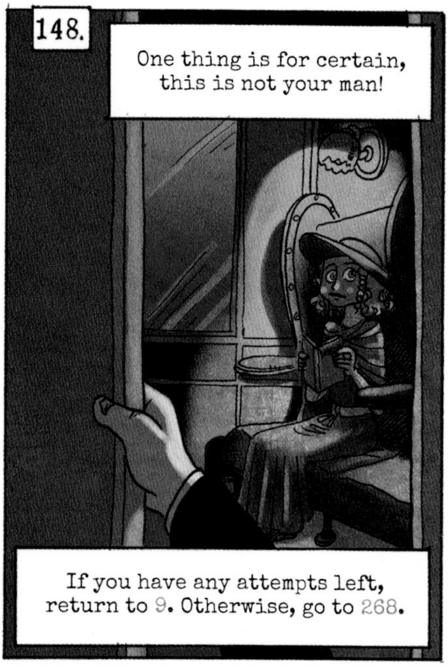
148.
One thing is for certain, this is not your man!
If you have any attempts left, return to 9. Otherwise, go to 268.

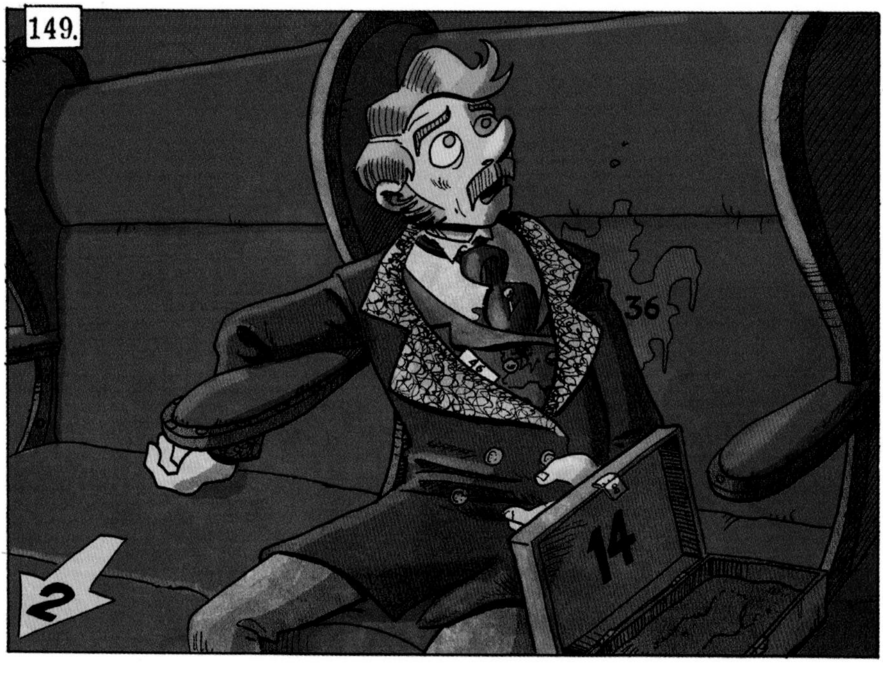
149.
36
14
2

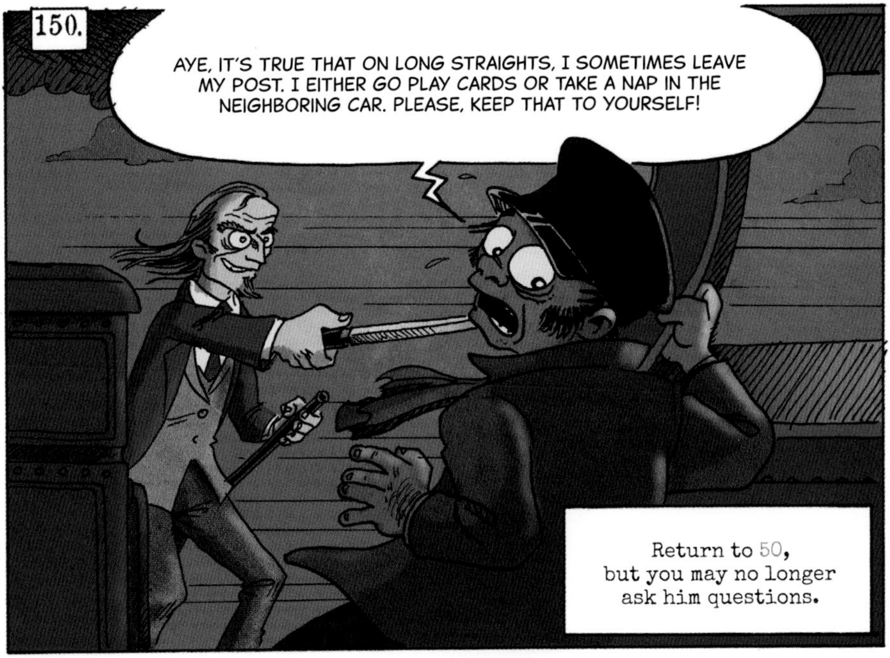
150.
AYE, IT'S TRUE THAT ON LONG STRAIGHTS, I SOMETIMES LEAVE MY POST. I EITHER GO PLAY CARDS OR TAKE A NAP IN THE NEIGHBORING CAR. PLEASE, KEEP THAT TO YOURSELF!
Return to 50, but you may no longer ask him questions.

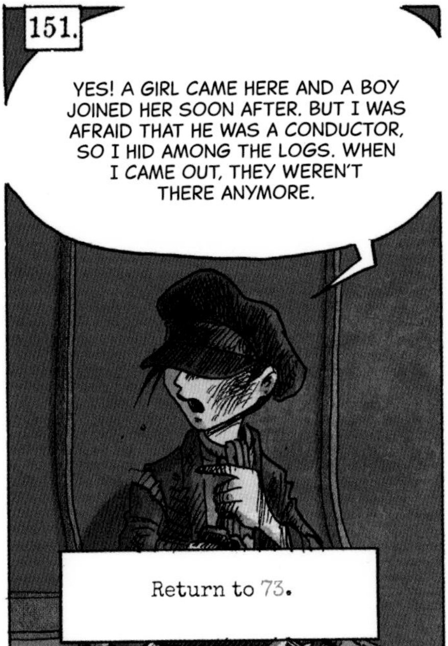
151.
YES! A GIRL CAME HERE AND A BOY JOINED HER SOON AFTER. BUT I WAS AFRAID THAT HE WAS A CONDUCTOR, SO I HID AMONG THE LOGS. WHEN I CAME OUT, THEY WEREN'T THERE ANYMORE.
Return to 73.

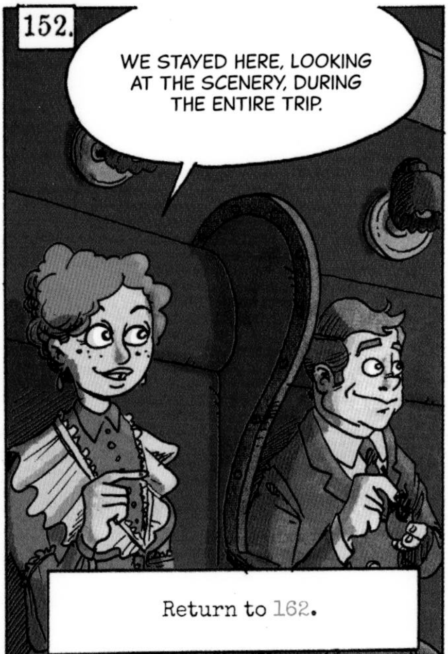
152.
WE STAYED HERE, LOOKING AT THE SCENERY, DURING THE ENTIRE TRIP.
Return to 162.

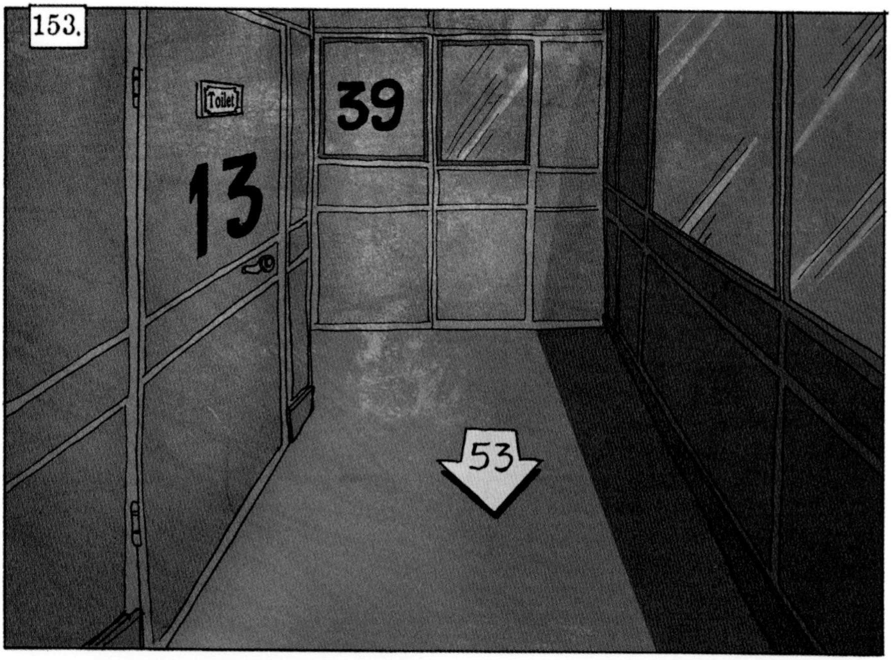
153.
Toilet
13
39
53

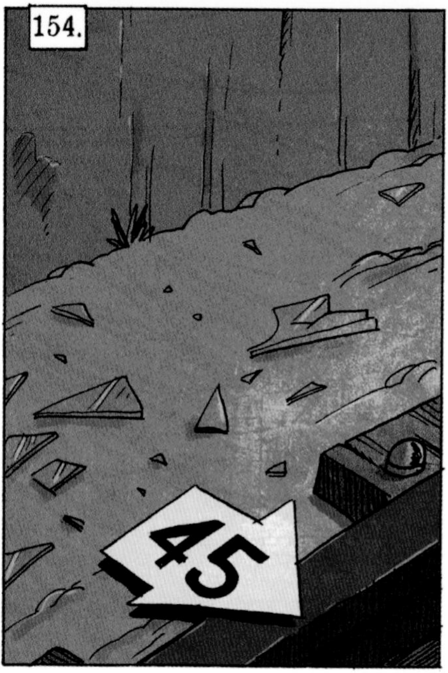
154.
45

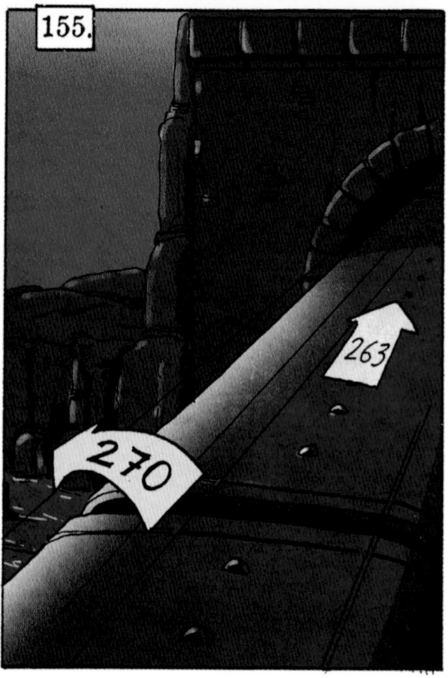
155.
263
270

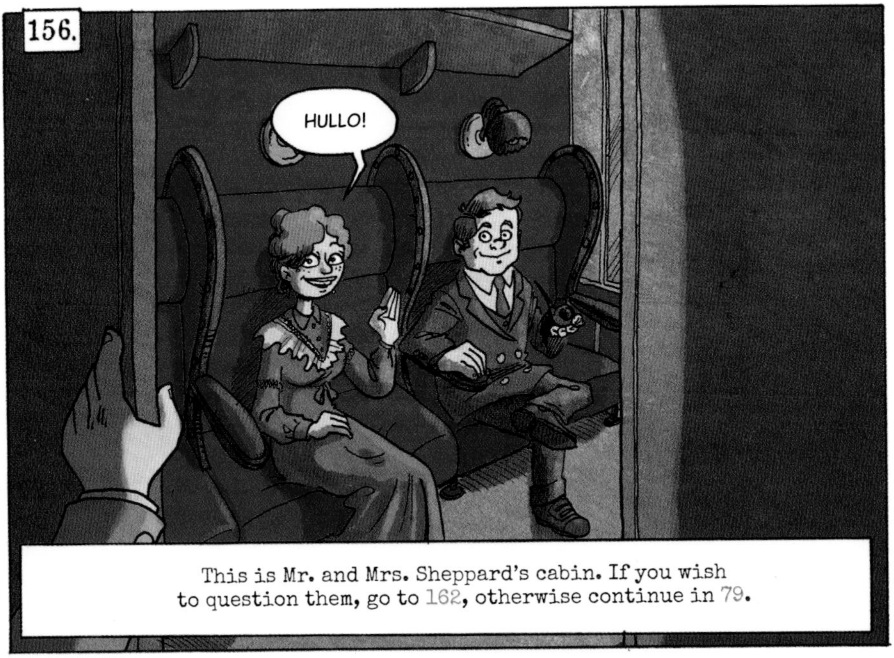
156.
HULLO!
This is Mr. and Mrs. Sheppard's cabin. If you wish to question them, go to 162, otherwise continue in 79.

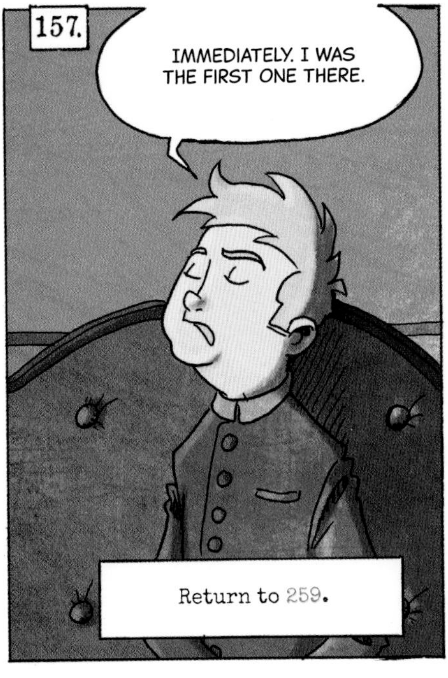
157.
IMMEDIATELY. I WAS THE FIRST ONE THERE.
Return to 259.

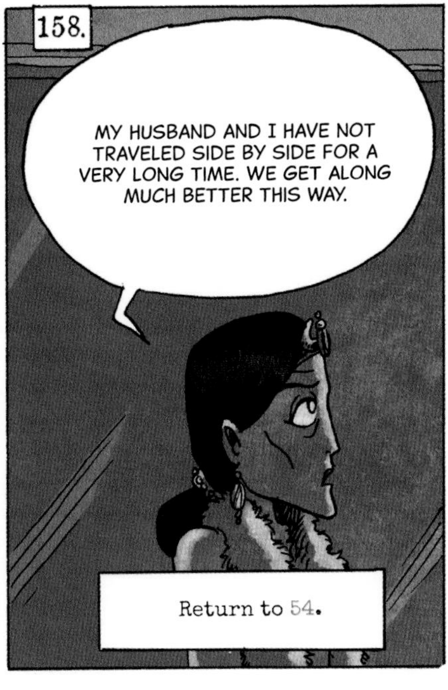
158.
MY HUSBAND AND I HAVE NOT TRAVELED SIDE BY SIDE FOR A VERY LONG TIME. WE GET ALONG MUCH BETTER THIS WAY.
Return to 54.

159.

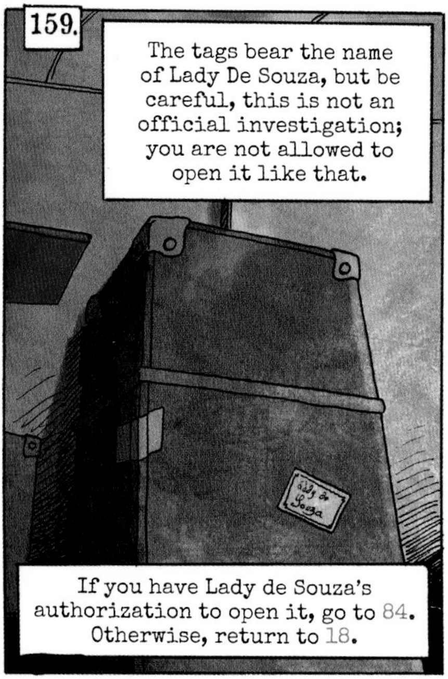
The tags bear the name of Lady De Souza, but be careful, this is not an official investigation; you are not allowed to open it like that.
If you have Lady de Souza's authorization to open it, go to 84. Otherwise, return to 18.

160.

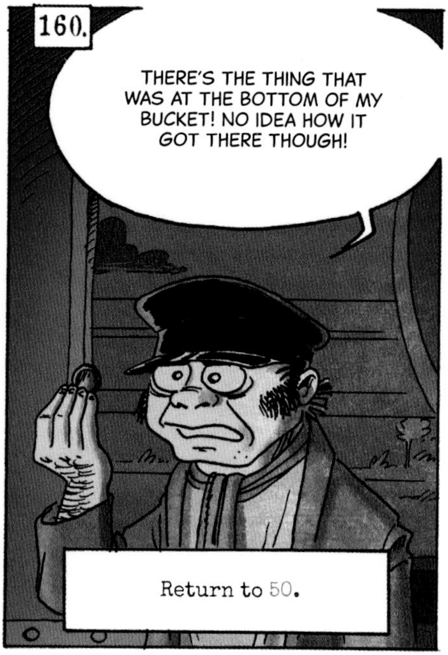
THERE'S THE THING THAT WAS AT THE BOTTOM OF MY BUCKET! NO IDEA HOW IT GOT THERE THOUGH!
Return to 50.

161.

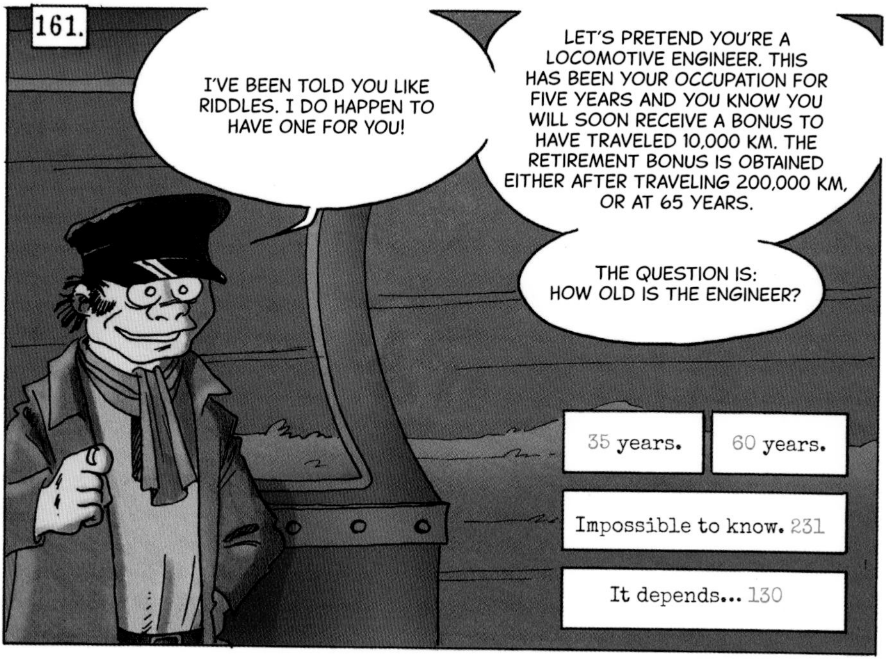
I'VE BEEN TOLD YOU LIKE RIDDLES. I DO HAPPEN TO HAVE ONE FOR YOU!
LET'S PRETEND YOU'RE A LOCOMOTIVE ENGINEER. THIS HAS BEEN YOUR OCCUPATION FOR FIVE YEARS AND YOU KNOW YOU WILL SOON RECEIVE A BONUS TO HAVE TRAVELED 10,000 KM. THE RETIREMENT BONUS IS OBTAINED EITHER AFTER TRAVELING 200,000 KM, OR AT 65 YEARS.
THE QUESTION IS: HOW OLD IS THE ENGINEER?
35 years.
60 years.
Impossible to know. 231
It depends... 130

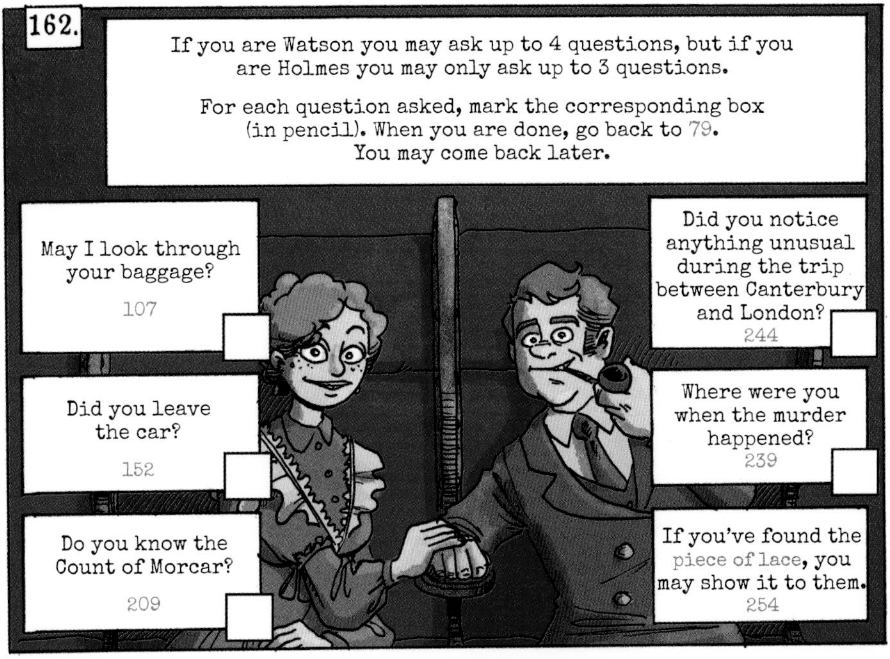
162.
If you are Watson you may ask up to 4 questions, but if you are Holmes you may only ask up to 3 questions.
For each question asked, mark the corresponding box (in pencil). When you are done, go back to 79. You may come back later.
May I look through your baggage? 107
Did you leave the car? 152
Do you know the Count of Morcar? 209
Did you notice anything unusual during the trip between Canterbury and London? 244
Where were you when the murder happened? 239
If you've found the piece of lace, you may show it to them. 254

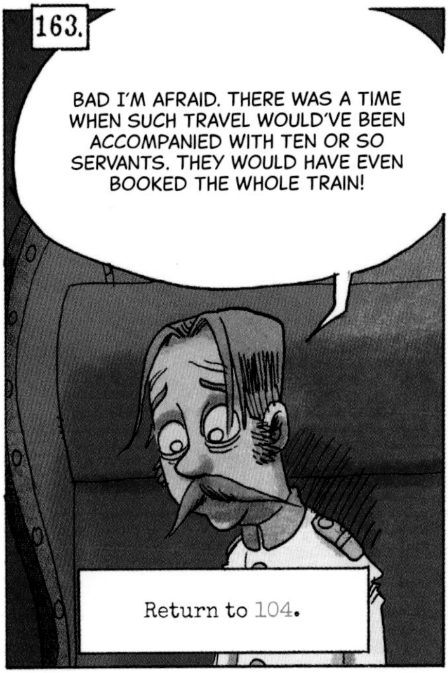
163.
BAD I'M AFRAID. THERE WAS A TIME WHEN SUCH TRAVEL WOULD'VE BEEN ACCOMPANIED WITH TEN OR SO SERVANTS. THEY WOULD HAVE EVEN BOOKED THE WHOLE TRAIN!
Return to 104.

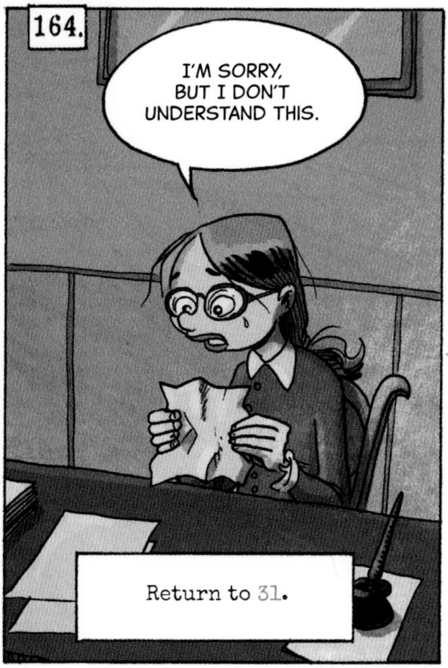
164.
I'M SORRY, BUT I DON'T UNDERSTAND THIS.
Return to 31.

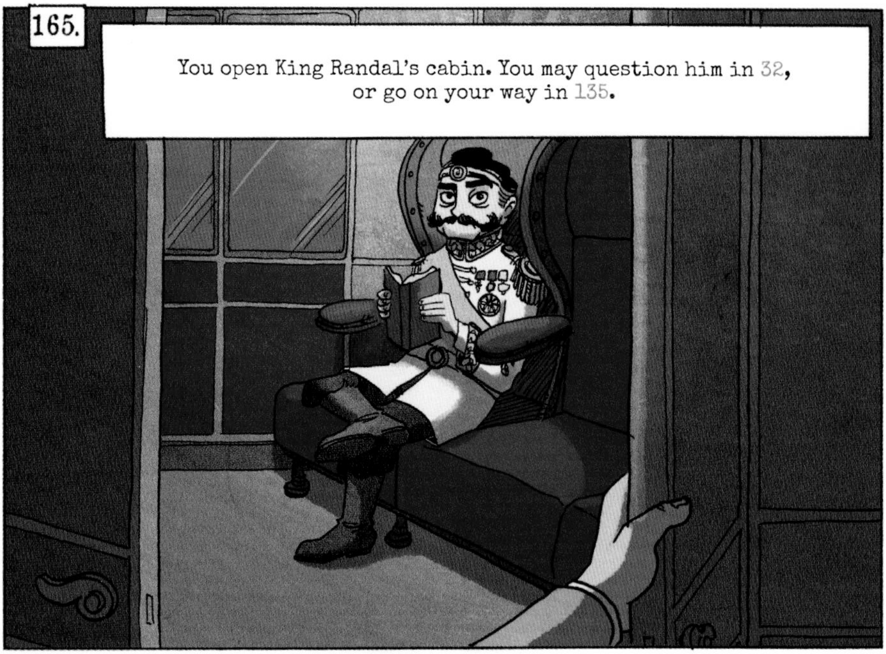
165.
You open King Randal's cabin. You may question him in 32, or go on your way in 135.

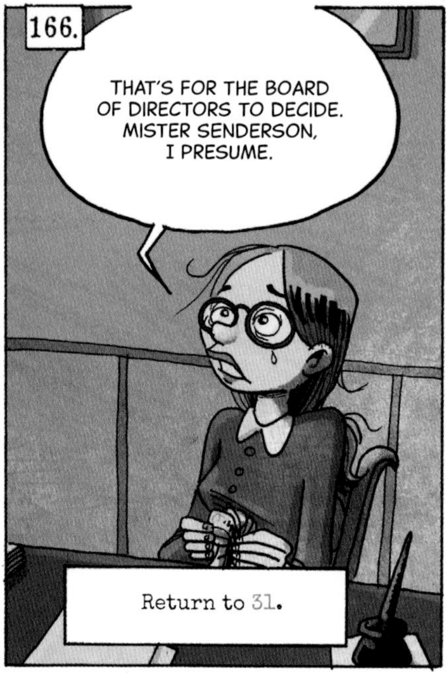
166.
THAT'S FOR THE BOARD OF DIRECTORS TO DECIDE. MISTER SENDERSON, I PRESUME.
Return to 31.

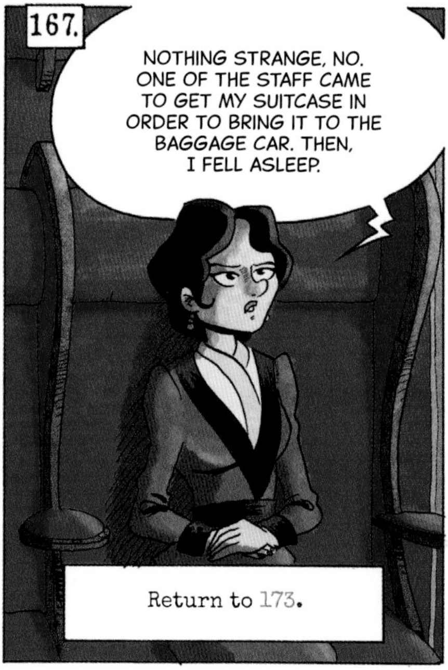
167.
NOTHING STRANGE, NO. ONE OF THE STAFF CAME TO GET MY SUITCASE IN ORDER TO BRING IT TO THE BAGGAGE CAR. THEN, I FELL ASLEEP.
Return to 173.

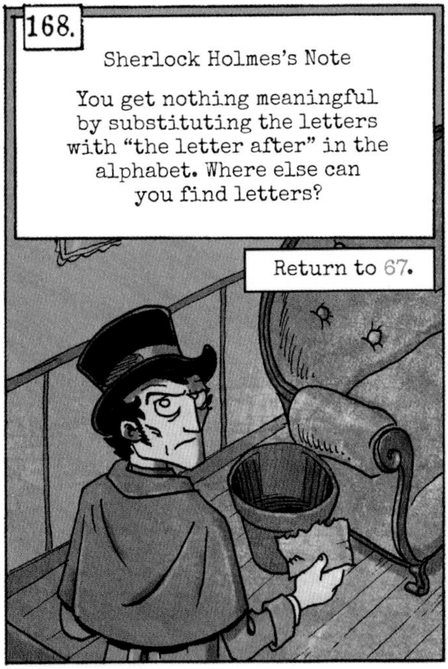
168.
Sherlock Holmes's Note
You get nothing meaningful by substituting the letters with "the letter after" in the alphabet. Where else can you find letters?
Return to 67.

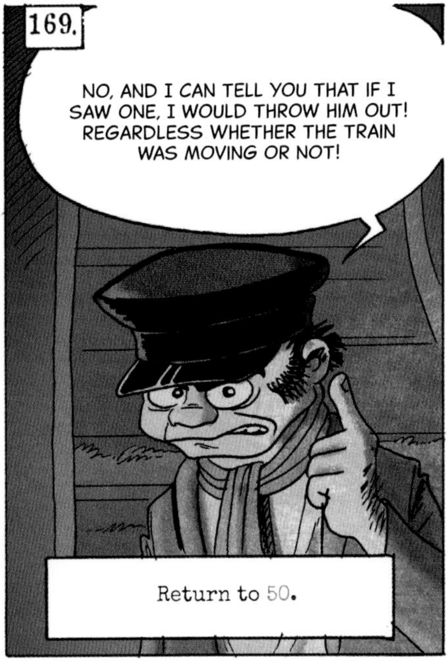
169.
NO, AND I CAN TELL YOU THAT IF I SAW ONE, I WOULD THROW HIM OUT! REGARDLESS WHETHER THE TRAIN WAS MOVING OR NOT!
Return to 50.

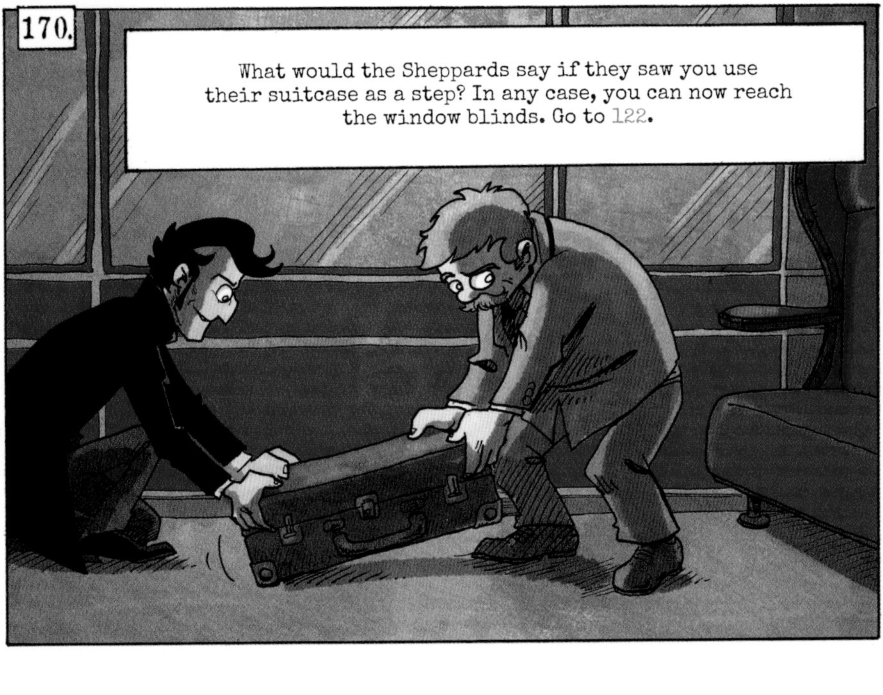
170.
What would the Sheppards say if they saw you use their suitcase as a step? In any case, you can now reach the window blinds. Go to 122.

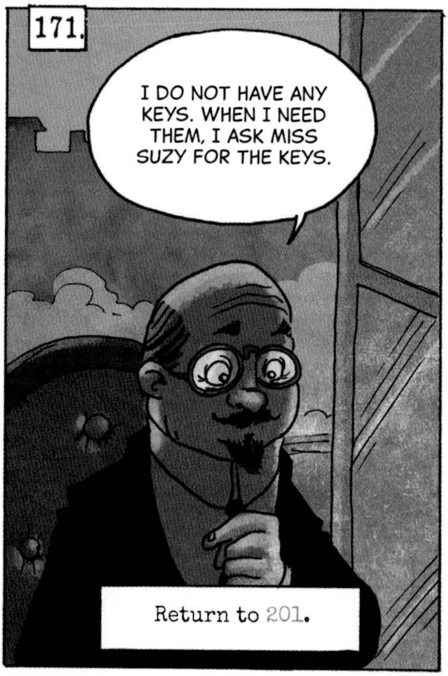
171.
I DO NOT HAVE ANY KEYS. WHEN I NEED THEM, I ASK MISS SUZY FOR THE KEYS.
Return to 201.

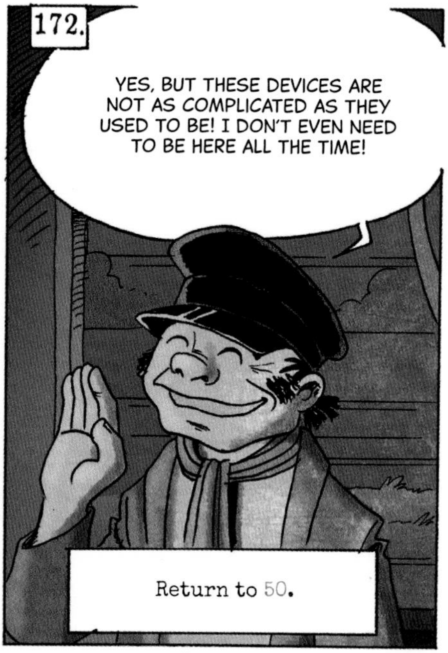
172.
YES, BUT THESE DEVICES ARE NOT AS COMPLICATED AS THEY USED TO BE! I DON'T EVEN NEED TO BE HERE ALL THE TIME!
Return to 50.

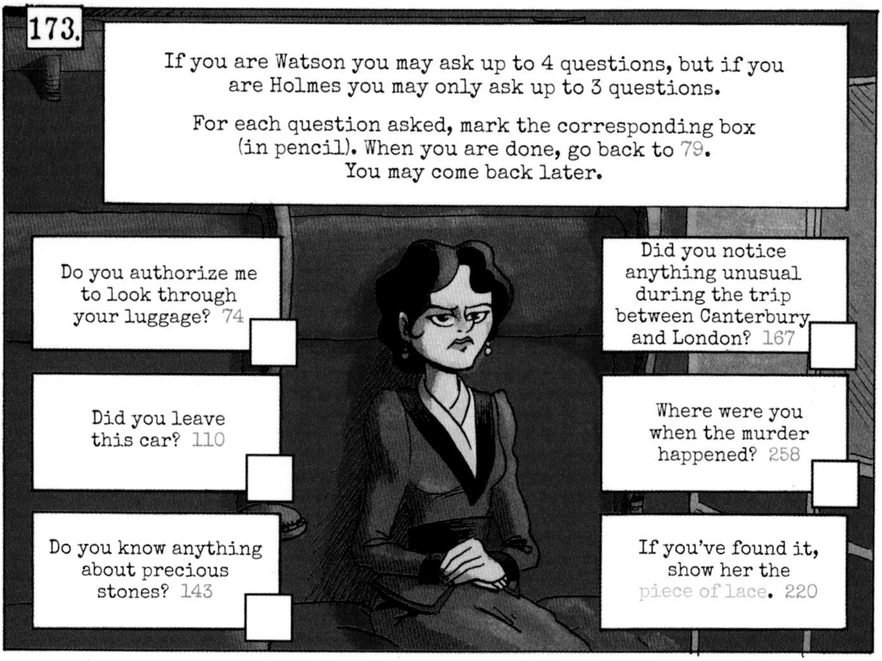
173.
If you are Watson you may ask up to 4 questions, but if you are Holmes you may only ask up to 3 questions.
For each question asked, mark the corresponding box (in pencil). When you are done, go back to 79. You may come back later.
Do you authorize me to look through your luggage? 74
Did you notice anything unusual during the trip between Canterbury and London? 167
Did you leave this car? 110
Where were you when the murder happened? 258
Do you know anything about precious stones? 143
If you've found it, show her the piece of lace. 220

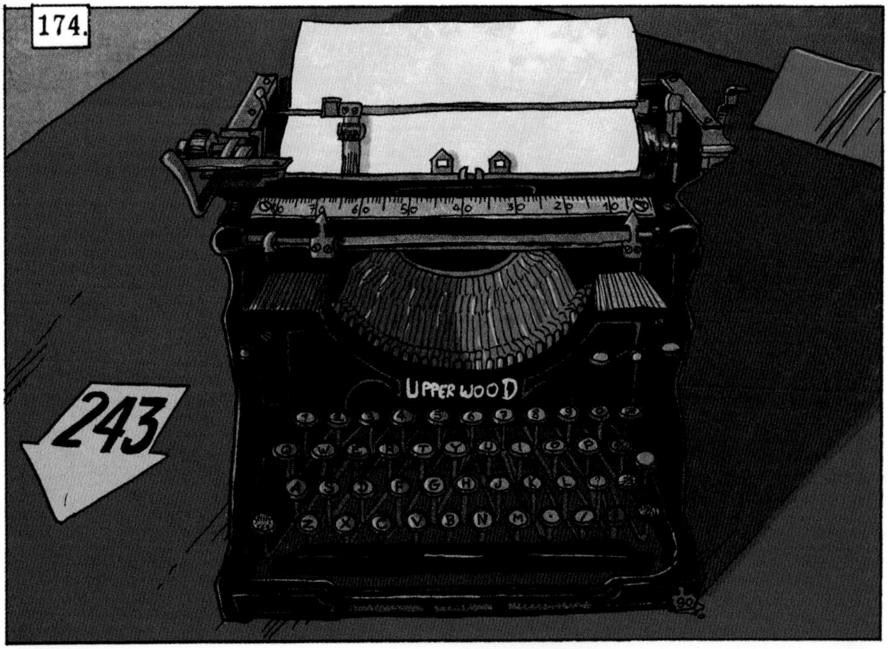
174.
243
UPPERWOOD

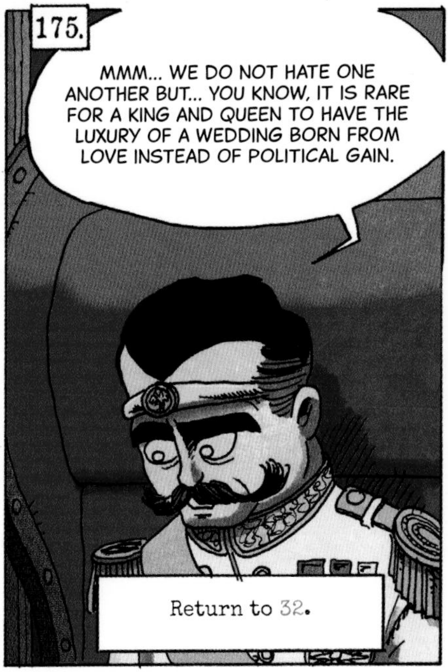
175.
MMM... WE DO NOT HATE ONE ANOTHER BUT... YOU KNOW, IT IS RARE FOR A KING AND QUEEN TO HAVE THE LUXURY OF A WEDDING BORN FROM LOVE INSTEAD OF POLITICAL GAIN.
Return to 32.

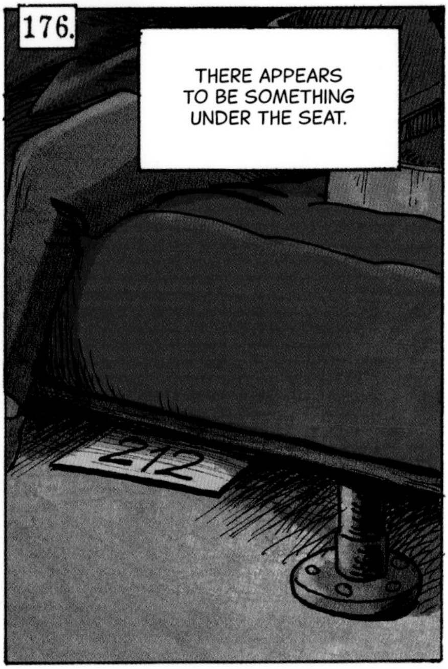
176.
THERE APPEARS TO BE SOMETHING UNDER THE SEAT.
212

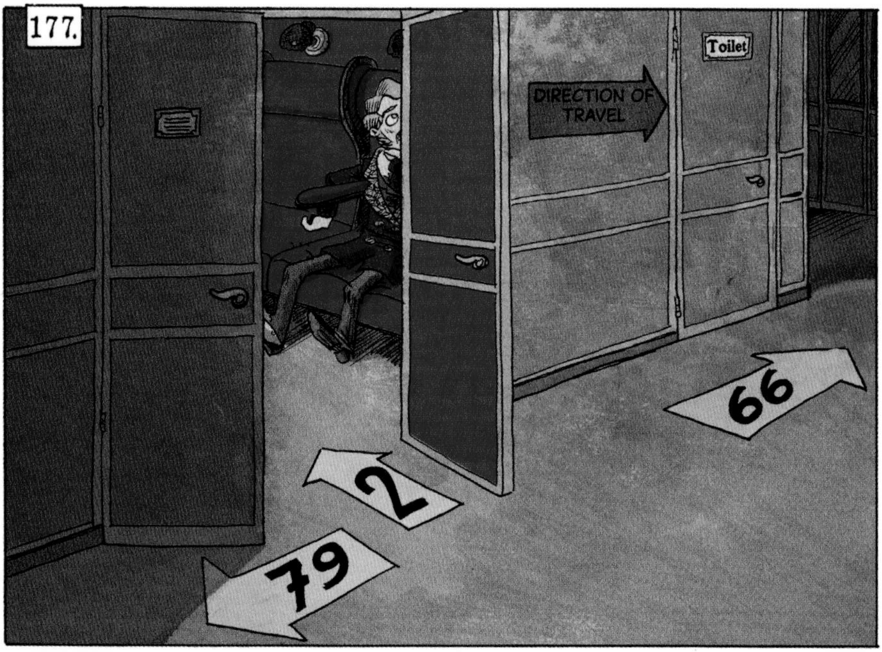
177.
Toilet
DIRECTION OF TRAVEL
66
2
79

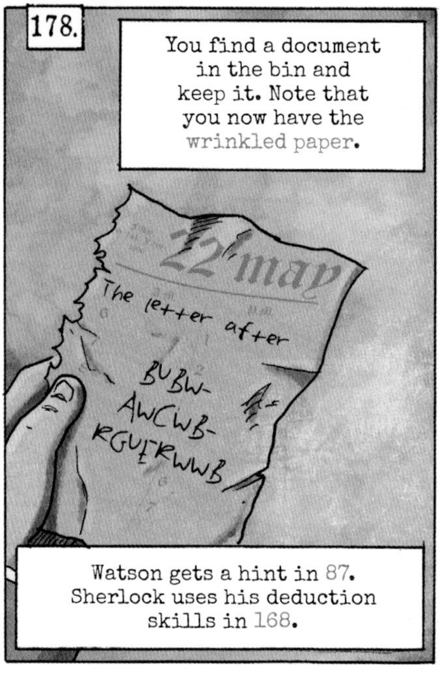
178.
You find a document in the bin and keep it. Note that you now have the wrinkled paper.
22 may
The letter after
BUBW-
AWCWB-
RGUERWWB
Watson gets a hint in 87. Sherlock uses his deduction skills in 168.

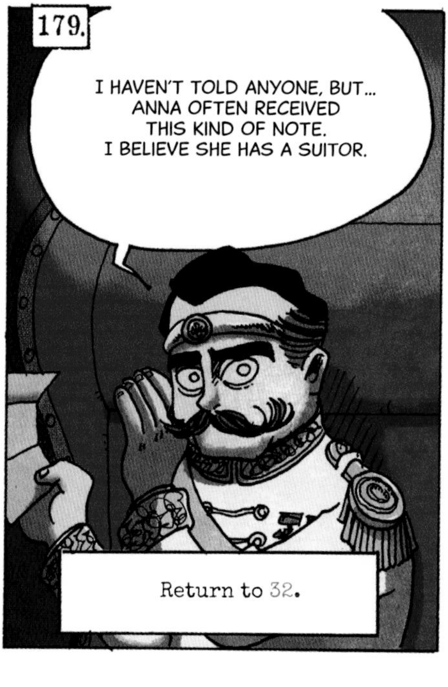
179.
I HAVEN'T TOLD ANYONE, BUT... ANNA OFTEN RECEIVED THIS KIND OF NOTE. I BELIEVE SHE HAS A SUITOR.
Return to 32.

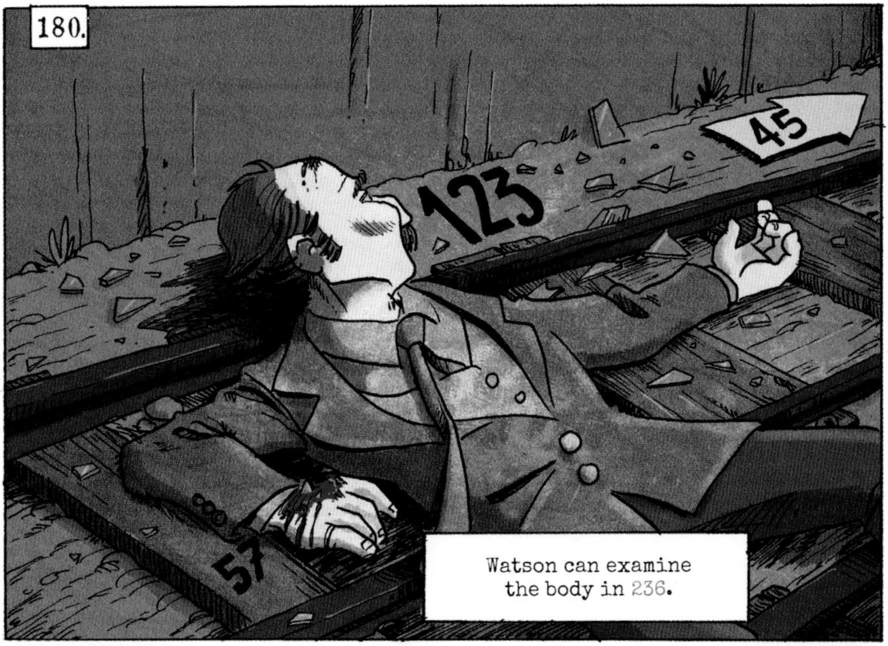
180.
45
123
57
Watson can examine the body in 236.

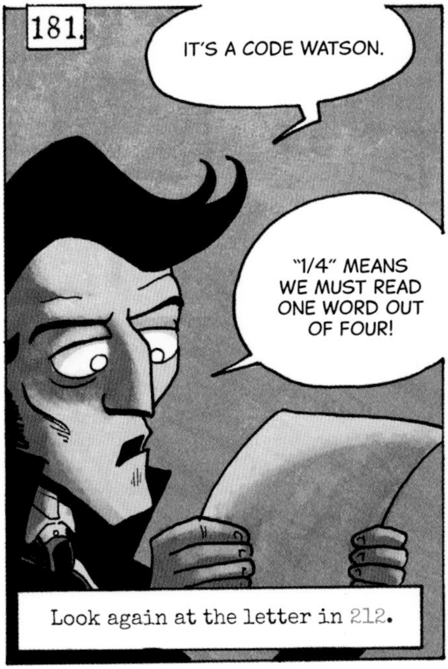
181.
IT'S A CODE WATSON.
"1/4" MEANS WE MUST READ ONE WORD OUT OF FOUR!
Look again at the letter in 212.

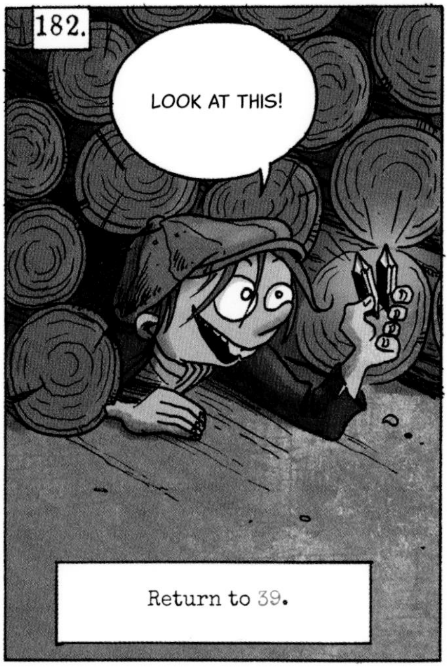
182.
LOOK AT THIS!
Return to 39.

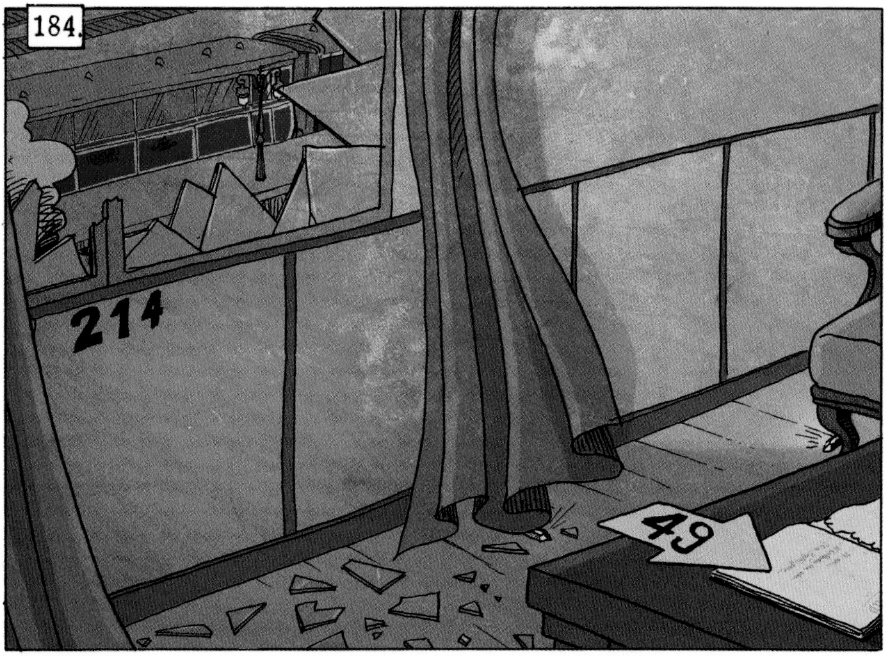
184.
214
49

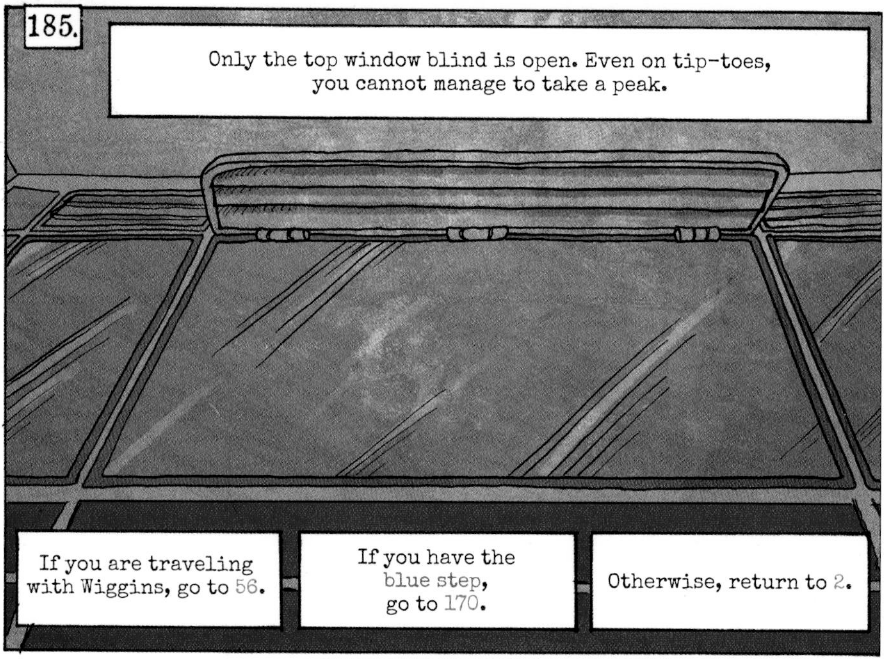
185.
Only the top window blind is open. Even on tip-toes, you cannot manage to take a peak.
If you are traveling with Wiggins, go to 56.
If you have the blue step, go to 170.
Otherwise, return to 2.

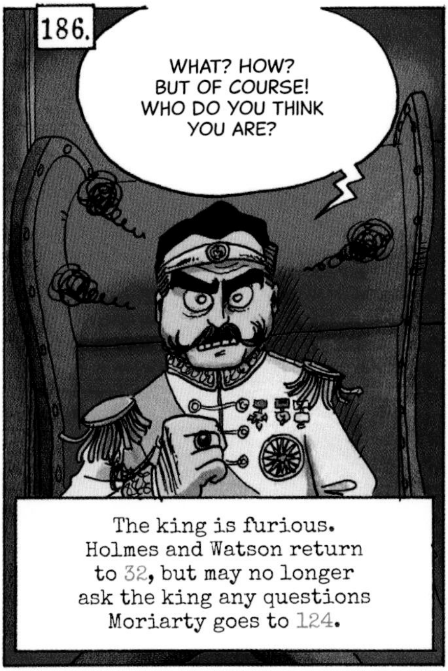
186.
WHAT? HOW? BUT OF COURSE! WHO DO YOU THINK YOU ARE?
The king is furious. Holmes and Watson return to 32, but may no longer ask the king any questions Moriarty goes to 124.

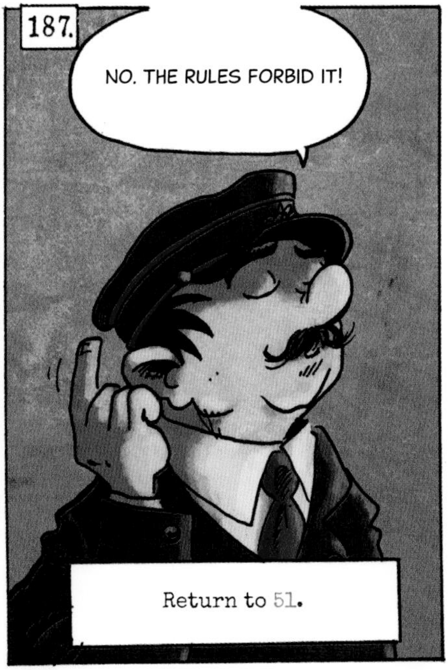
187.
NO. THE RULES FORBID IT!
Return to 51.

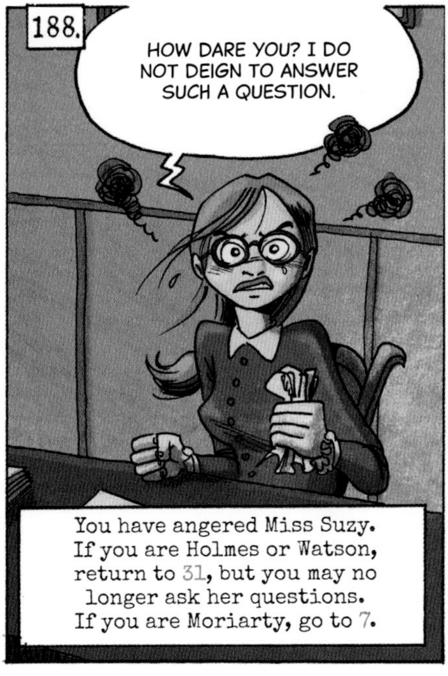
188.
HOW DARE YOU? I DO NOT DEIGN TO ANSWER SUCH A QUESTION.
You have angered Miss Suzy. If you are Holmes or Watson, return to 31, but you may no longer ask her questions. If you are Moriarty, go to 7.

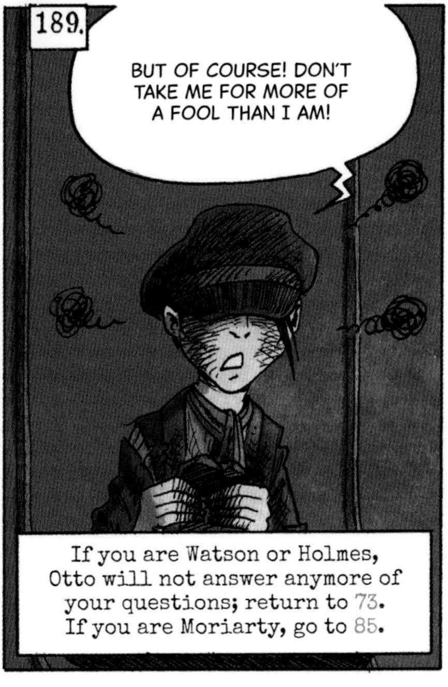
189.
BUT OF COURSE! DON'T TAKE ME FOR MORE OF A FOOL THAN I AM!
If you are Watson or Holmes, Otto will not answer anymore of your questions; return to 73. If you are Moriarty, go to 85.

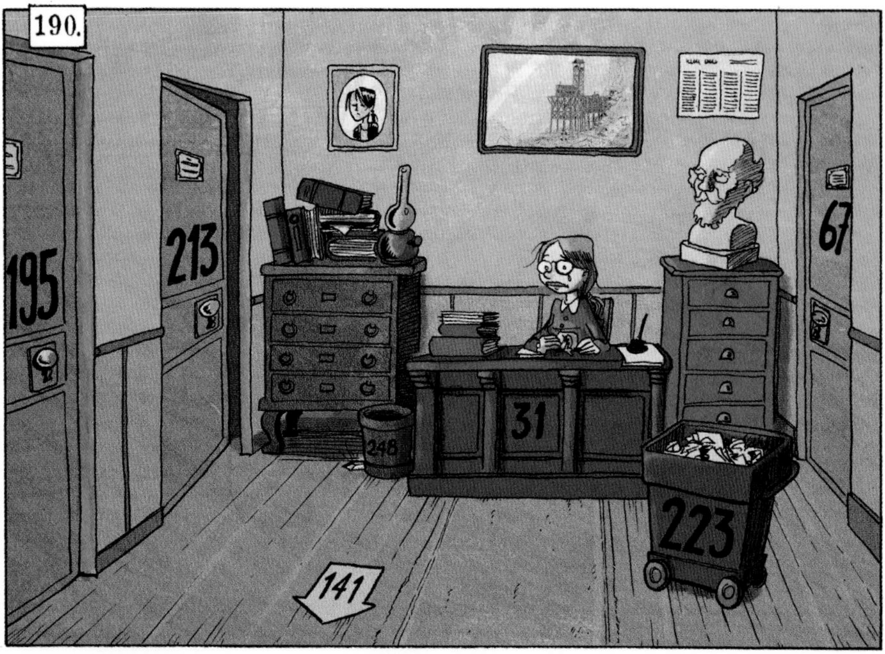
190.
195
213
67
31
248
223
141

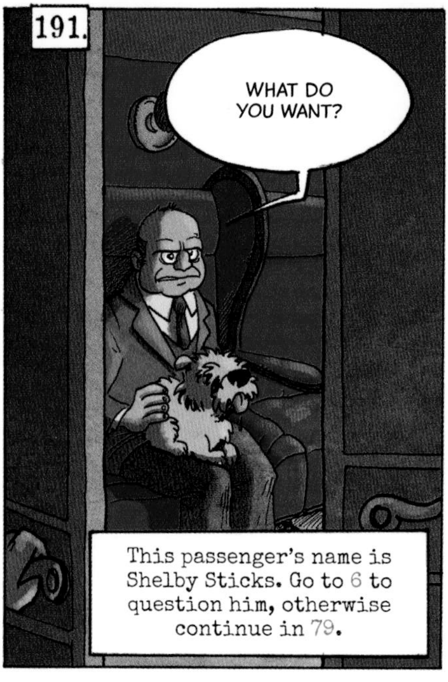
191.
WHAT DO YOU WANT?
This passenger's name is Shelby Sticks. Go to 6 to question him, otherwise continue in 79.

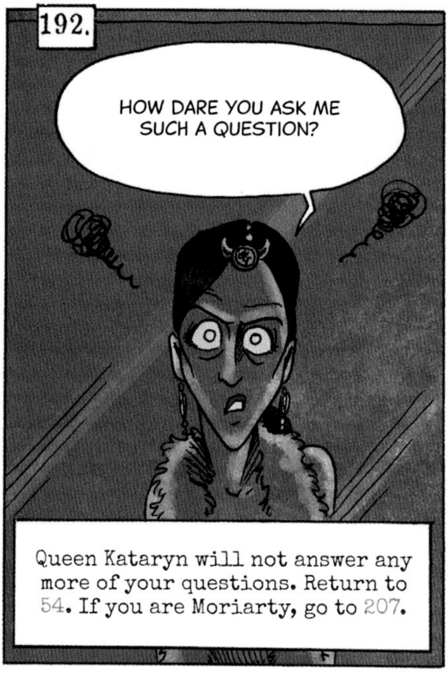
192.
HOW DARE YOU ASK ME SUCH A QUESTION?
Queen Kataryn will not answer any more of your questions. Return to 54. If you are Moriarty, go to 207.

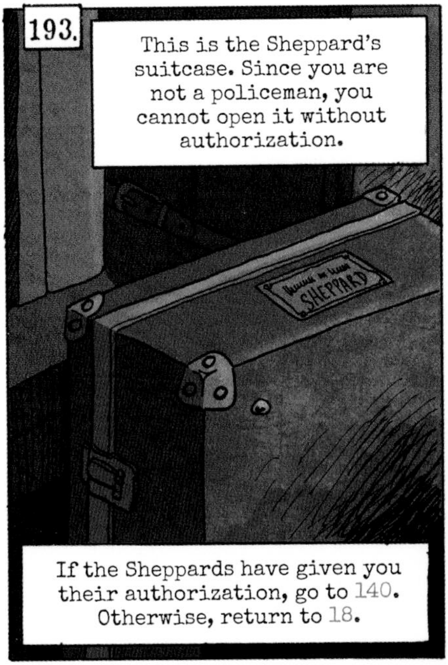
193.
This is the Sheppard's suitcase. Since you are not a policeman, you cannot open it without authorization.
SHEPPARD
If the Sheppards have given you their authorization, go to 140. Otherwise, return to 18.

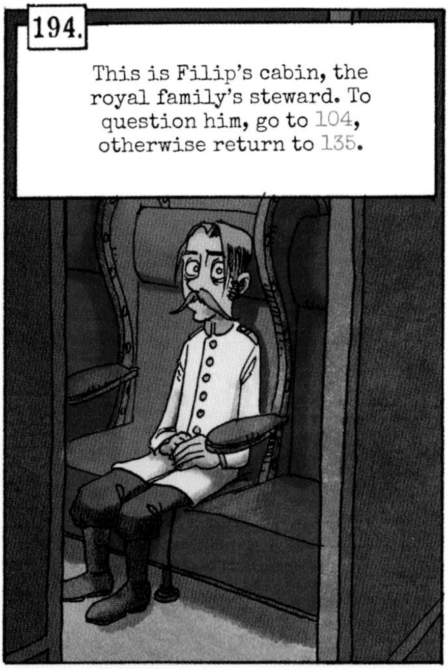
194.
This is Filip's cabin, the royal family's steward. To question him, go to 104, otherwise return to 135.

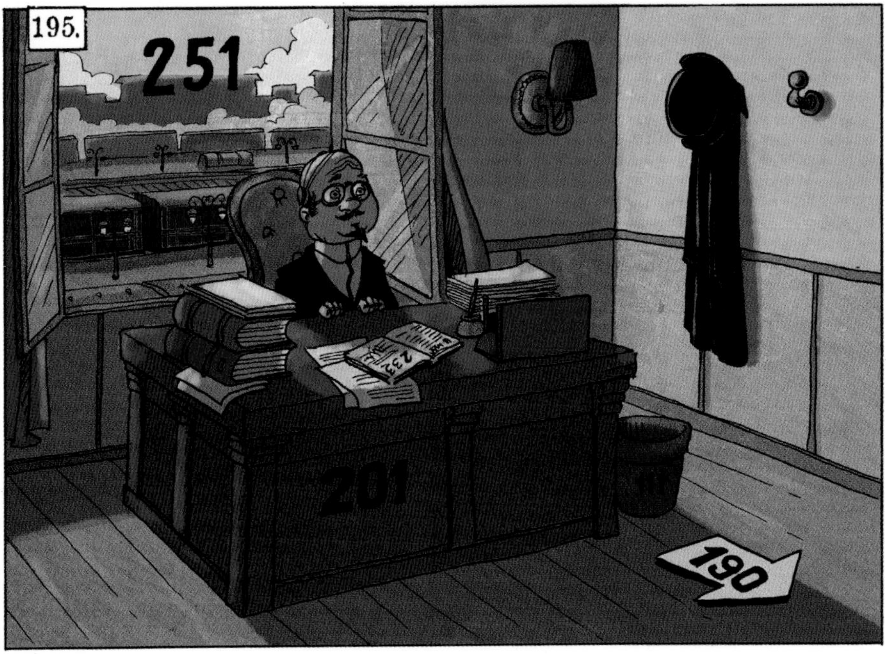
195.
251
233
201
190

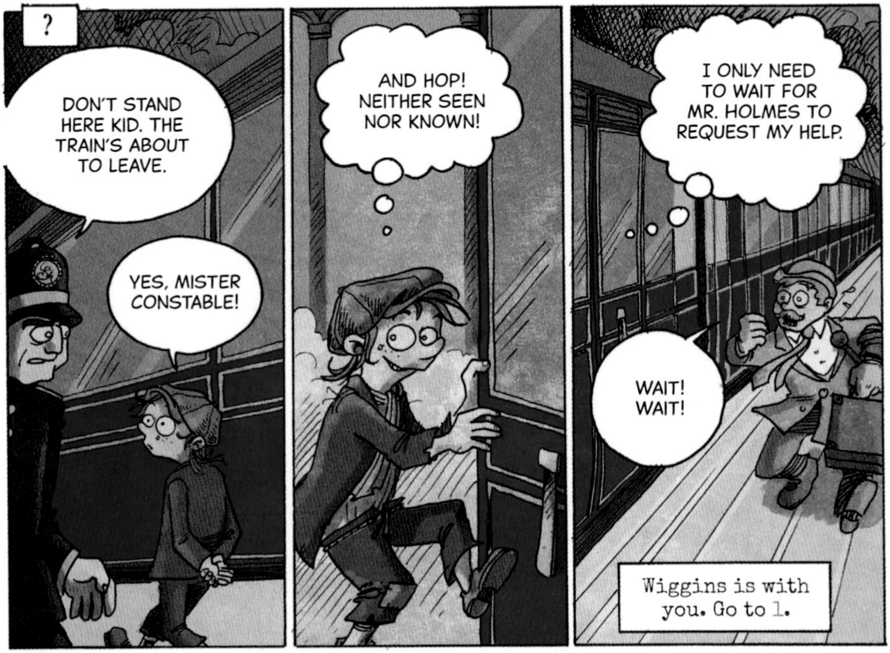
?
DON'T STAND HERE KID. THE TRAIN'S ABOUT TO LEAVE.
YES, MISTER CONSTABLE!
AND HOP! NEITHER SEEN NOR KNOWN!
I ONLY NEED TO WAIT FOR MR. HOLMES TO REQUEST MY HELP.
WAIT! WAIT!
Wiggins is with you. Go to 1.

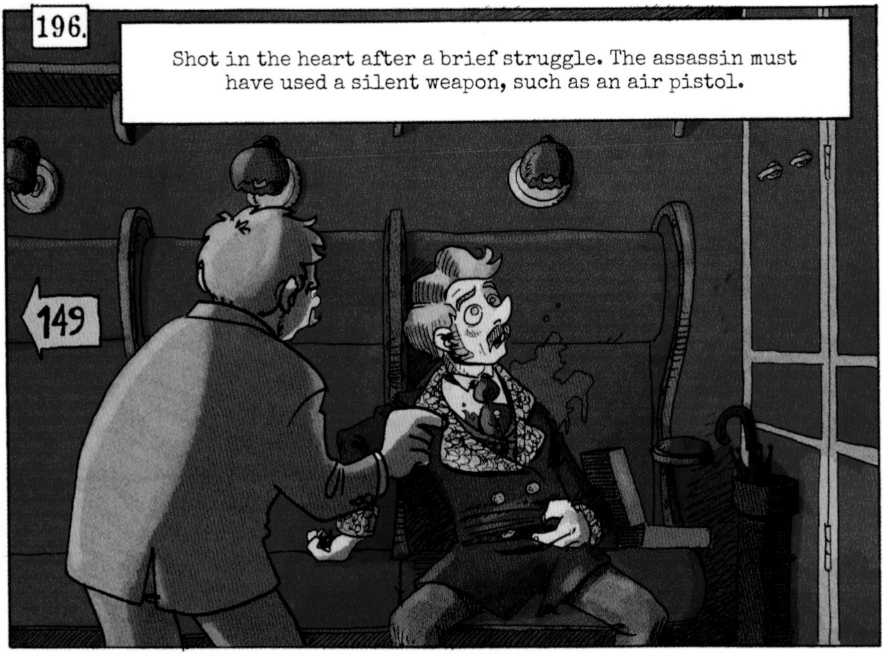
196.
Shot in the heart after a brief struggle. The assassin must have used a silent weapon, such as an air pistol.
149

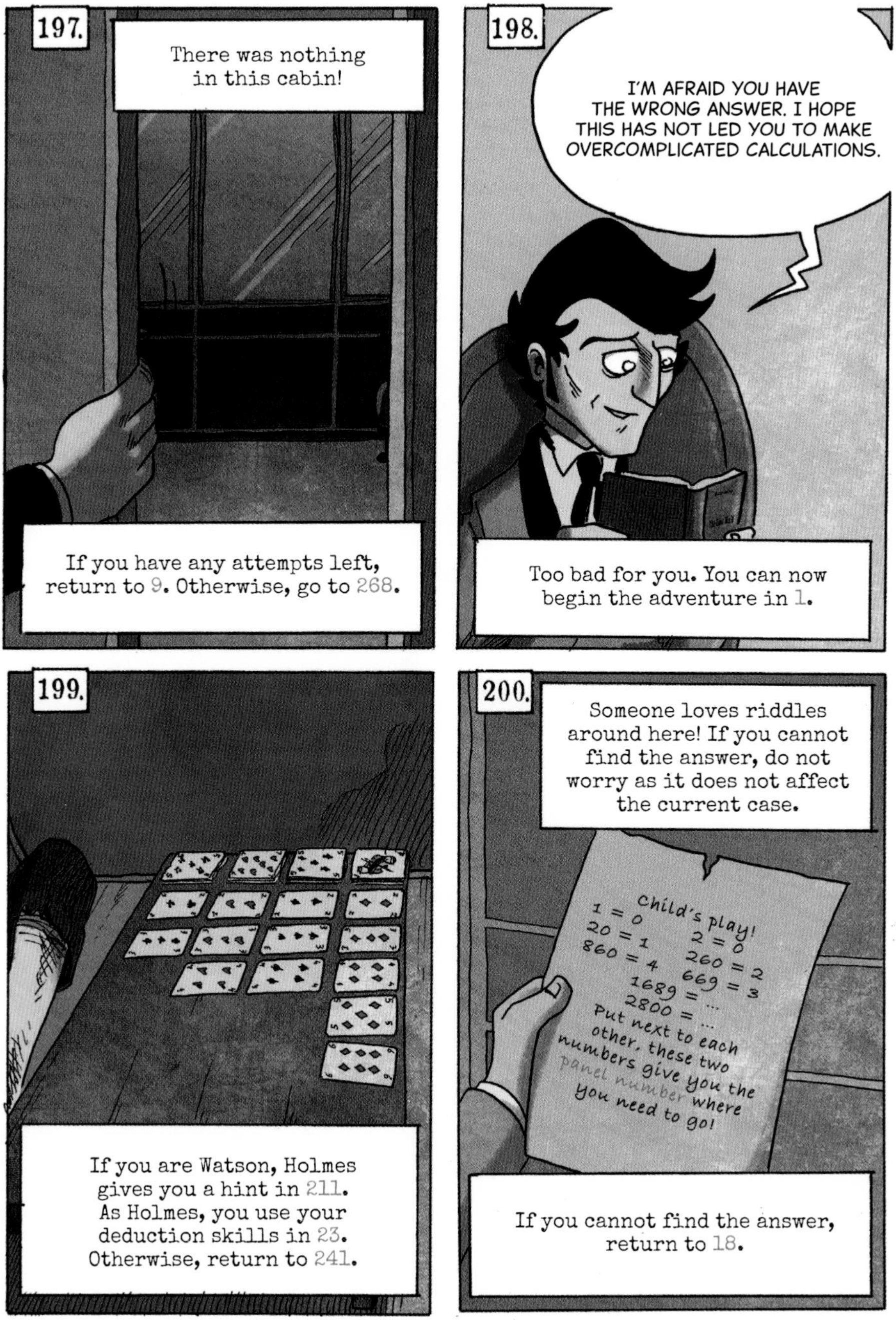
197.
There was nothing in this cabin!
If you have any attempts left, return to 9. Otherwise, go to 268.
198.
I'M AFRAID YOU HAVE THE WRONG ANSWER. I HOPE THIS HAS NOT LED YOU TO MAKE OVERCOMPLICATED CALCULATIONS.
Too bad for you. You can now begin the adventure in 1.
199.
If you are Watson, Holmes gives you a hint in 211. As Holmes, you use your deduction skills in 23. Otherwise, return to 241.
200.
Someone loves riddles around here! If you cannot find the answer, do not worry as it does not affect the current case.
Child's play!
1 = 0 2 = 0
20 = 1 260 = 2
860 = 4 669 = 3
1689 = ...
2800 = ...
Put next to each other, these two numbers give you the panel number where you need to go!
If you cannot find the answer, return to 18.

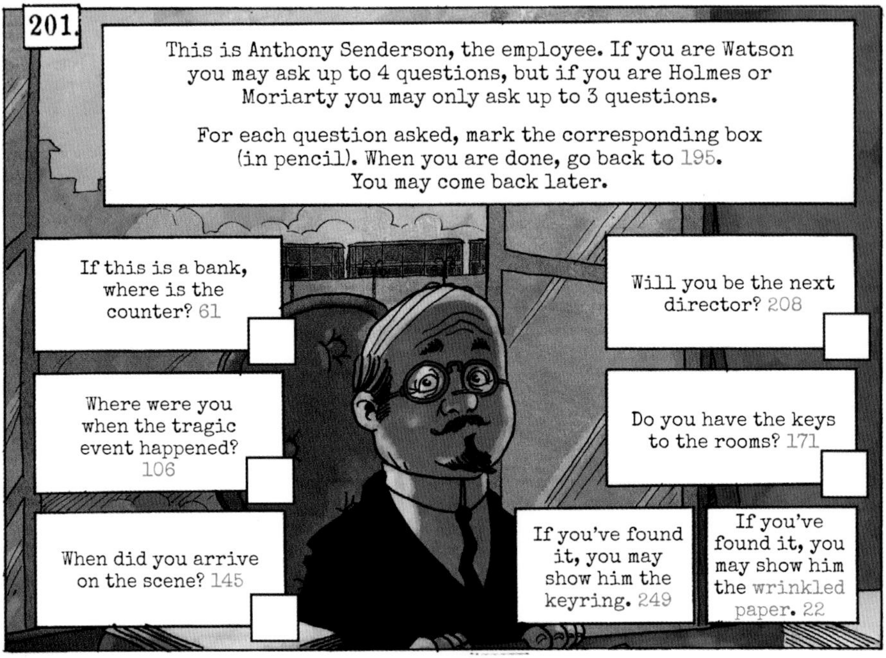

201.
This is Anthony Senderson, the employee. If you are Watson you may ask up to 4 questions, but if you are Holmes or Moriarty you may only ask up to 3 questions.
For each question asked, mark the corresponding box (in pencil). When you are done, go back to 195. You may come back later.
If this is a bank, where is the counter? 61
Where were you when the tragic event happened? 106
When did you arrive on the scene? 145
Will you be the next director? 208
Do you have the keys to the rooms? 171
If you've found it, you may show him the keyring. 249
If you've found it, you may show him the wrinkled paper. 22

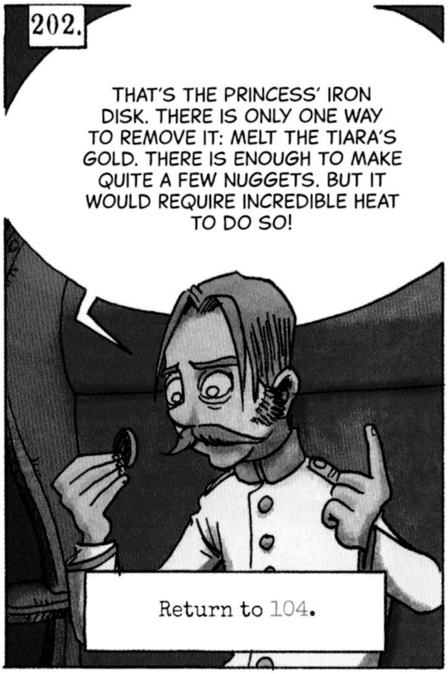

202.
THAT'S THE PRINCESS' IRON DISK. THERE IS ONLY ONE WAY TO REMOVE IT: MELT THE TIARA'S GOLD. THERE IS ENOUGH TO MAKE QUITE A FEW NUGGETS. BUT IT WOULD REQUIRE INCREDIBLE HEAT TO DO SO!
Return to 104.

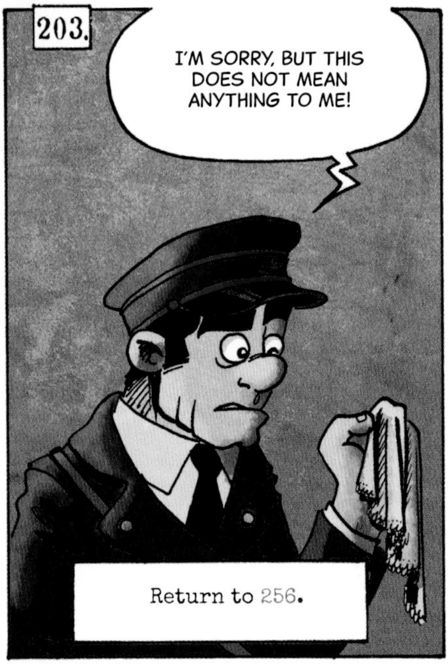

203.
I'M SORRY, BUT THIS DOES NOT MEAN ANYTHING TO ME!
Return to 256.

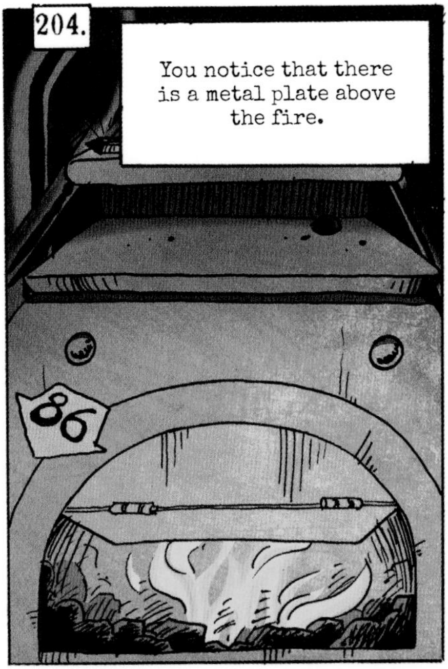
204.
You notice that there is a metal plate above the fire.
86

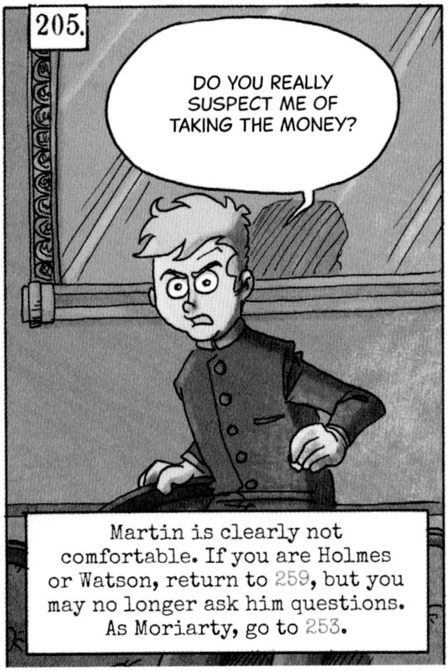
205.
DO YOU REALLY SUSPECT ME OF TAKING THE MONEY?
Martin is clearly not comfortable. If you are Holmes or Watson, return to 259, but you may no longer ask him questions. As Moriarty, go to 253.

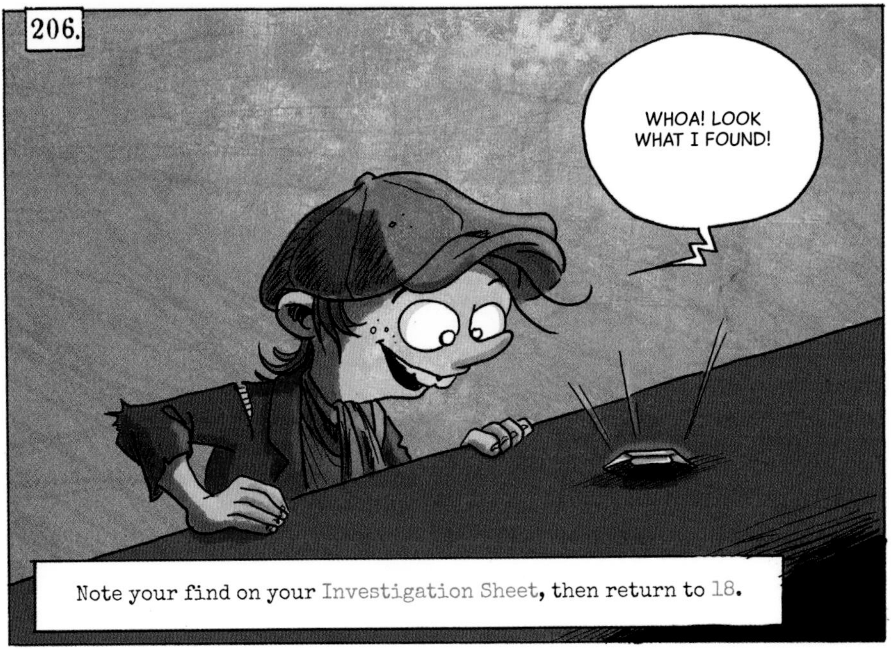
206.
WHOA! LOOK WHAT I FOUND!
Note your find on your Investigation Sheet, then return to 18.

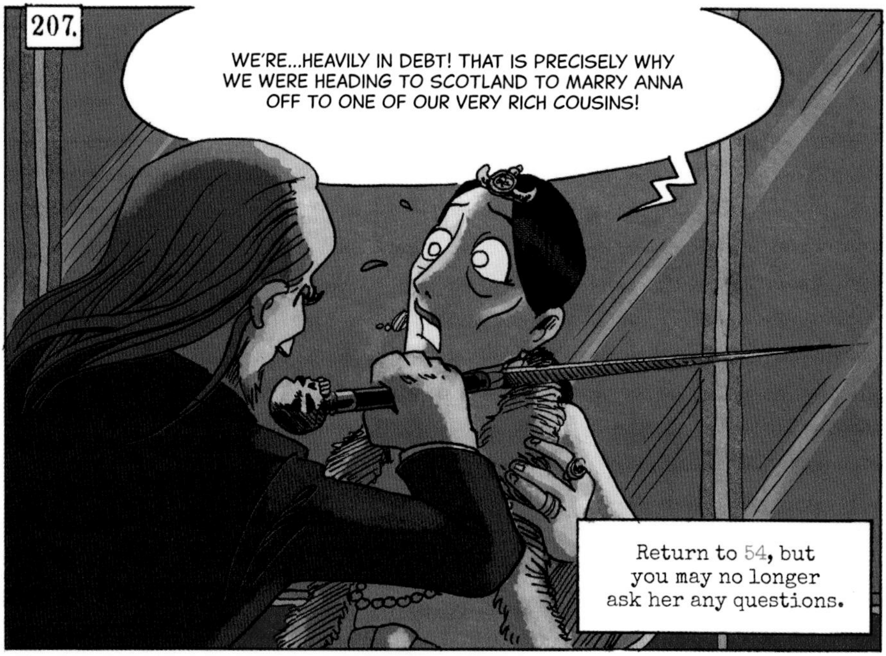
207.
WE'RE...HEAVILY IN DEBT! THAT IS PRECISELY WHY WE WERE HEADING TO SCOTLAND TO MARRY ANNA OFF TO ONE OF OUR VERY RICH COUSINS!
Return to 54, but you may no longer ask her any questions.

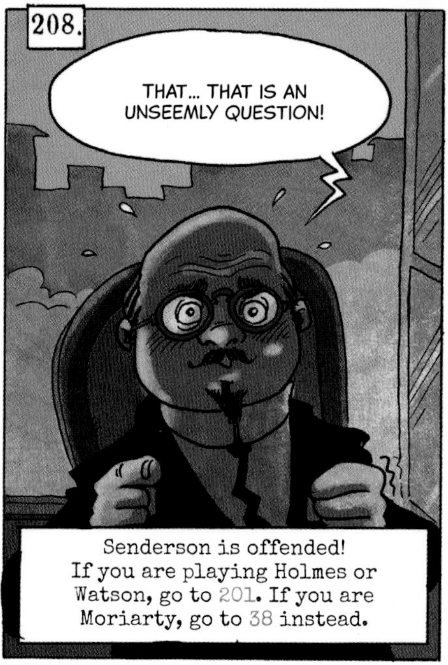
208.
THAT... THAT IS AN UNSEEMLY QUESTION!
Senderson is offended! If you are playing Holmes or Watson, go to 201. If you are Moriarty, go to 38 instead.

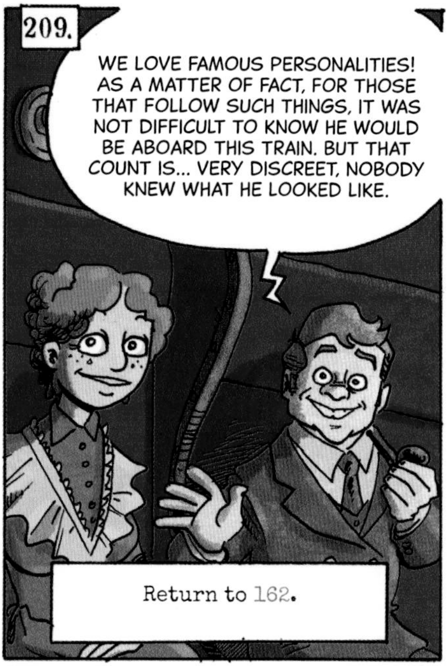
209.
WE LOVE FAMOUS PERSONALITIES! AS A MATTER OF FACT, FOR THOSE THAT FOLLOW SUCH THINGS, IT WAS NOT DIFFICULT TO KNOW HE WOULD BE ABOARD THIS TRAIN. BUT THAT COUNT IS... VERY DISCREET, NOBODY KNEW WHAT HE LOOKED LIKE.
Return to 162.

210.

If you are Watson, go to 262.
As Holmes, go to 48.
Otherwise, return to 184.

211.

LOOK, THESE CARDS ARE PERFECTLY CLEAN.

I DO NOT KNOW WHO STARTED THIS GAME, BUT IT CANNOT BE THAT BOY.

Return to 241.

212.

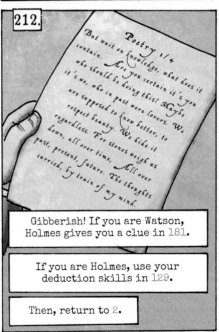

Poetry 1/4

But wait on knowledge, what does it contain. Are you certain it's you who should be doing this? Maybe it's we, who in past were lovers. We are supposed to know better, to respect beauty. We hide it regardless. For stones weigh us down, all over time. All over past, present, future. The thoughts carried by train of my mind.

Gibberish! If you are Watson, Holmes gives you a clue in 181.

If you are Holmes, use your deduction skills in 129.

Then, return to 2.

213.

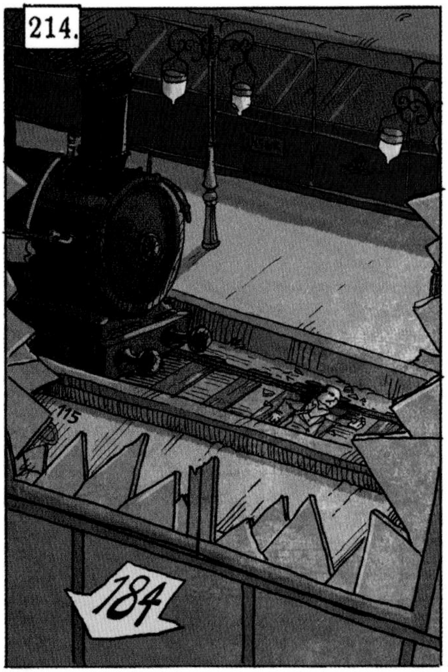
214.
115
184

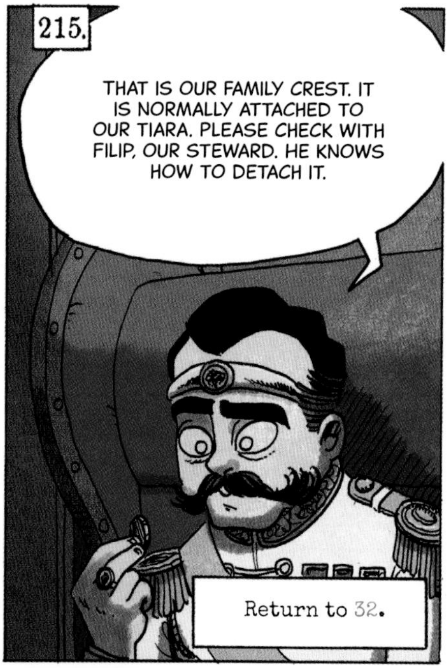
215.
THAT IS OUR FAMILY CREST. IT IS NORMALLY ATTACHED TO OUR TIARA. PLEASE CHECK WITH FILIP, OUR STEWARD. HE KNOWS HOW TO DETACH IT.
Return to 32.

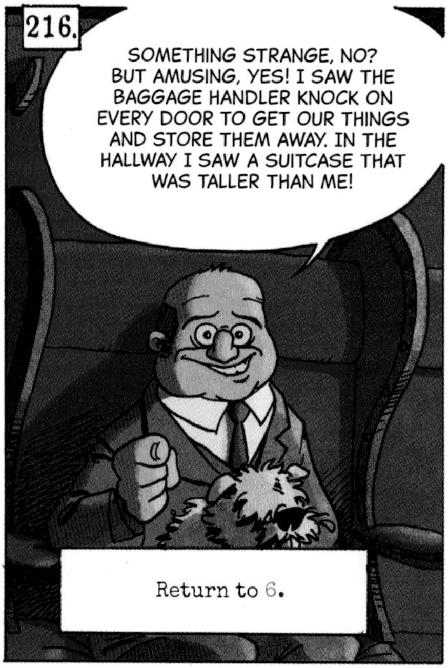
216.
SOMETHING STRANGE, NO? BUT AMUSING, YES! I SAW THE BAGGAGE HANDLER KNOCK ON EVERY DOOR TO GET OUR THINGS AND STORE THEM AWAY. IN THE HALLWAY I SAW A SUITCASE THAT WAS TALLER THAN ME!
Return to 6.

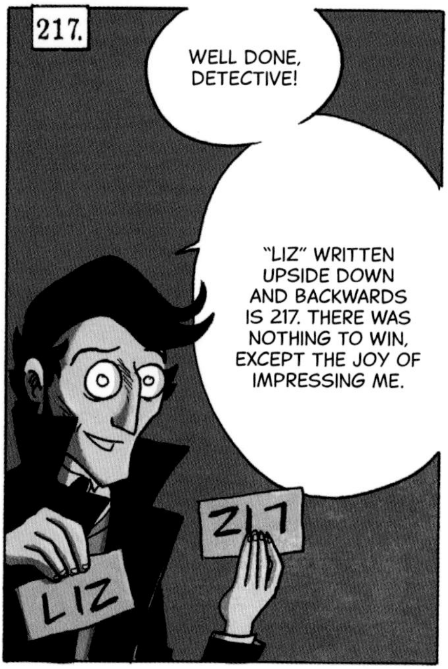
217.
WELL DONE, DETECTIVE!
"LIZ" WRITTEN UPSIDE DOWN AND BACKWARDS IS 217. THERE WAS NOTHING TO WIN, EXCEPT THE JOY OF IMPRESSING ME.
217
LIZ

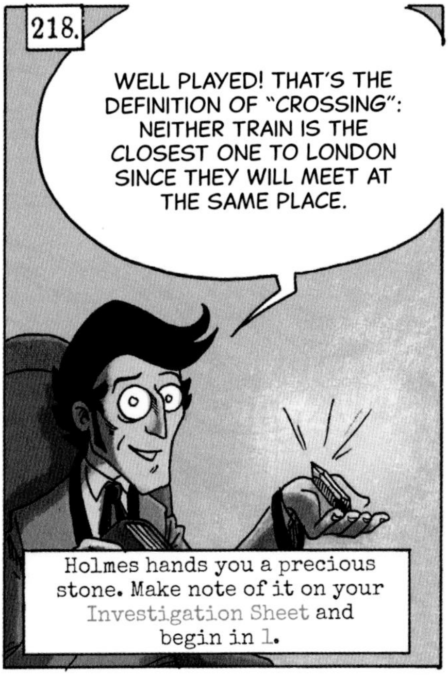
218.
WELL PLAYED! THAT'S THE DEFINITION OF "CROSSING": NEITHER TRAIN IS THE CLOSEST ONE TO LONDON SINCE THEY WILL MEET AT THE SAME PLACE.
Holmes hands you a precious stone. Make note of it on your Investigation Sheet and begin in 1.

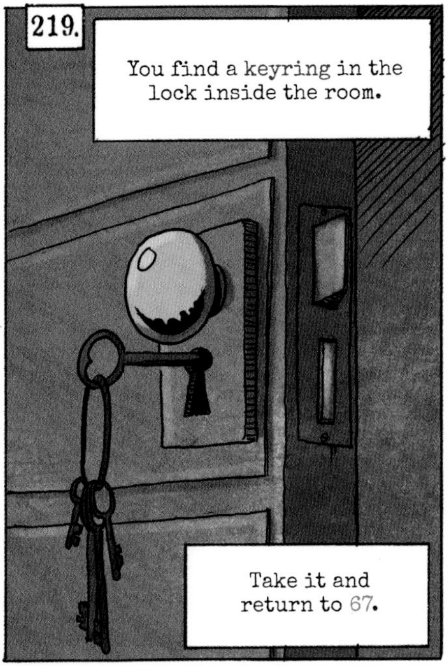
219.
You find a keyring in the lock inside the room.
Take it and return to 67.

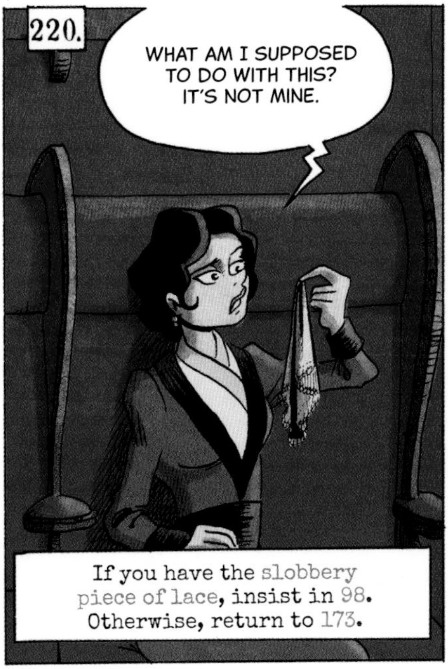
220.
WHAT AM I SUPPOSED TO DO WITH THIS? IT'S NOT MINE.
If you have the slobbery piece of lace, insist in 98. Otherwise, return to 173.

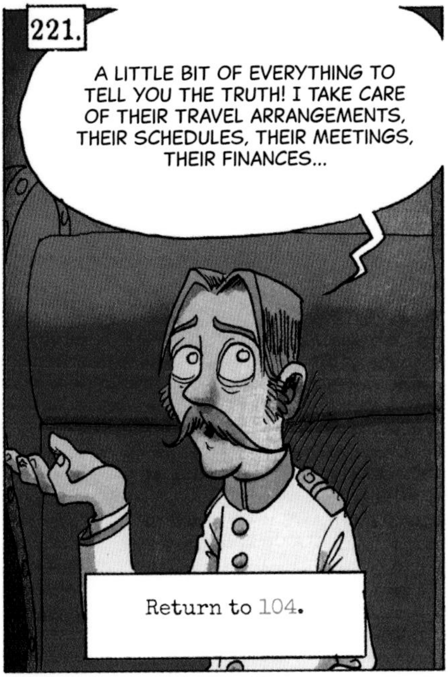
221.
A LITTLE BIT OF EVERYTHING TO TELL YOU THE TRUTH! I TAKE CARE OF THEIR TRAVEL ARRANGEMENTS, THEIR SCHEDULES, THEIR MEETINGS, THEIR FINANCES...
Return to 104.

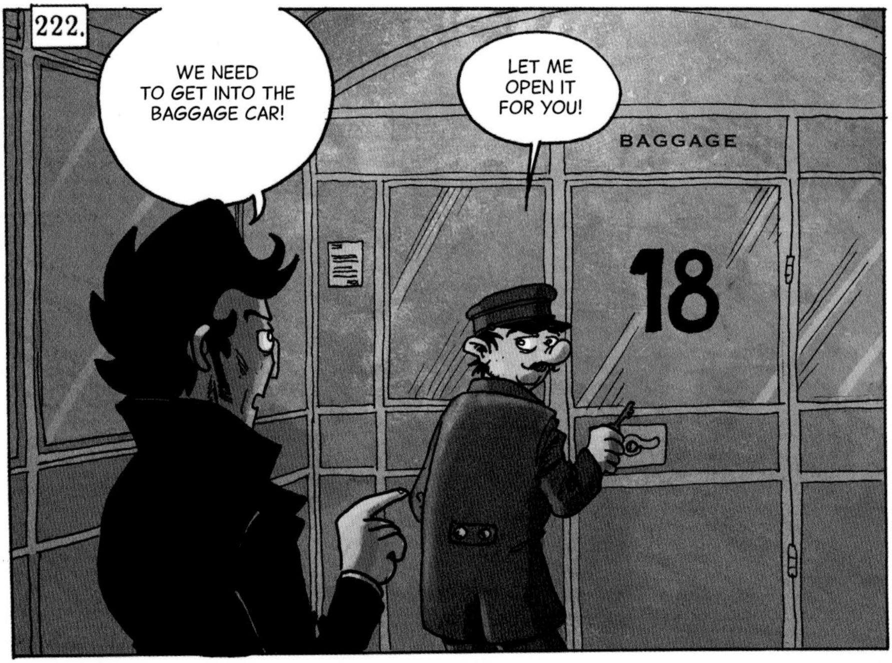
222.
WE NEED TO GET INTO THE BAGGAGE CAR!
LET ME OPEN IT FOR YOU!
BAGGAGE
18

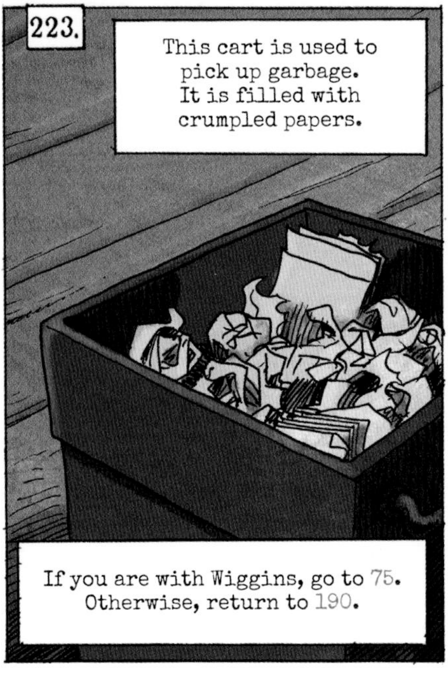
223.
This cart is used to pick up garbage. It is filled with crumpled papers.
If you are with Wiggins, go to 75. Otherwise, return to 190.

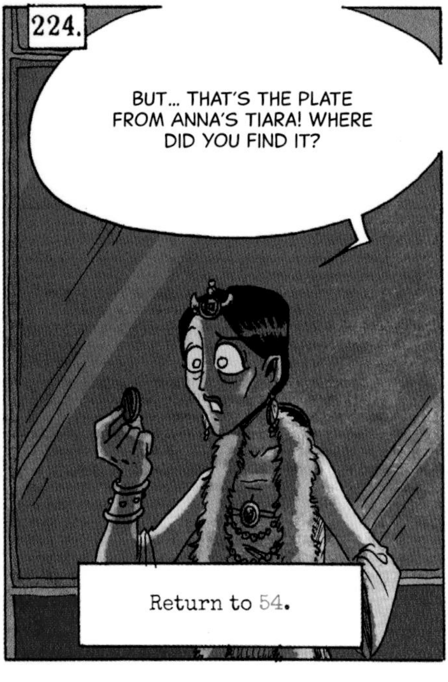
224.
BUT... THAT'S THE PLATE FROM ANNA'S TIARA! WHERE DID YOU FIND IT?
Return to 54.

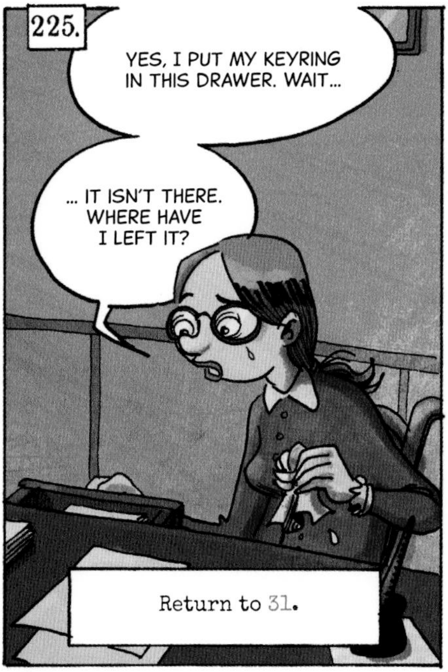
225.
YES, I PUT MY KEYRING IN THIS DRAWER. WAIT...
... IT ISN'T THERE. WHERE HAVE I LEFT IT?
Return to 31.

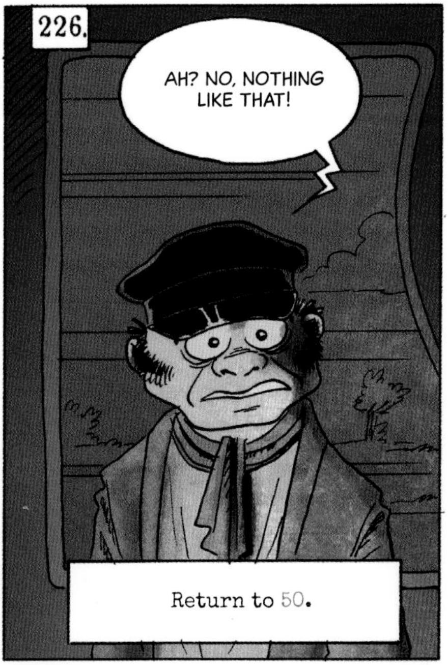
226.
AH? NO, NOTHING LIKE THAT!
Return to 50.

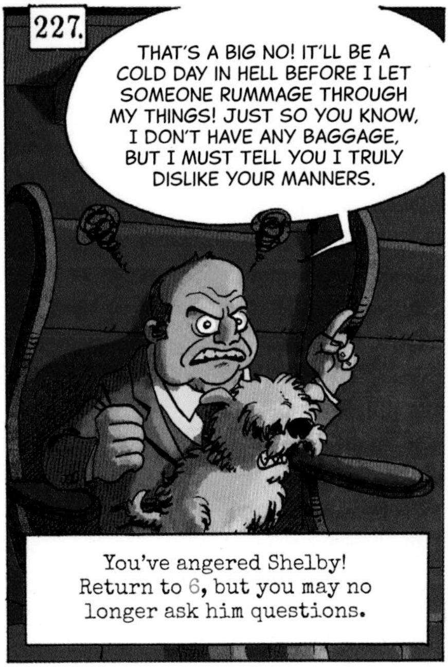
227.
THAT'S A BIG NO! IT'LL BE A COLD DAY IN HELL BEFORE I LET SOMEONE RUMMAGE THROUGH MY THINGS! JUST SO YOU KNOW, I DON'T HAVE ANY BAGGAGE, BUT I MUST TELL YOU I TRULY DISLIKE YOUR MANNERS.
You've angered Shelby! Return to 6, but you may no longer ask him questions.

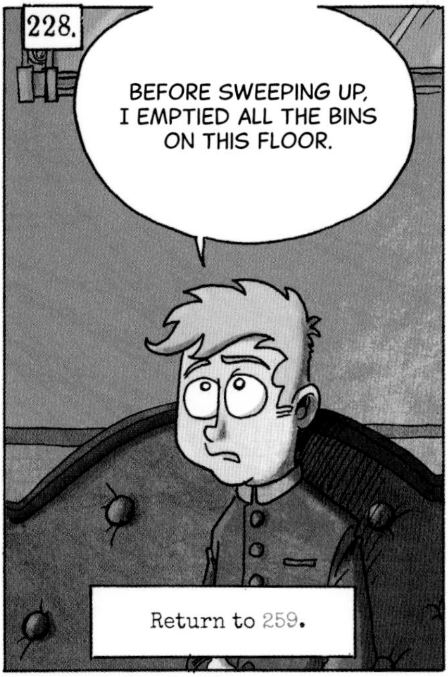
228.
BEFORE SWEEPING UP, I EMPTIED ALL THE BINS ON THIS FLOOR.
Return to 259.

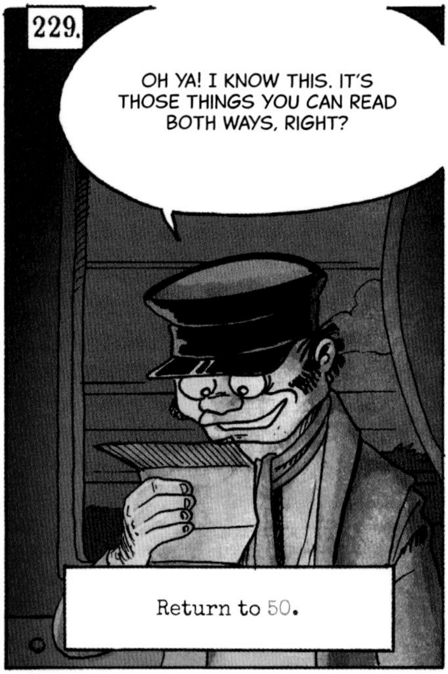
229.
OH YA! I KNOW THIS. IT'S THOSE THINGS YOU CAN READ BOTH WAYS, RIGHT?
Return to 50.

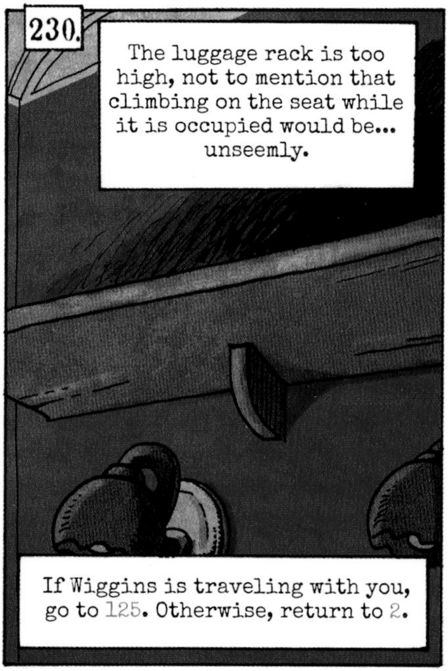
230.
The luggage rack is too high, not to mention that climbing on the seat while it is occupied would be... unseemly.
If Wiggins is traveling with you, go to 125. Otherwise, return to 2.

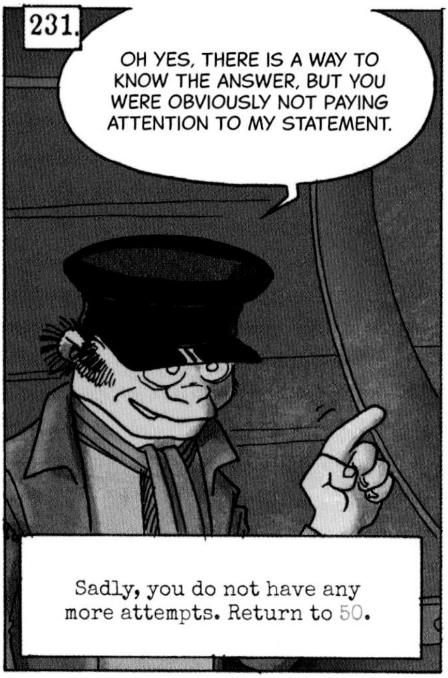
231.
OH YES, THERE IS A WAY TO KNOW THE ANSWER, BUT YOU WERE OBVIOUSLY NOT PAYING ATTENTION TO MY STATEMENT.
Sadly, you do not have any more attempts. Return to 50.

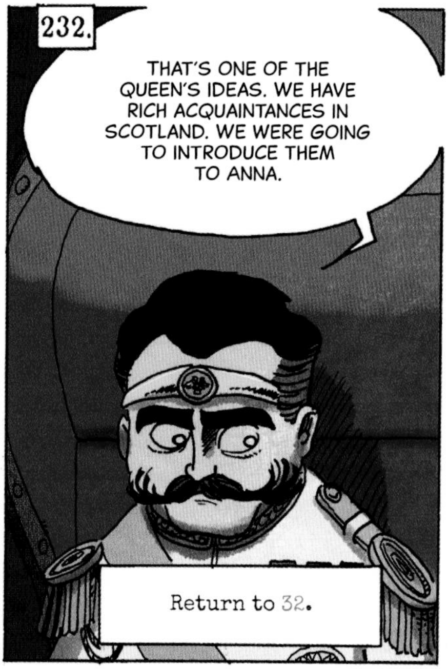
232.
THAT'S ONE OF THE QUEEN'S IDEAS. WE HAVE RICH ACQUAINTANCES IN SCOTLAND. WE WERE GOING TO INTRODUCE THEM TO ANNA.
Return to 32.

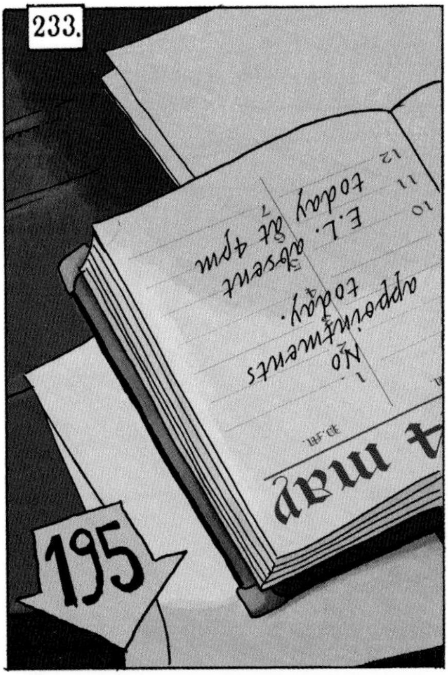
233.
No appointments today.
E.L. absent today at 4pm
195

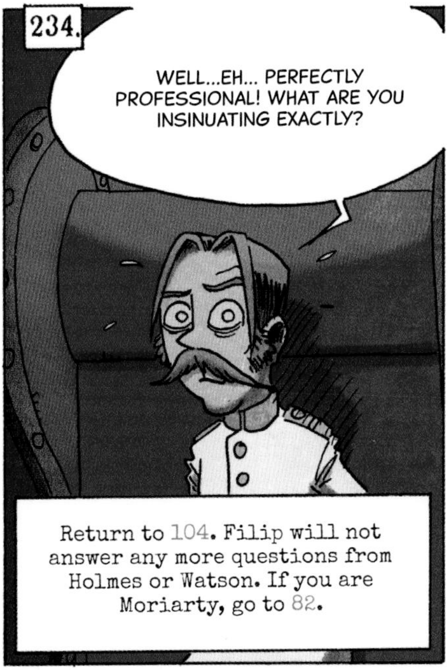
234.
WELL...EH... PERFECTLY PROFESSIONAL! WHAT ARE YOU INSINUATING EXACTLY?
Return to 104. Filip will not answer any more questions from Holmes or Watson. If you are Moriarty, go to 82.

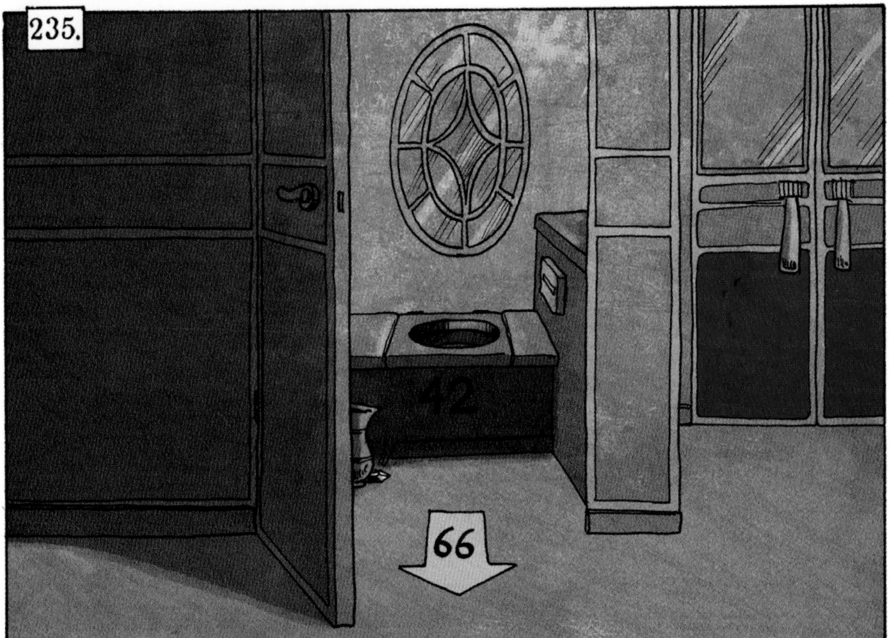
235.
42
66

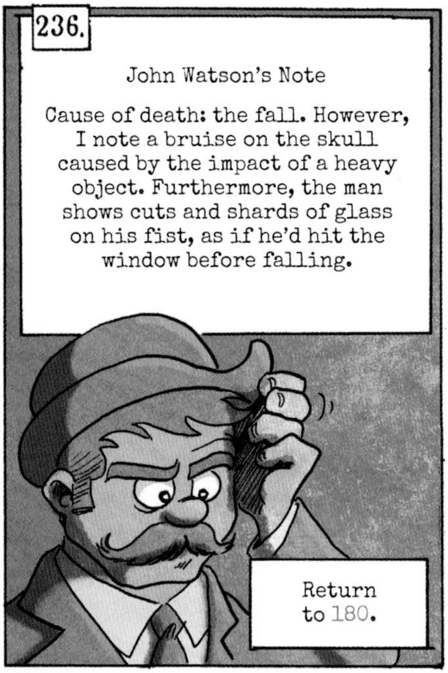
236.
John Watson's Note
Cause of death: the fall. However, I note a bruise on the skull caused by the impact of a heavy object. Furthermore, the man shows cuts and shards of glass on his fist, as if he'd hit the window before falling.
Return to 180.

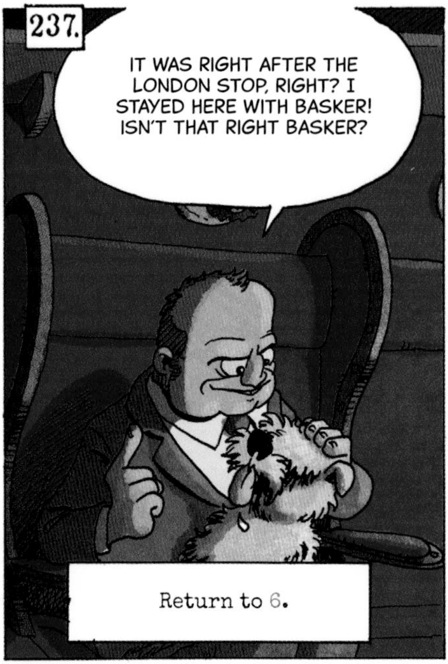
237.
IT WAS RIGHT AFTER THE LONDON STOP, RIGHT? I STAYED HERE WITH BASKER! ISN'T THAT RIGHT BASKER?
Return to 6.

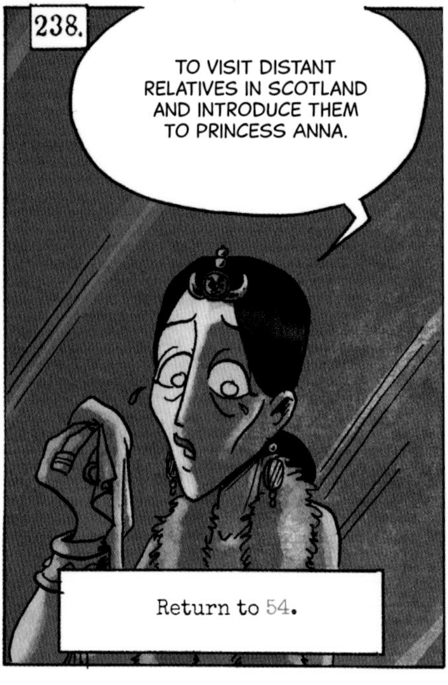
238.
TO VISIT DISTANT RELATIVES IN SCOTLAND AND INTRODUCE THEM TO PRINCESS ANNA.
Return to 54.

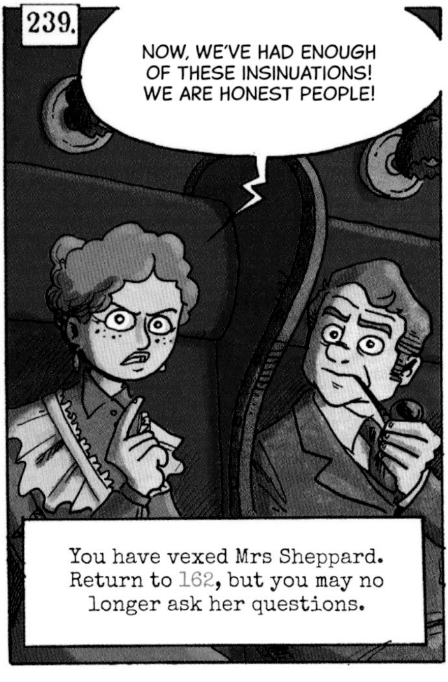
239.
NOW, WE'VE HAD ENOUGH OF THESE INSINUATIONS! WE ARE HONEST PEOPLE!
You have vexed Mrs Sheppard. Return to 162, but you may no longer ask her questions.

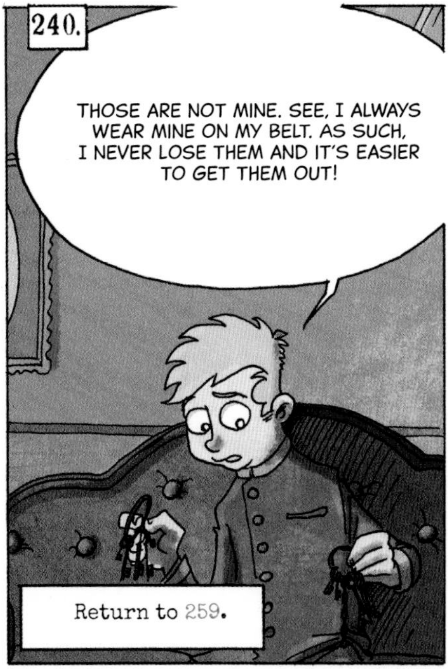
240.
THOSE ARE NOT MINE. SEE, I ALWAYS WEAR MINE ON MY BELT. AS SUCH, I NEVER LOSE THEM AND IT'S EASIER TO GET THEM OUT!
Return to 259.

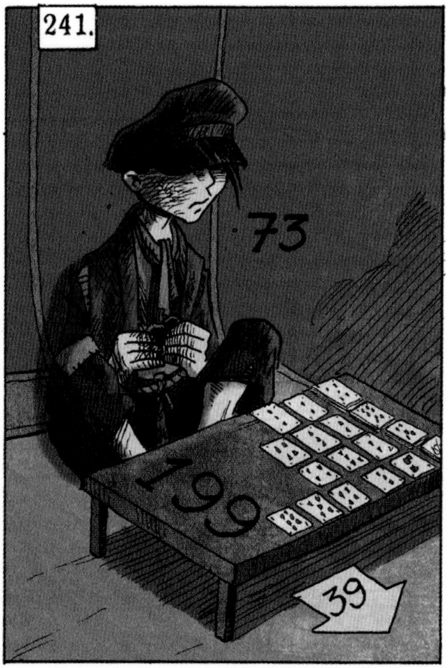
241.
73
199
39

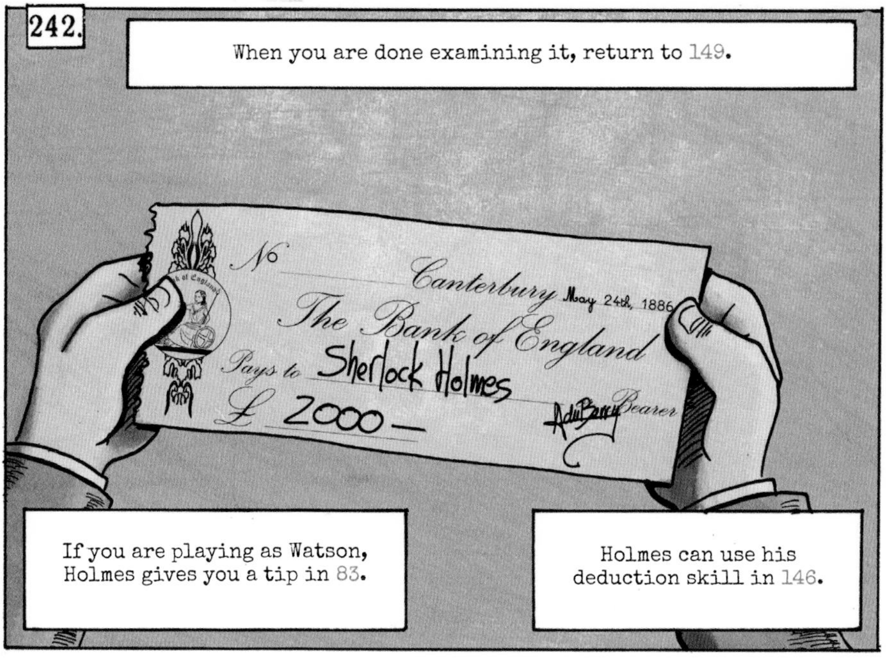
242.
When you are done examining it, return to 149.
No
Canterbury May 24th, 1886
The Bank of England
Pays to Sherlock Holmes
£ 2000 —
Bearer
If you are playing as Watson, Holmes gives you a tip in 83.
Holmes can use his deduction skill in 146.

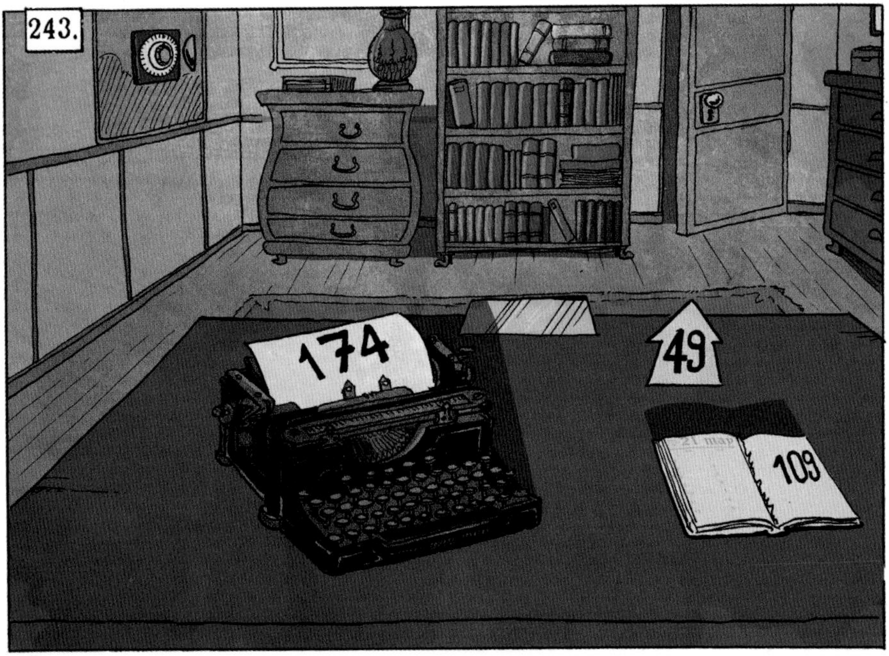
243.
174
49
109

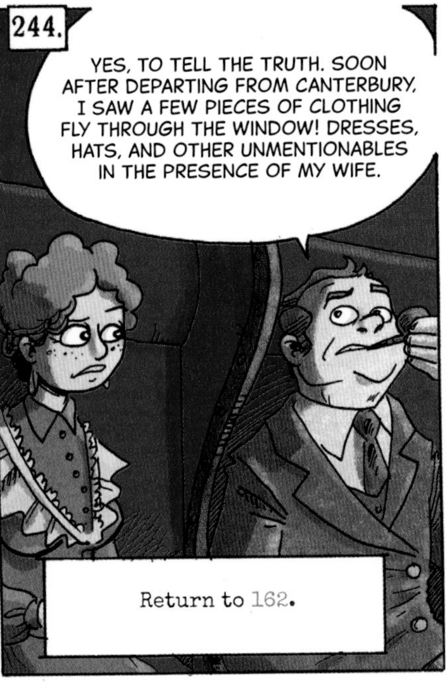
244.
YES, TO TELL THE TRUTH. SOON AFTER DEPARTING FROM CANTERBURY, I SAW A FEW PIECES OF CLOTHING FLY THROUGH THE WINDOW! DRESSES, HATS, AND OTHER UNMENTIONABLES IN THE PRESENCE OF MY WIFE.
Return to 162.

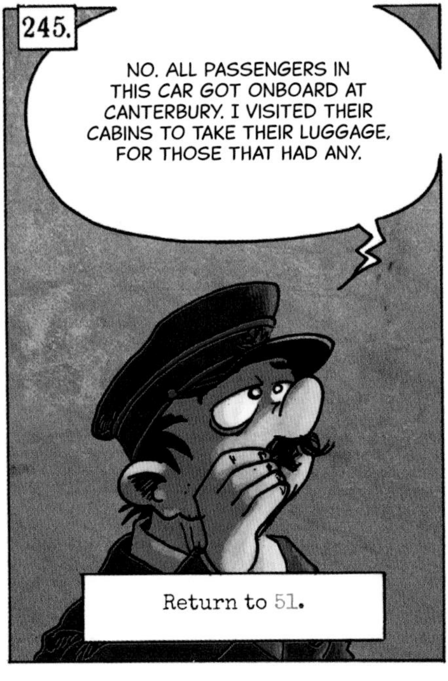
245.
NO. ALL PASSENGERS IN THIS CAR GOT ONBOARD AT CANTERBURY. I VISITED THEIR CABINS TO TAKE THEIR LUGGAGE, FOR THOSE THAT HAD ANY.
Return to 51.

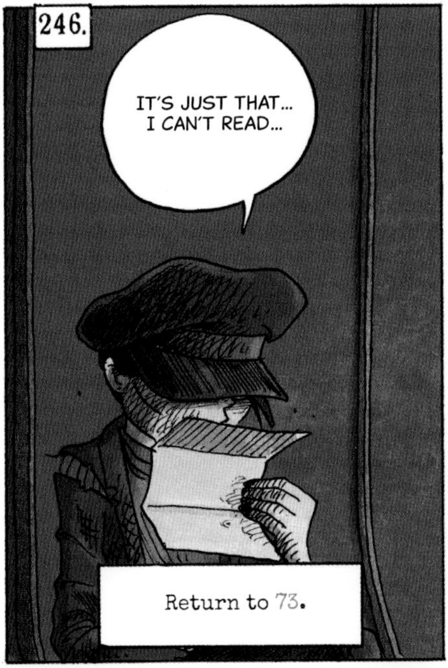
246.
IT'S JUST THAT... I CAN'T READ...
Return to 73.

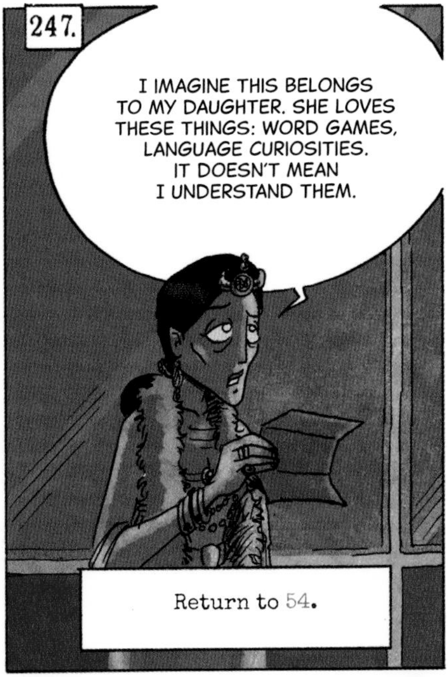
247.
I IMAGINE THIS BELONGS TO MY DAUGHTER. SHE LOVES THESE THINGS: WORD GAMES, LANGUAGE CURIOSITIES. IT DOESN'T MEAN I UNDERSTAND THEM.
Return to 54.

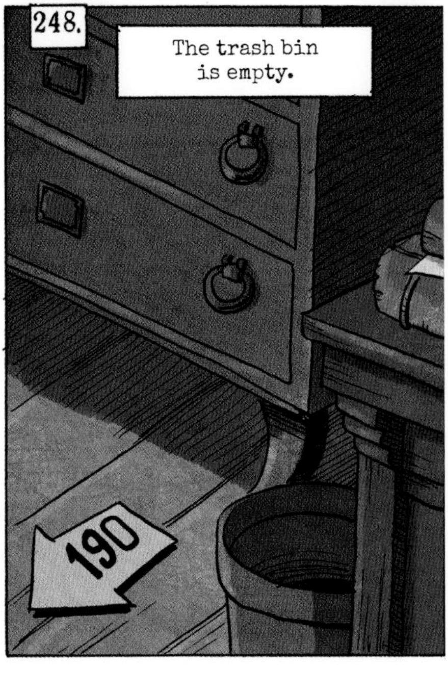
248.
The trash bin is empty.
190

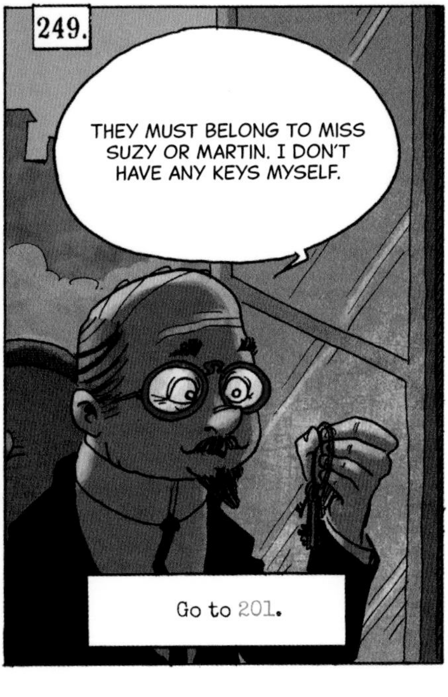
249.
THEY MUST BELONG TO MISS SUZY OR MARTIN. I DON'T HAVE ANY KEYS MYSELF.
Go to 201.

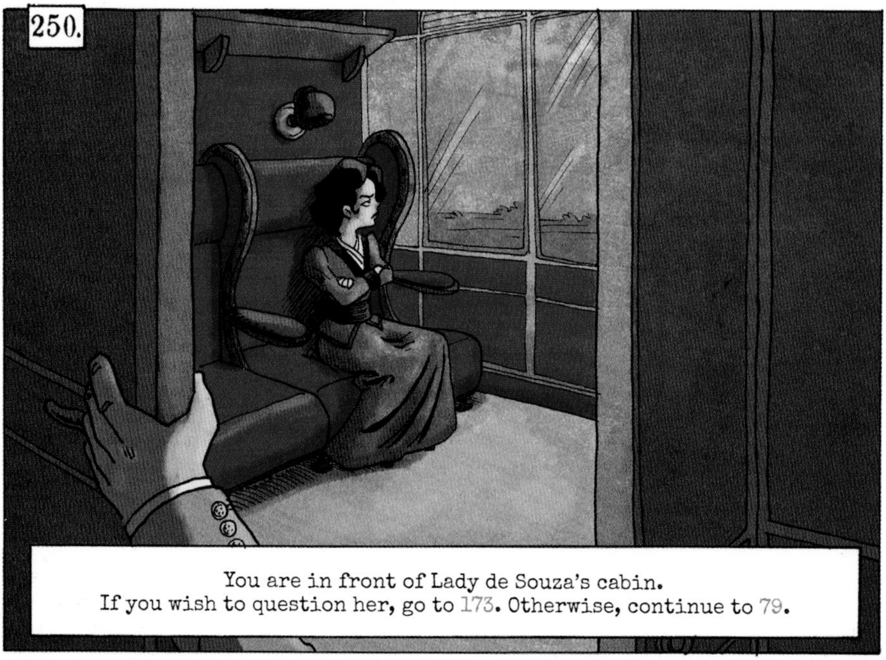
250.
You are in front of Lady de Souza's cabin.
If you wish to question her, go to 173. Otherwise, continue to 79.

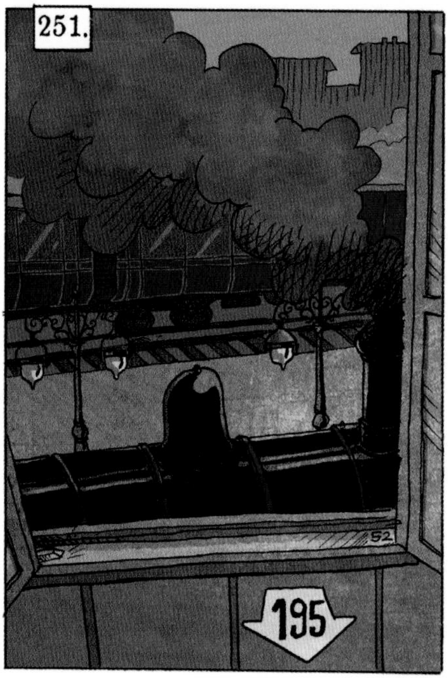
251.
52
195

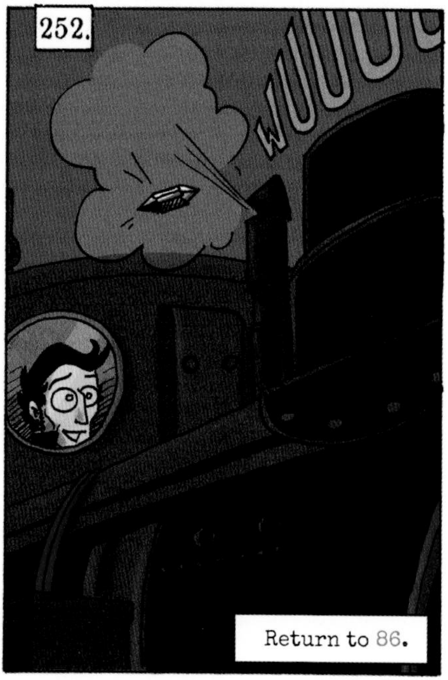
252.
Return to 86.

253.

254.

255.

(253 panel speech) YES, I ENVIED ALL THAT MONEY! I SOMETIMES SPIED ON THE BOSS THROUGH THE KEYHOLE TO LOOK AT HIM HANDLING ALL THOSE BILLS!

Return to 259,
but you may no longer
ask him questions.

(254 panel speech) YES, THESE ARE THE KIND OF SMALL THINGS WE SAW AFTER OUR DEPARTURE FROM CANTERBURY. IT IS AS IF SOMEONE WAS THROWING THEM OUT THE WINDOW OF ANOTHER CABIN.

Return to 162.

(255 panel speech) IN THE BAGGAGE CAR, TO PUT AWAY DOCTOR WATSON'S SUITCASE.

Return to 51.

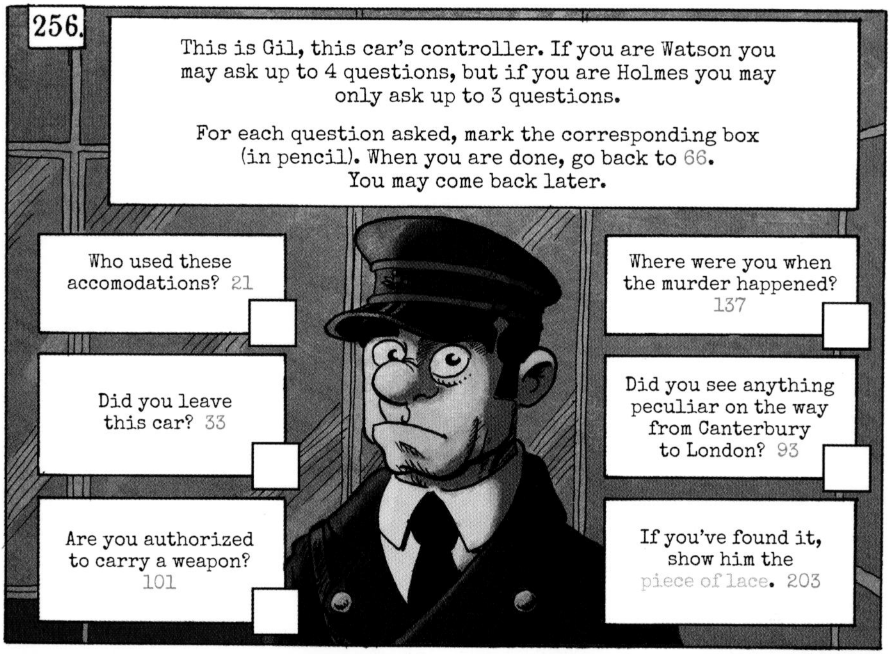
256.
This is Gil, this car's controller. If you are Watson you may ask up to 4 questions, but if you are Holmes you may only ask up to 3 questions.
For each question asked, mark the corresponding box (in pencil). When you are done, go back to 66. You may come back later.
Who used these accomodations? 21
Did you leave this car? 33
Are you authorized to carry a weapon? 101
Where were you when the murder happened? 137
Did you see anything peculiar on the way from Canterbury to London? 93
If you've found it, show him the piece of lace. 203

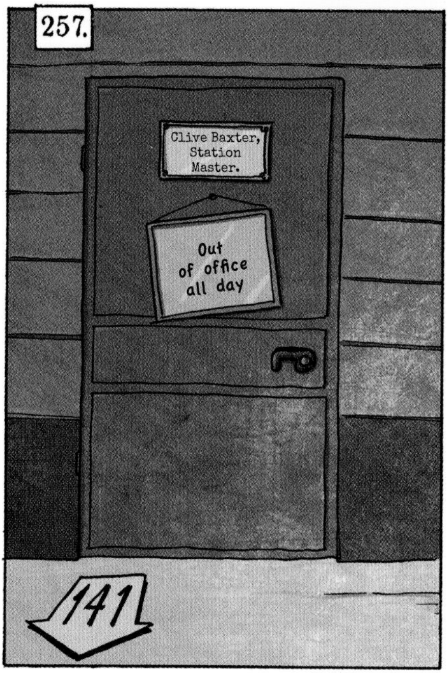
257.
Clive Baxter, Station Master.
Out of office all day
141

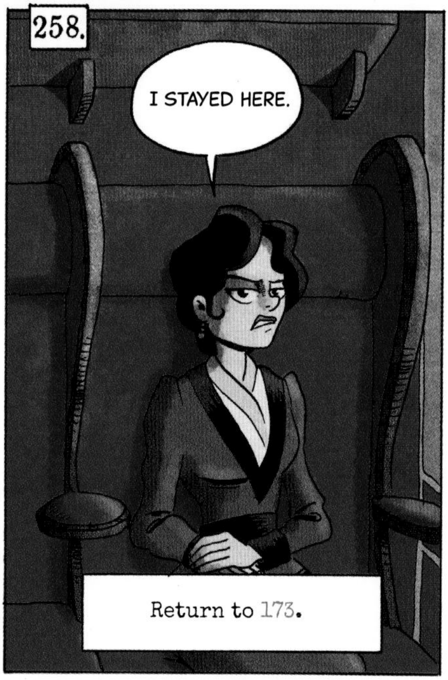
258.
I STAYED HERE.
Return to 173.

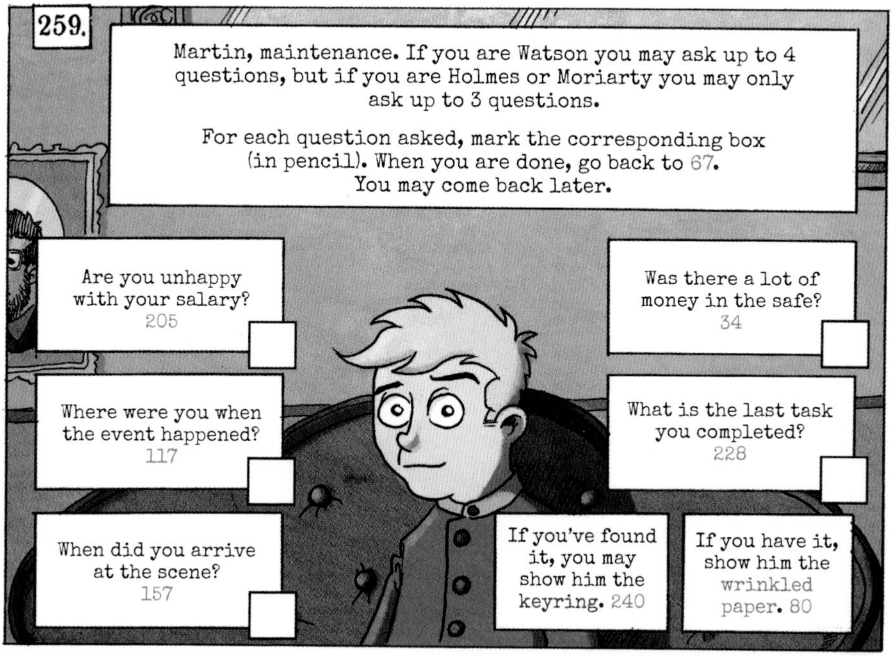
259.
Martin, maintenance. If you are Watson you may ask up to 4 questions, but if you are Holmes or Moriarty you may only ask up to 3 questions.
For each question asked, mark the corresponding box (in pencil). When you are done, go back to 67. You may come back later.
Are you unhappy with your salary? 205
Where were you when the event happened? 117
When did you arrive at the scene? 157
Was there a lot of money in the safe? 34
What is the last task you completed? 228
If you've found it, you may show him the keyring. 240
If you have it, show him the wrinkled paper. 80

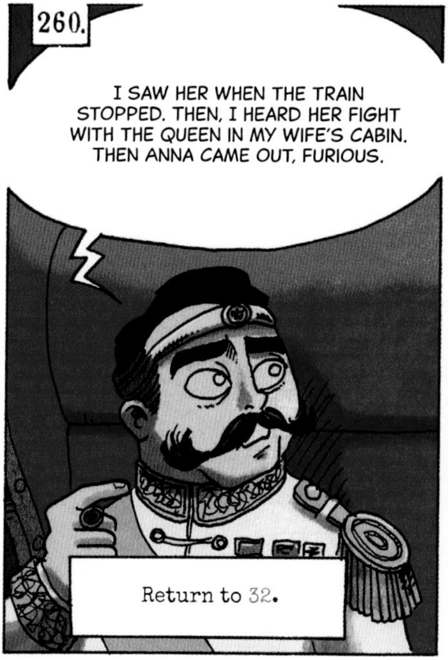
260.
I SAW HER WHEN THE TRAIN STOPPED. THEN, I HEARD HER FIGHT WITH THE QUEEN IN MY WIFE'S CABIN. THEN ANNA CAME OUT, FURIOUS.
Return to 32.

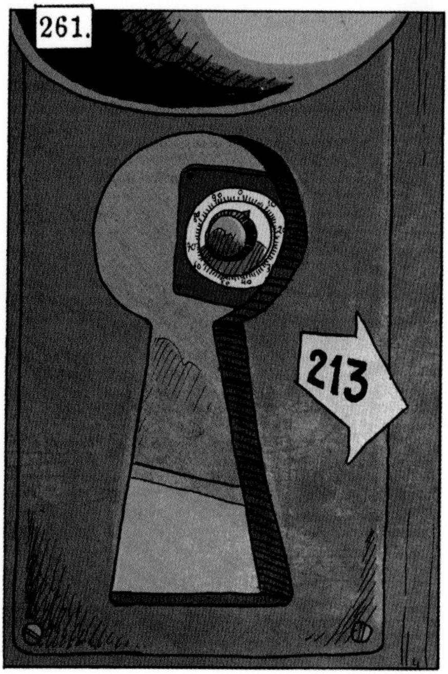
261.
213

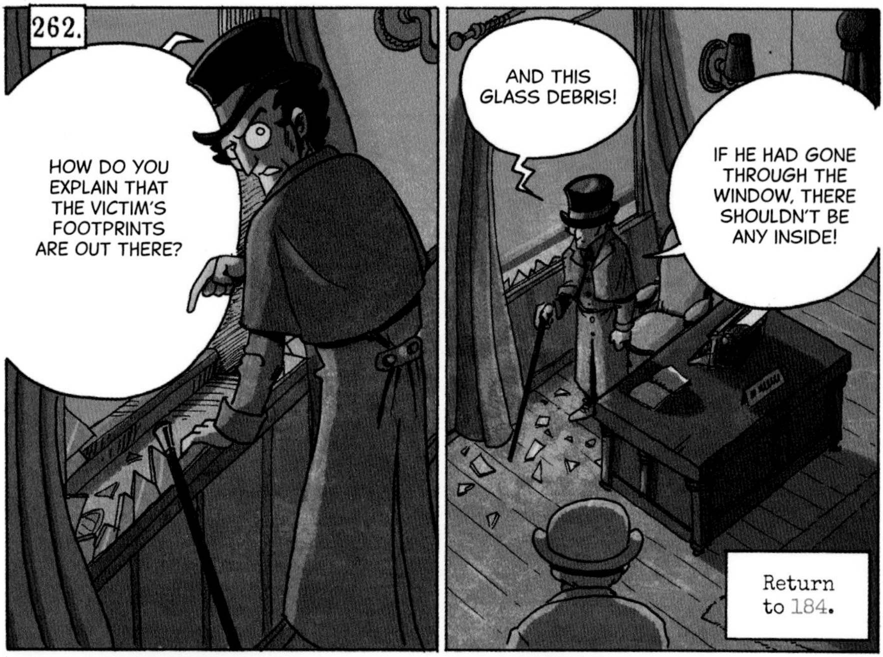
262.
HOW DO YOU EXPLAIN THAT THE VICTIM'S FOOTPRINTS ARE OUT THERE?
AND THIS GLASS DEBRIS!
IF HE HAD GONE THROUGH THE WINDOW, THERE SHOULDN'T BE ANY INSIDE!
Return to 184.

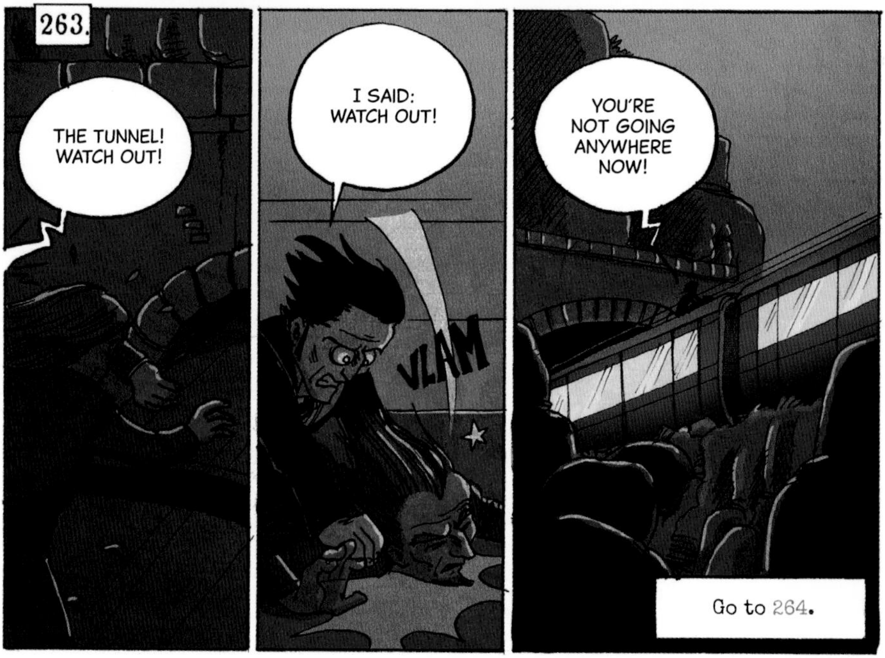
263.
THE TUNNEL! WATCH OUT!
I SAID: WATCH OUT!
VLAM
YOU'RE NOT GOING ANYWHERE NOW!
Go to 264.

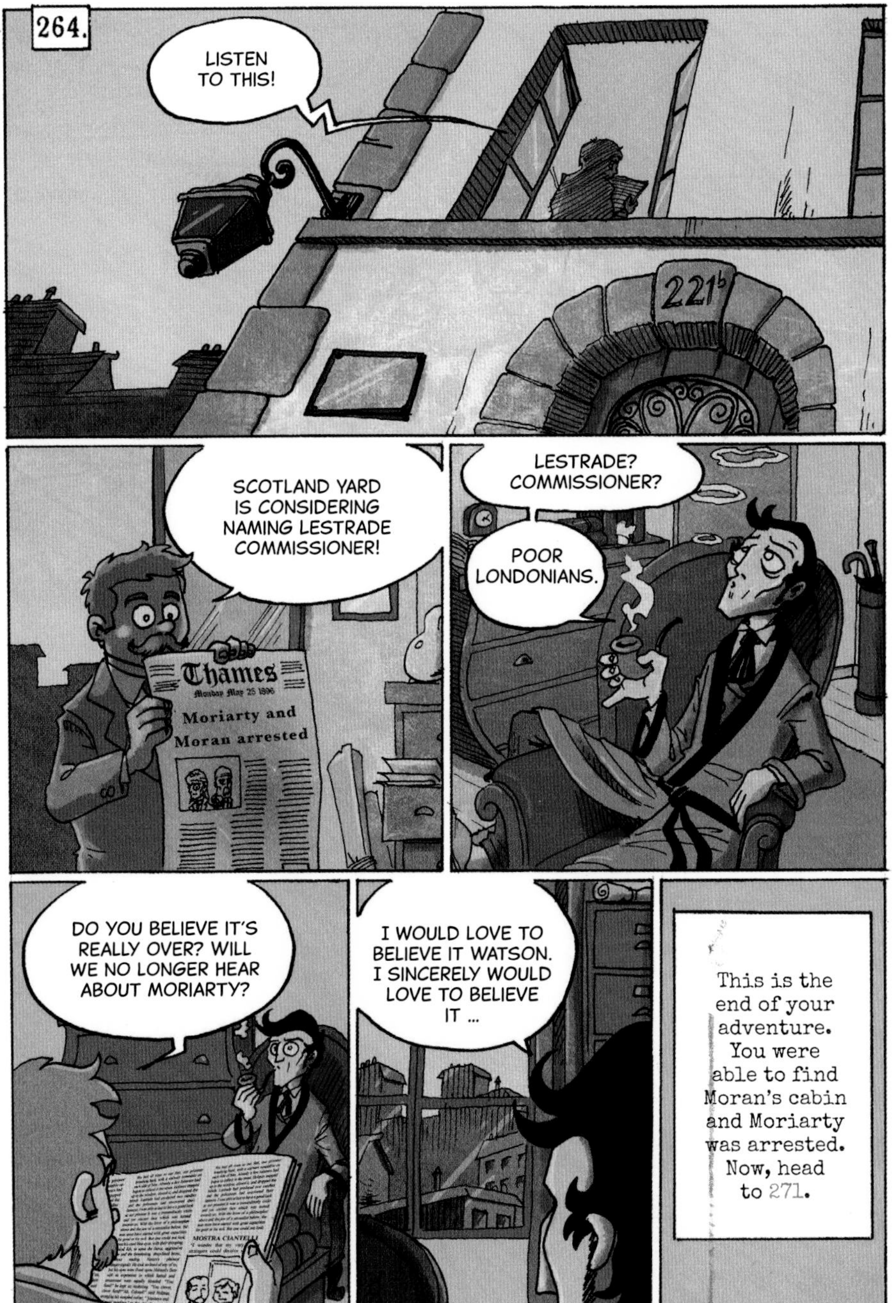
264.
LISTEN TO THIS!
221b
SCOTLAND YARD IS CONSIDERING NAMING LESTRADE COMMISSIONER!
Thames
Monday May 25 1896
Moriarty and Moran arrested
LESTRADE? COMMISSIONER?
POOR LONDONIANS.
DO YOU BELIEVE IT'S REALLY OVER? WILL WE NO LONGER HEAR ABOUT MORIARTY?
I WOULD LOVE TO BELIEVE IT WATSON. I SINCERELY WOULD LOVE TO BELIEVE IT ...
This is the end of your adventure. You were able to find Moran's cabin and Moriarty was arrested. Now, head to 271.

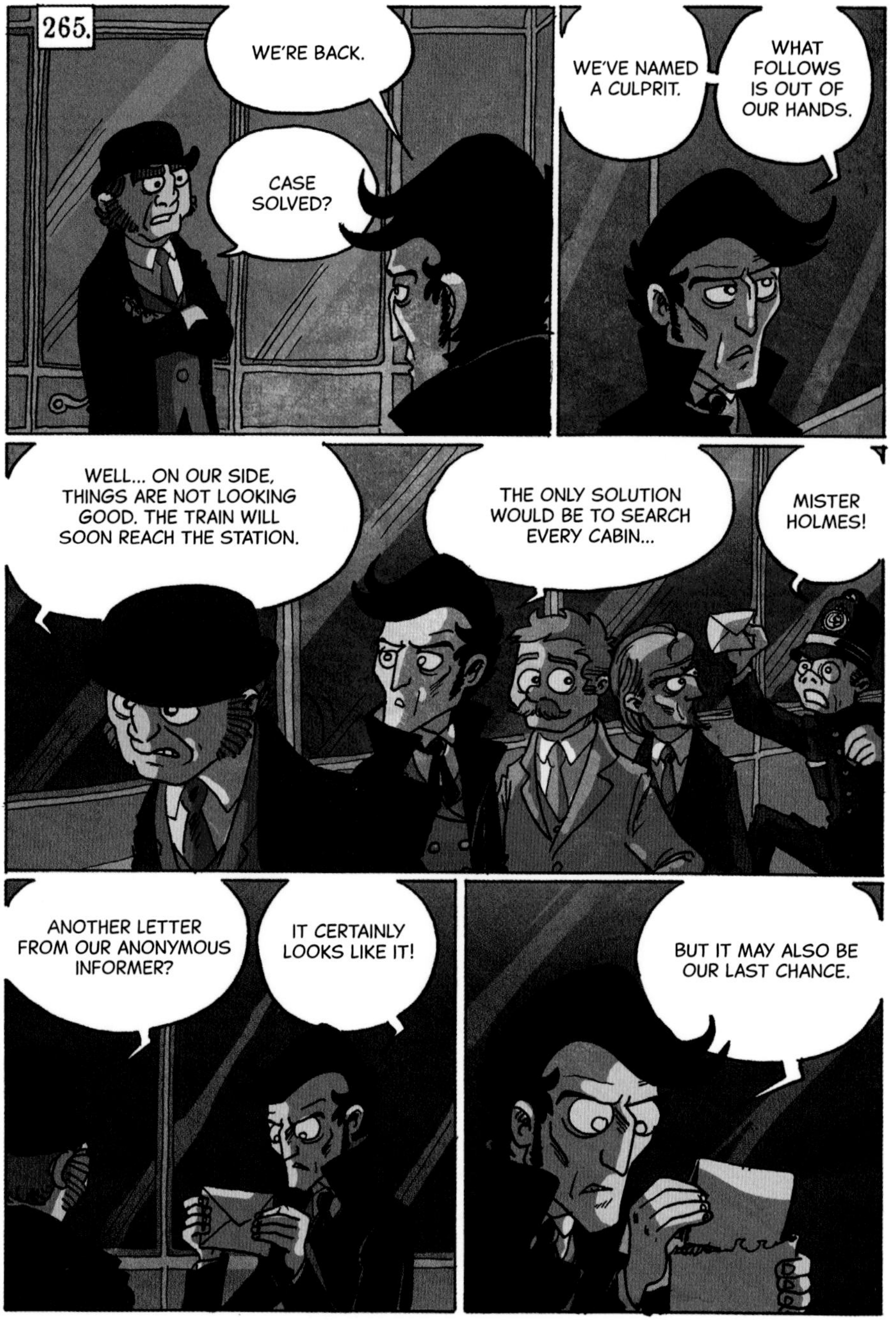
265.
WE'RE BACK.
CASE SOLVED?
WE'VE NAMED A CULPRIT.
WHAT FOLLOWS IS OUT OF OUR HANDS.
WELL... ON OUR SIDE, THINGS ARE NOT LOOKING GOOD. THE TRAIN WILL SOON REACH THE STATION.
THE ONLY SOLUTION WOULD BE TO SEARCH EVERY CABIN...
MISTER HOLMES!
ANOTHER LETTER FROM OUR ANONYMOUS INFORMER?
IT CERTAINLY LOOKS LIKE IT!
BUT IT MAY ALSO BE OUR LAST CHANCE.

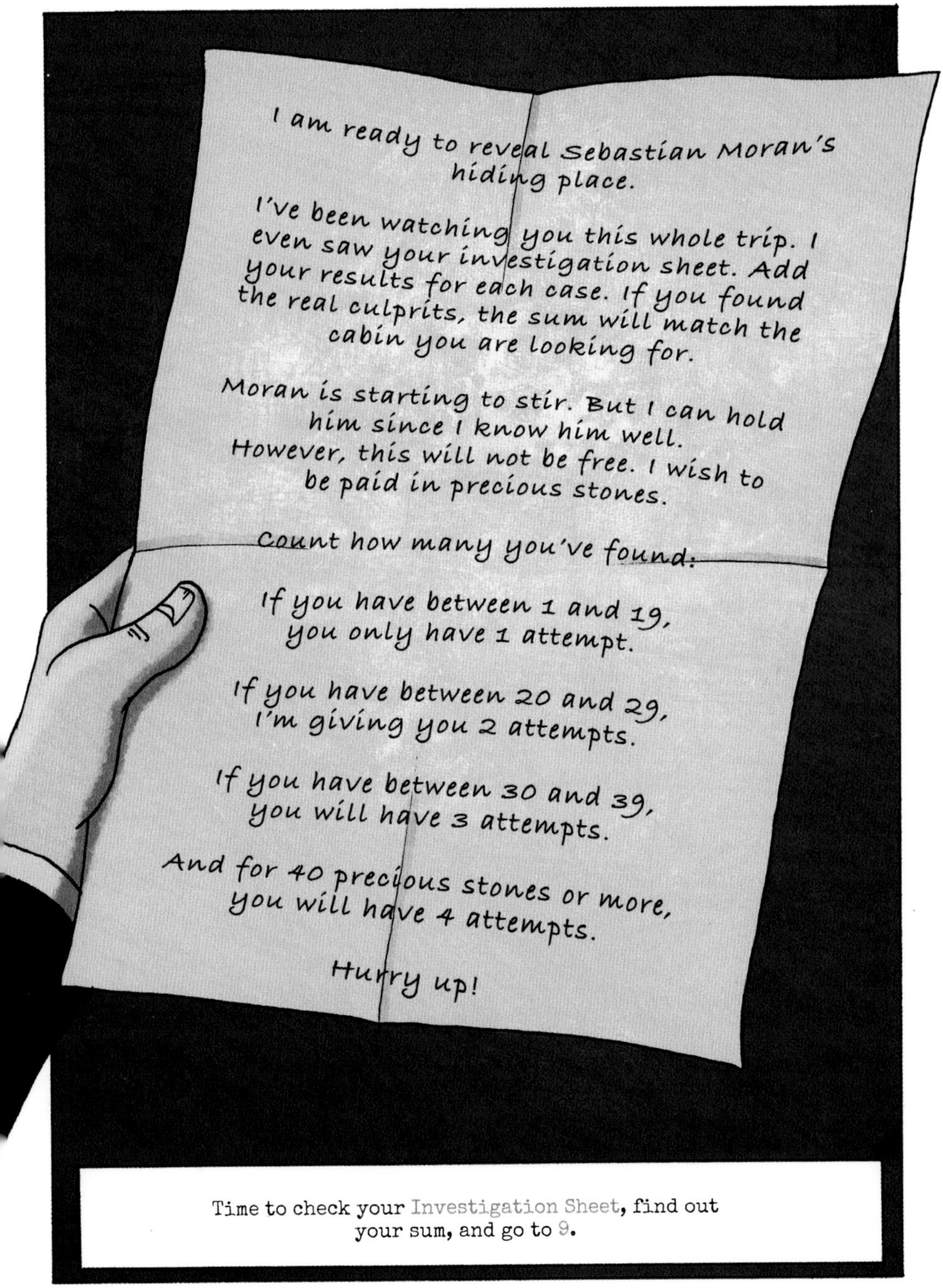
I am ready to reveal Sebastian Moran's hiding place.
I've been watching you this whole trip. I even saw your investigation sheet. Add your results for each case. If you found the real culprits, the sum will match the cabin you are looking for.
Moran is starting to stir. But I can hold him since I know him well.
However, this will not be free. I wish to be paid in precious stones.
Count how many you've found:
If you have between 1 and 19, you only have 1 attempt.
If you have between 20 and 29, I'm giving you 2 attempts.
If you have between 30 and 39, you will have 3 attempts.
And for 40 precious stones or more, you will have 4 attempts.
Hurry up!

Time to check your Investigation Sheet, find out your sum, and go to 9.

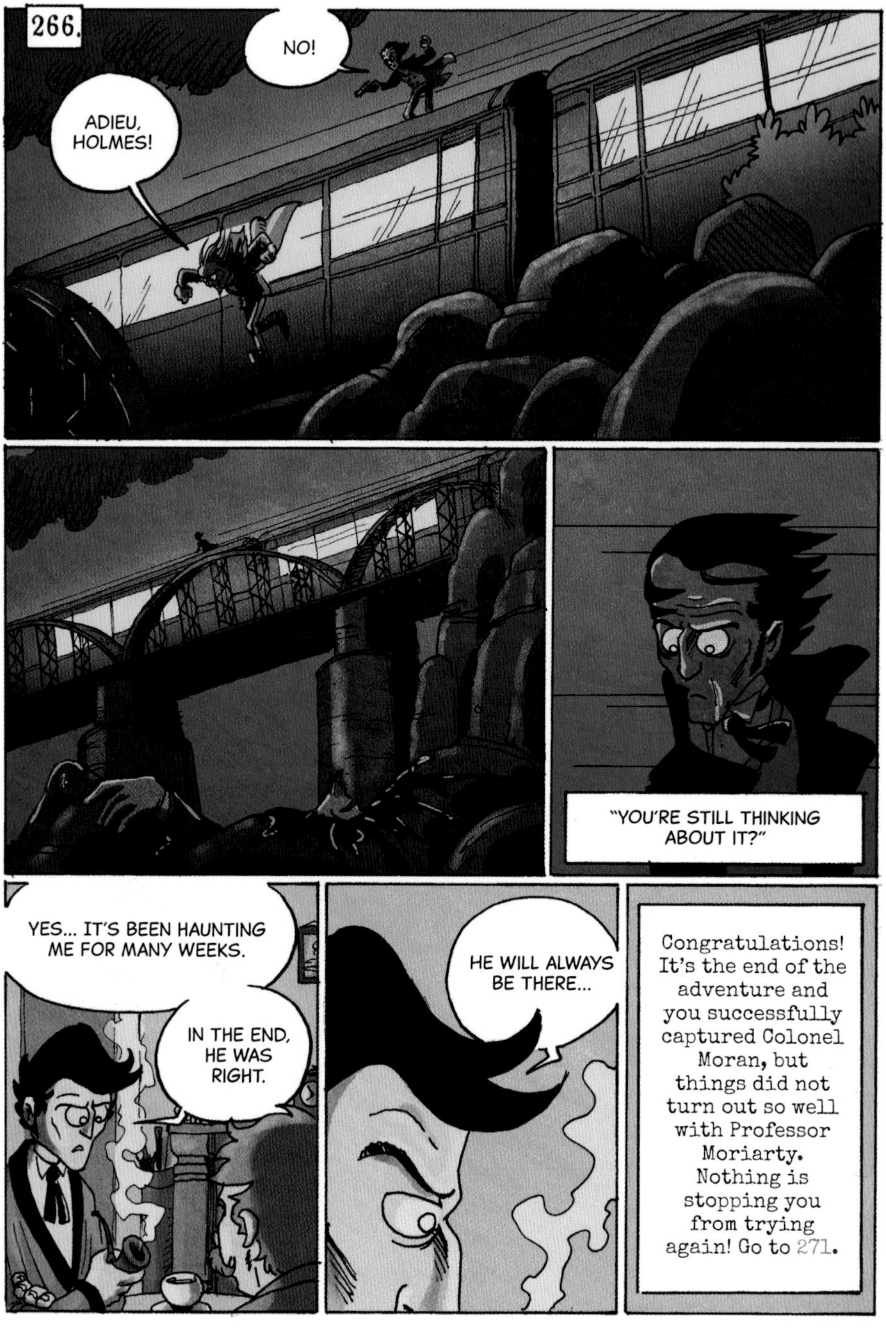
266.
NO!
ADIEU, HOLMES!
"YOU'RE STILL THINKING ABOUT IT?"
YES... IT'S BEEN HAUNTING ME FOR MANY WEEKS.
IN THE END, HE WAS RIGHT.
HE WILL ALWAYS BE THERE...
Congratulations! It's the end of the adventure and you successfully captured Colonel Moran, but things did not turn out so well with Professor Moriarty. Nothing is stopping you from trying again! Go to 271.

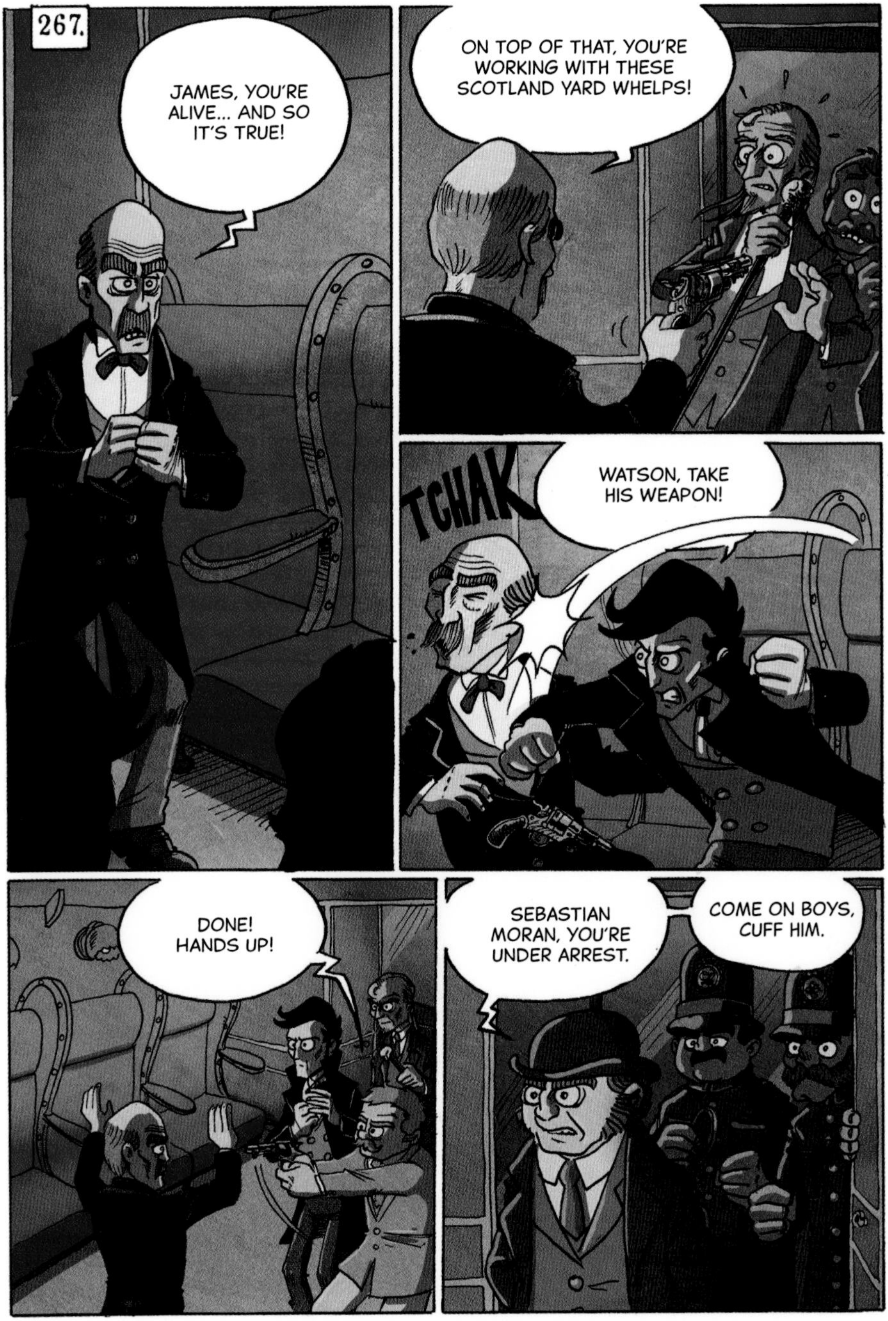
267.
JAMES, YOU'RE ALIVE... AND SO IT'S TRUE!
ON TOP OF THAT, YOU'RE WORKING WITH THESE SCOTLAND YARD WHELPS!
TCHAK
WATSON, TAKE HIS WEAPON!
DONE! HANDS UP!
SEBASTIAN MORAN, YOU'RE UNDER ARREST.
COME ON BOYS, CUFF HIM.

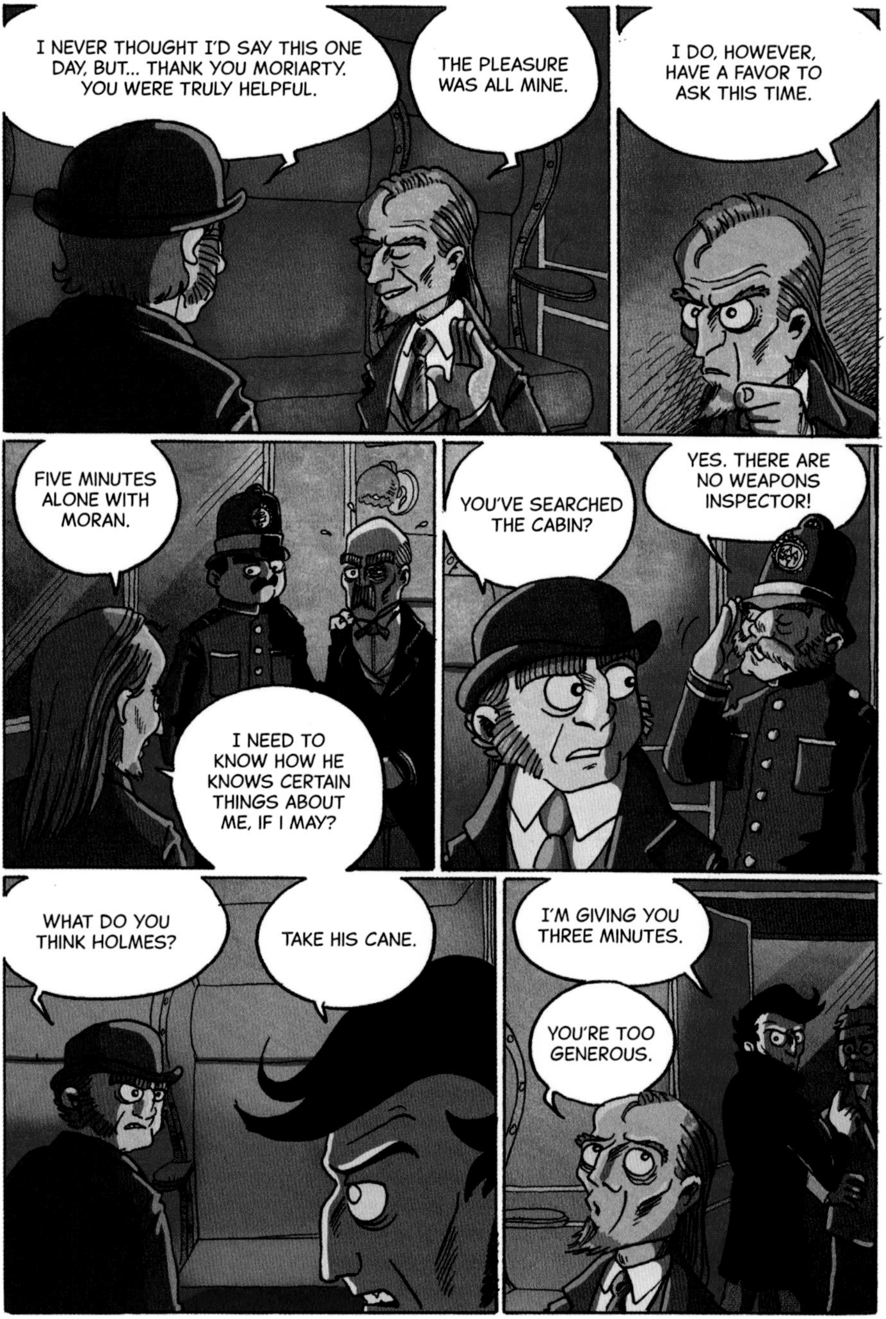
I NEVER THOUGHT I'D SAY THIS ONE DAY, BUT... THANK YOU MORIARTY. YOU WERE TRULY HELPFUL.
THE PLEASURE WAS ALL MINE.
I DO, HOWEVER, HAVE A FAVOR TO ASK THIS TIME.
FIVE MINUTES ALONE WITH MORAN.
I NEED TO KNOW HOW HE KNOWS CERTAIN THINGS ABOUT ME, IF I MAY?
YOU'VE SEARCHED THE CABIN?
YES. THERE ARE NO WEAPONS INSPECTOR!
WHAT DO YOU THINK HOLMES?
TAKE HIS CANE.
I'M GIVING YOU THREE MINUTES.
YOU'RE TOO GENEROUS.

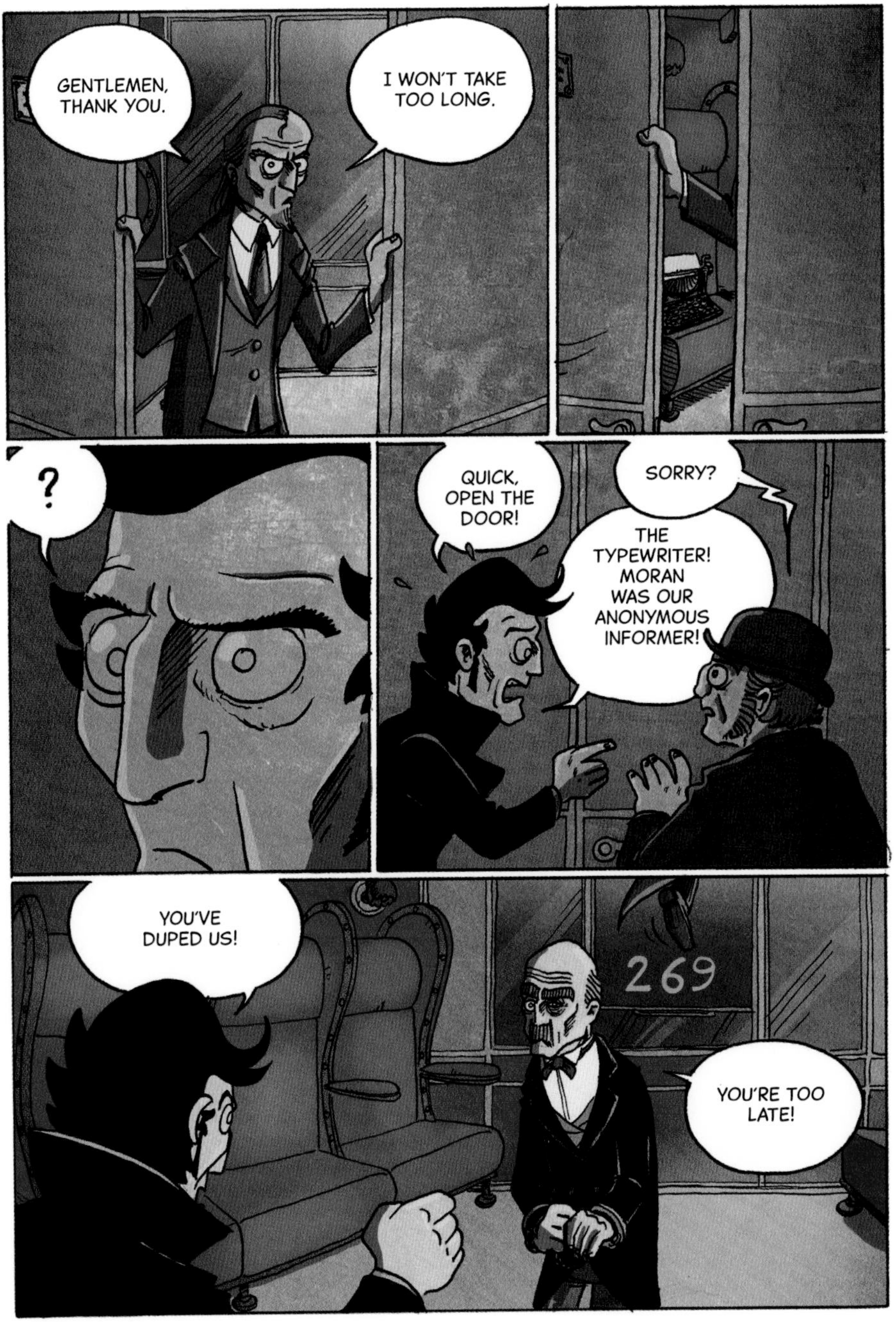
GENTLEMEN, THANK YOU.
I WON'T TAKE TOO LONG.
?
QUICK, OPEN THE DOOR!
SORRY?
THE TYPEWRITER! MORAN WAS OUR ANONYMOUS INFORMER!
YOU'VE DUPED US!
269
YOU'RE TOO LATE!

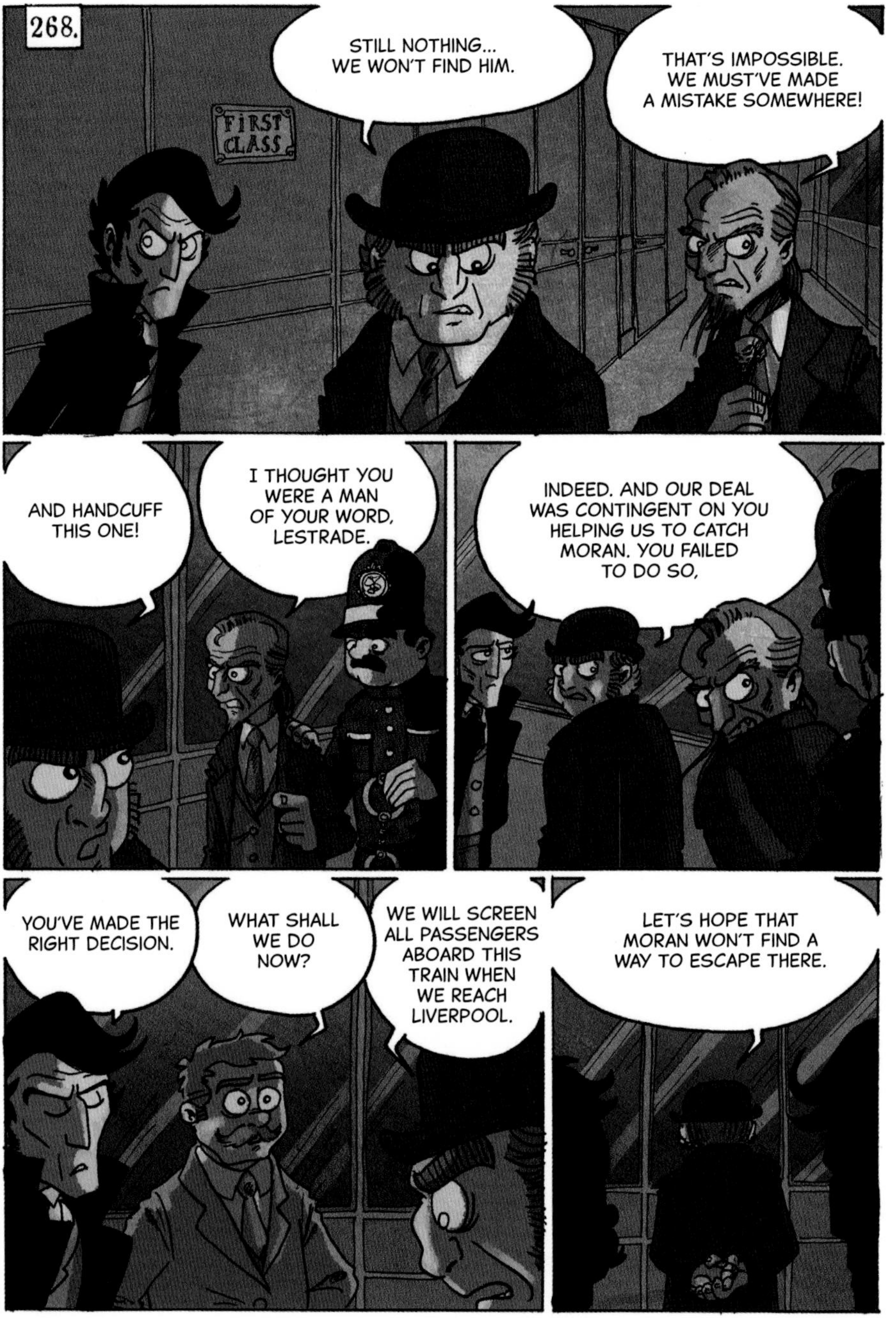
268.
STILL NOTHING... WE WON'T FIND HIM.
THAT'S IMPOSSIBLE. WE MUST'VE MADE A MISTAKE SOMEWHERE!
FIRST CLASS
AND HANDCUFF THIS ONE!
I THOUGHT YOU WERE A MAN OF YOUR WORD, LESTRADE.
INDEED. AND OUR DEAL WAS CONTINGENT ON YOU HELPING US TO CATCH MORAN. YOU FAILED TO DO SO,
YOU'VE MADE THE RIGHT DECISION.
WHAT SHALL WE DO NOW?
WE WILL SCREEN ALL PASSENGERS ABOARD THIS TRAIN WHEN WE REACH LIVERPOOL.
LET'S HOPE THAT MORAN WON'T FIND A WAY TO ESCAPE THERE.

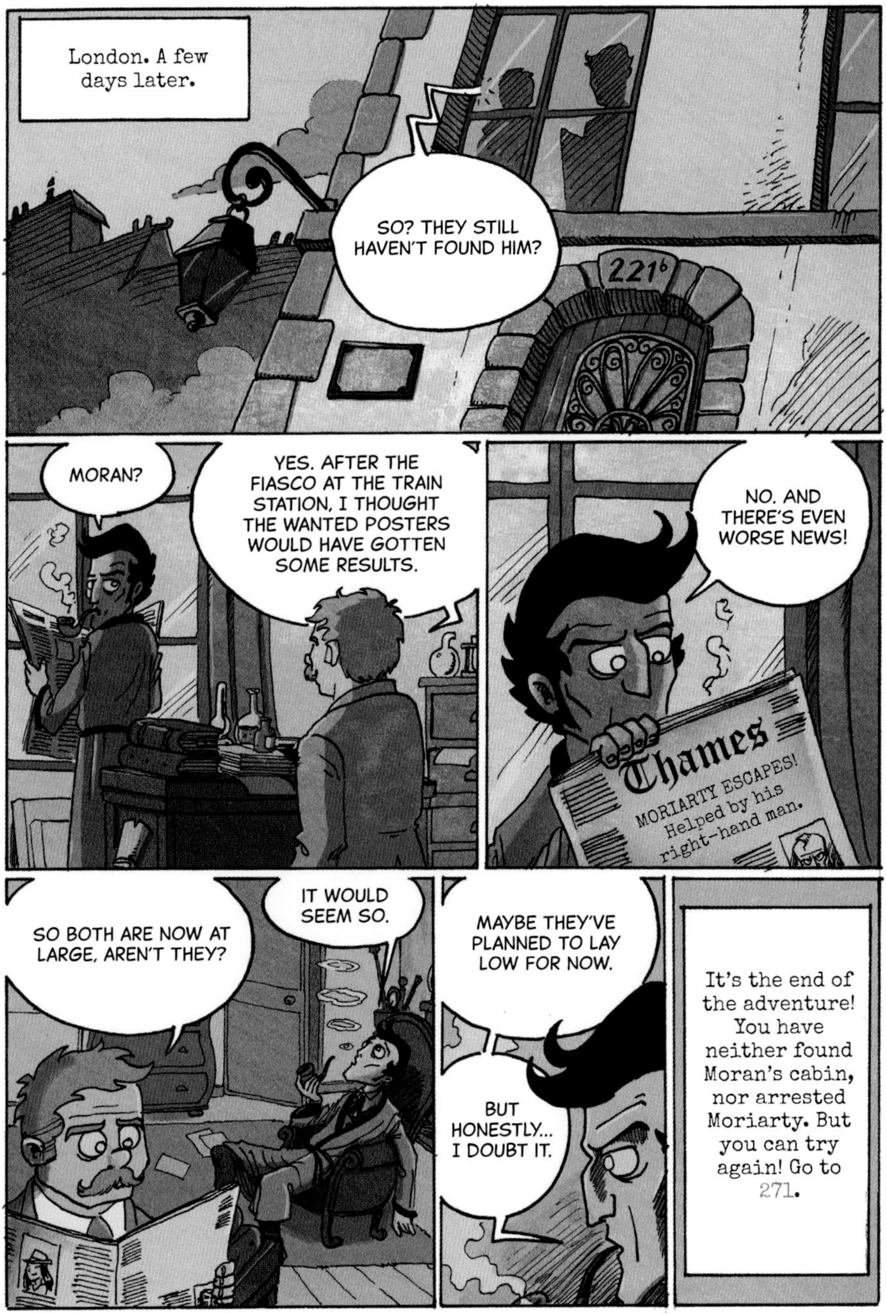
London. A few days later.
SO? THEY STILL HAVEN'T FOUND HIM?
221b
MORAN?
YES. AFTER THE FIASCO AT THE TRAIN STATION, I THOUGHT THE WANTED POSTERS WOULD HAVE GOTTEN SOME RESULTS.
NO. AND THERE'S EVEN WORSE NEWS!
Thames
MORIARTY ESCAPES!
MORIARTY Helped by his right-hand man.
SO BOTH ARE NOW AT LARGE, AREN'T THEY?
IT WOULD SEEM SO.
MAYBE THEY'VE PLANNED TO LAY LOW FOR NOW.
BUT HONESTLY... I DOUBT IT.
It's the end of the adventure! You have neither found Moran's cabin, nor arrested Moriarty. But you can try again! Go to 271.

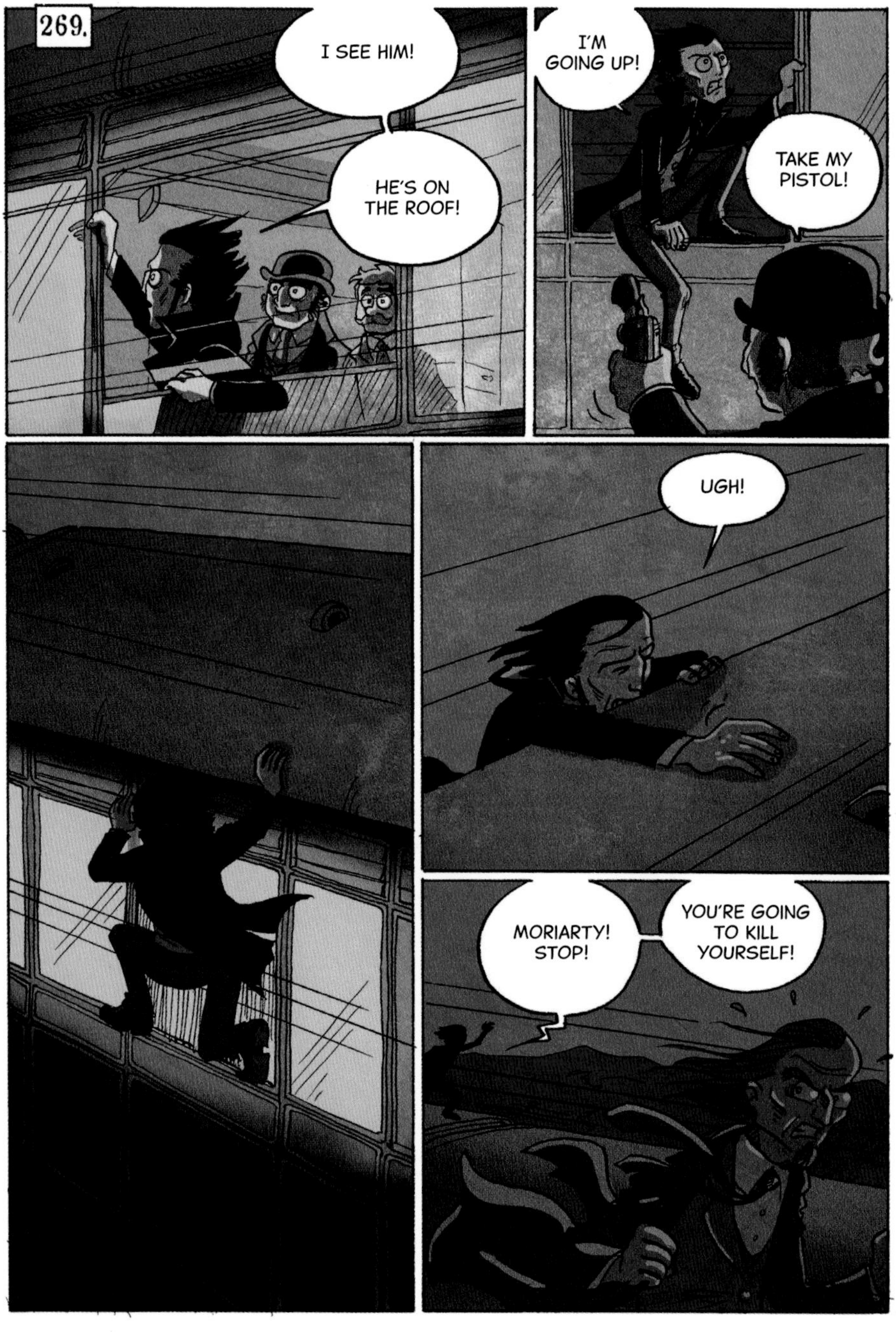
269.
I SEE HIM!
HE'S ON THE ROOF!
I'M GOING UP!
TAKE MY PISTOL!
UGH!
MORIARTY! STOP!
YOU'RE GOING TO KILL YOURSELF!

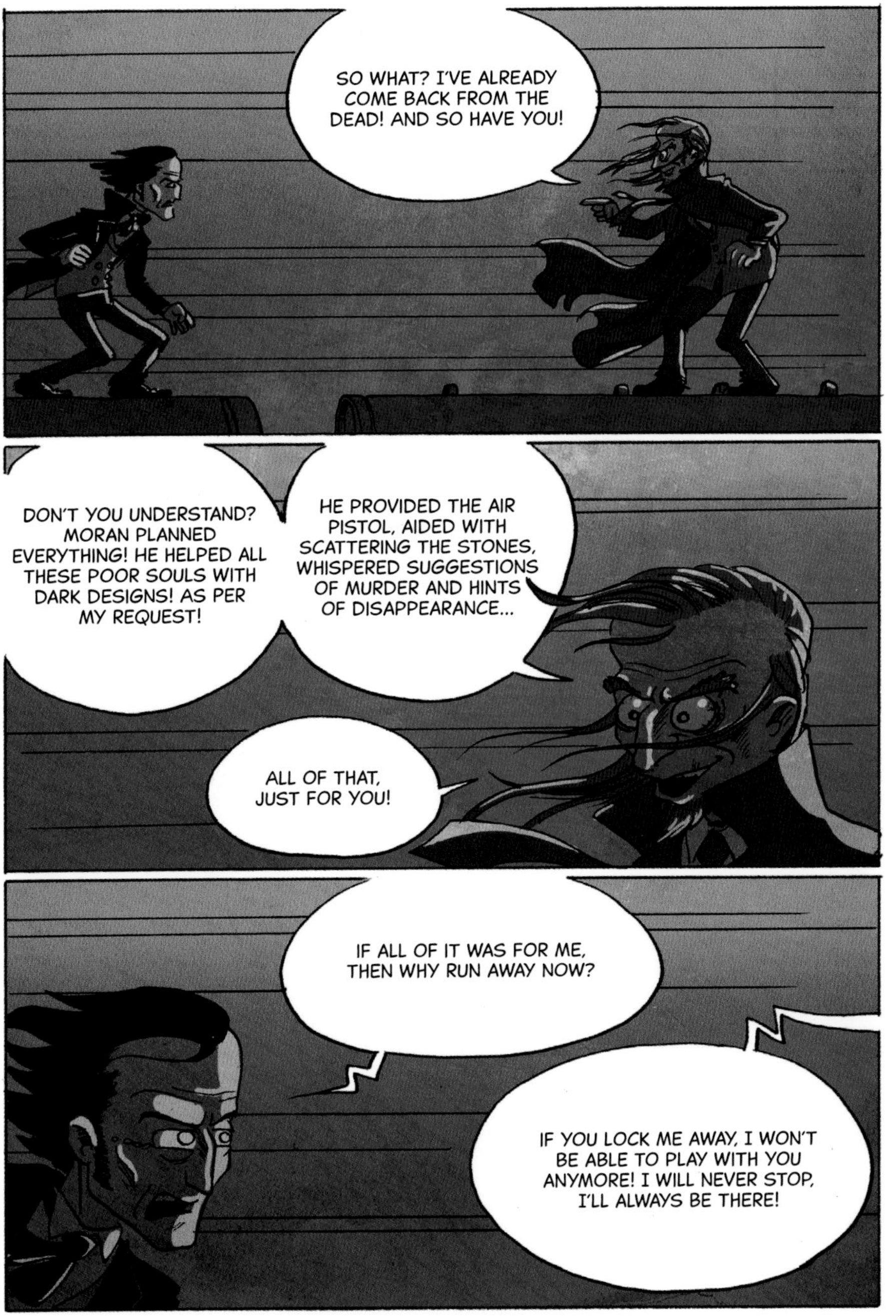
SO WHAT? I'VE ALREADY COME BACK FROM THE DEAD! AND SO HAVE YOU!
DON'T YOU UNDERSTAND? MORAN PLANNED EVERYTHING! HE HELPED ALL THESE POOR SOULS WITH DARK DESIGNS! AS PER MY REQUEST!
HE PROVIDED THE AIR PISTOL, AIDED WITH SCATTERING THE STONES, WHISPERED SUGGESTIONS OF MURDER AND HINTS OF DISAPPEARANCE...
ALL OF THAT, JUST FOR YOU!
IF ALL OF IT WAS FOR ME, THEN WHY RUN AWAY NOW?
IF YOU LOCK ME AWAY, I WON'T BE ABLE TO PLAY WITH YOU ANYMORE! I WILL NEVER STOP, I'LL ALWAYS BE THERE!

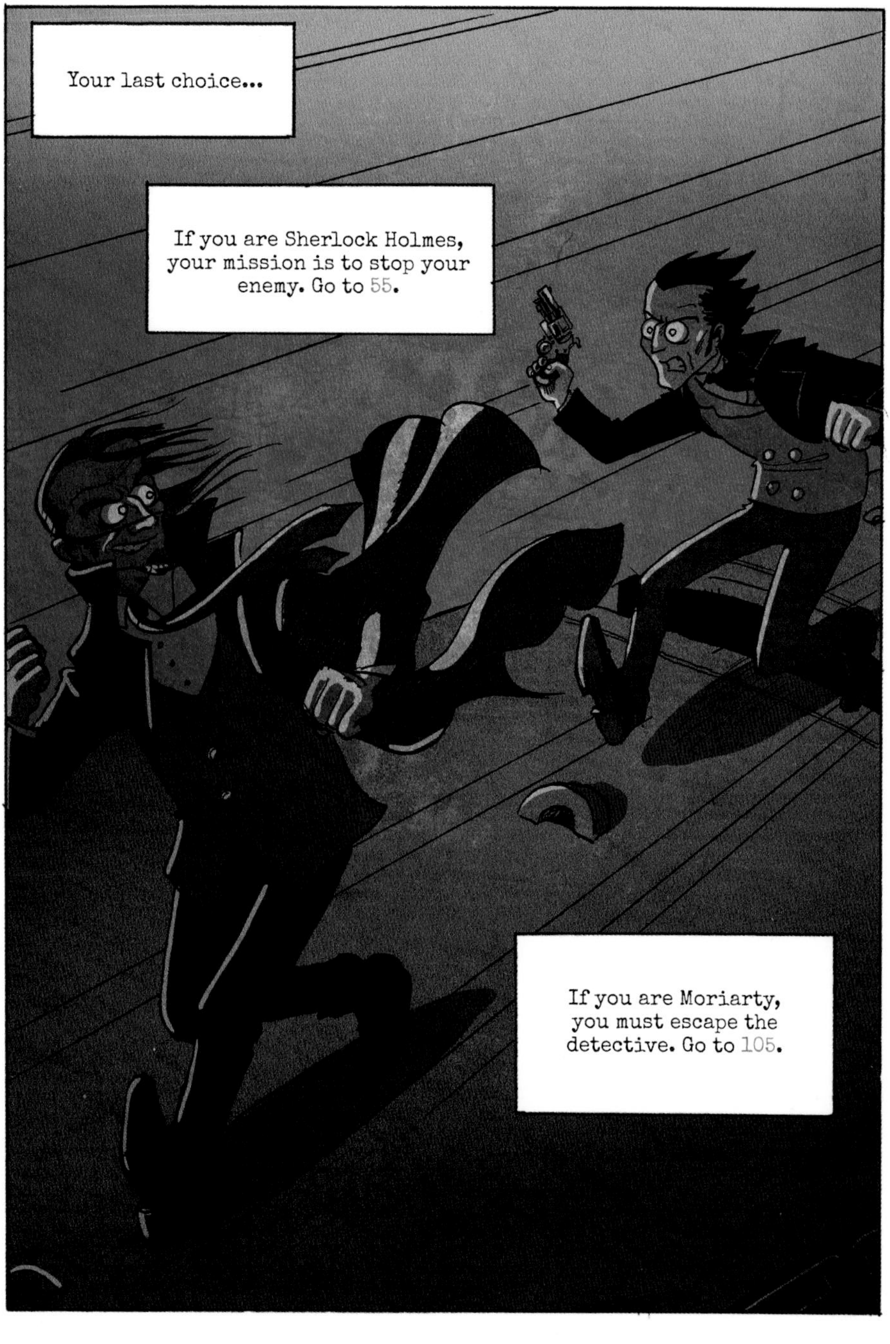
Your last choice...
If you are Sherlock Holmes, your mission is to stop your enemy. Go to 55.
If you are Moriarty, you must escape the detective. Go to 105.

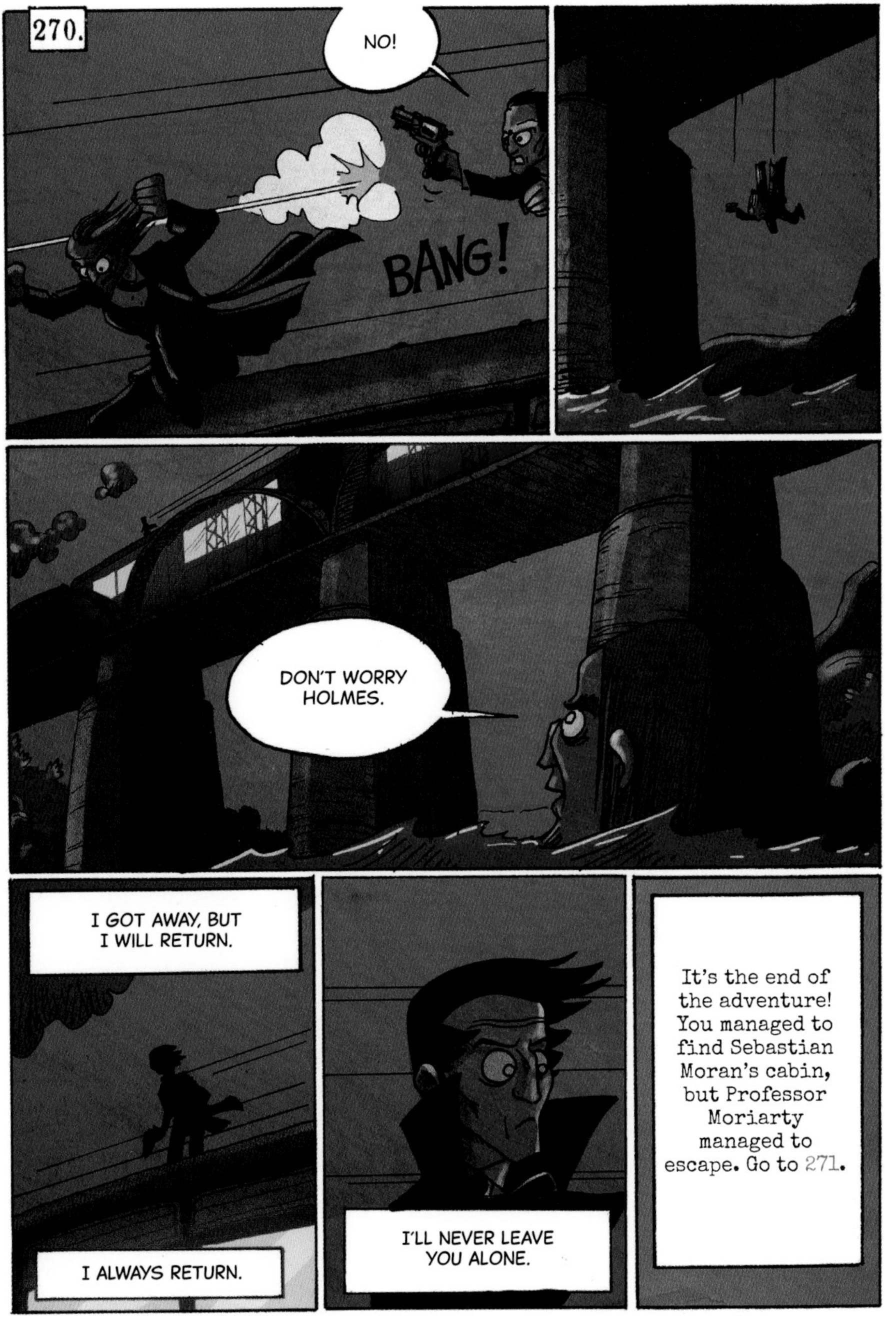

270.
NO!
BANG!
DON'T WORRY
HOLMES.
I GOT AWAY, BUT
I WILL RETURN.
I ALWAYS RETURN.
I'LL NEVER LEAVE
YOU ALONE.
It's the end of
the adventure!
You managed to
find Sebastian
Moran's cabin,
but Professor
Moriarty
managed to
escape. Go to 271.

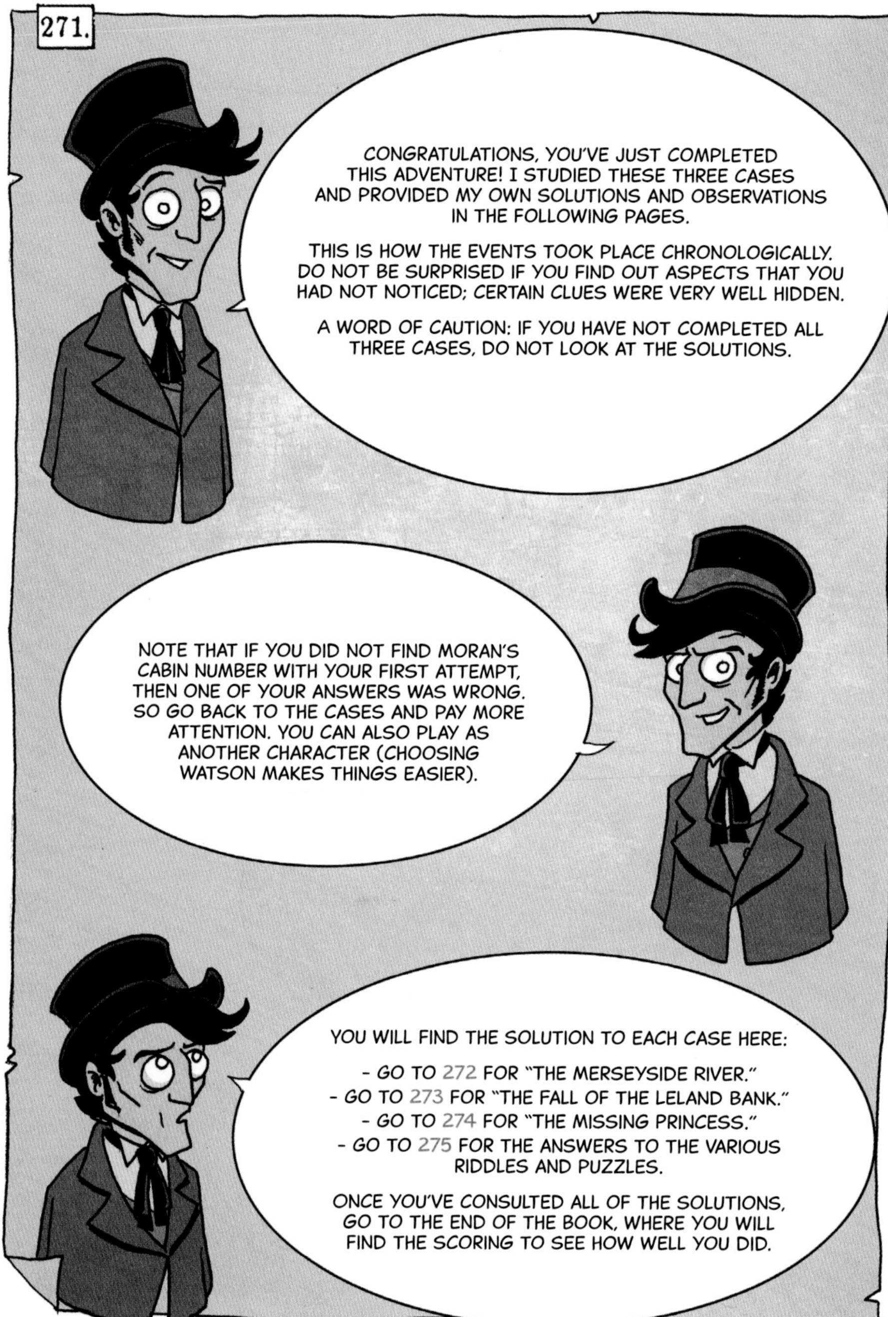
271.
CONGRATULATIONS, YOU'VE JUST COMPLETED THIS ADVENTURE! I STUDIED THESE THREE CASES AND PROVIDED MY OWN SOLUTIONS AND OBSERVATIONS IN THE FOLLOWING PAGES.
THIS IS HOW THE EVENTS TOOK PLACE CHRONOLOGICALLY. DO NOT BE SURPRISED IF YOU FIND OUT ASPECTS THAT YOU HAD NOT NOTICED; CERTAIN CLUES WERE VERY WELL HIDDEN.
A WORD OF CAUTION: IF YOU HAVE NOT COMPLETED ALL THREE CASES, DO NOT LOOK AT THE SOLUTIONS.
NOTE THAT IF YOU DID NOT FIND MORAN'S CABIN NUMBER WITH YOUR FIRST ATTEMPT, THEN ONE OF YOUR ANSWERS WAS WRONG. SO GO BACK TO THE CASES AND PAY MORE ATTENTION. YOU CAN ALSO PLAY AS ANOTHER CHARACTER (CHOOSING WATSON MAKES THINGS EASIER).
YOU WILL FIND THE SOLUTION TO EACH CASE HERE:
- GO TO 272 FOR "THE MERSEYSIDE RIVER."
- GO TO 273 FOR "THE FALL OF THE LELAND BANK."
- GO TO 274 FOR "THE MISSING PRINCESS."
- GO TO 275 FOR THE ANSWERS TO THE VARIOUS RIDDLES AND PUZZLES.
ONCE YOU'VE CONSULTED ALL OF THE SOLUTIONS, GO TO THE END OF THE BOOK, WHERE YOU WILL FIND THE SCORING TO SEE HOW WELL YOU DID.

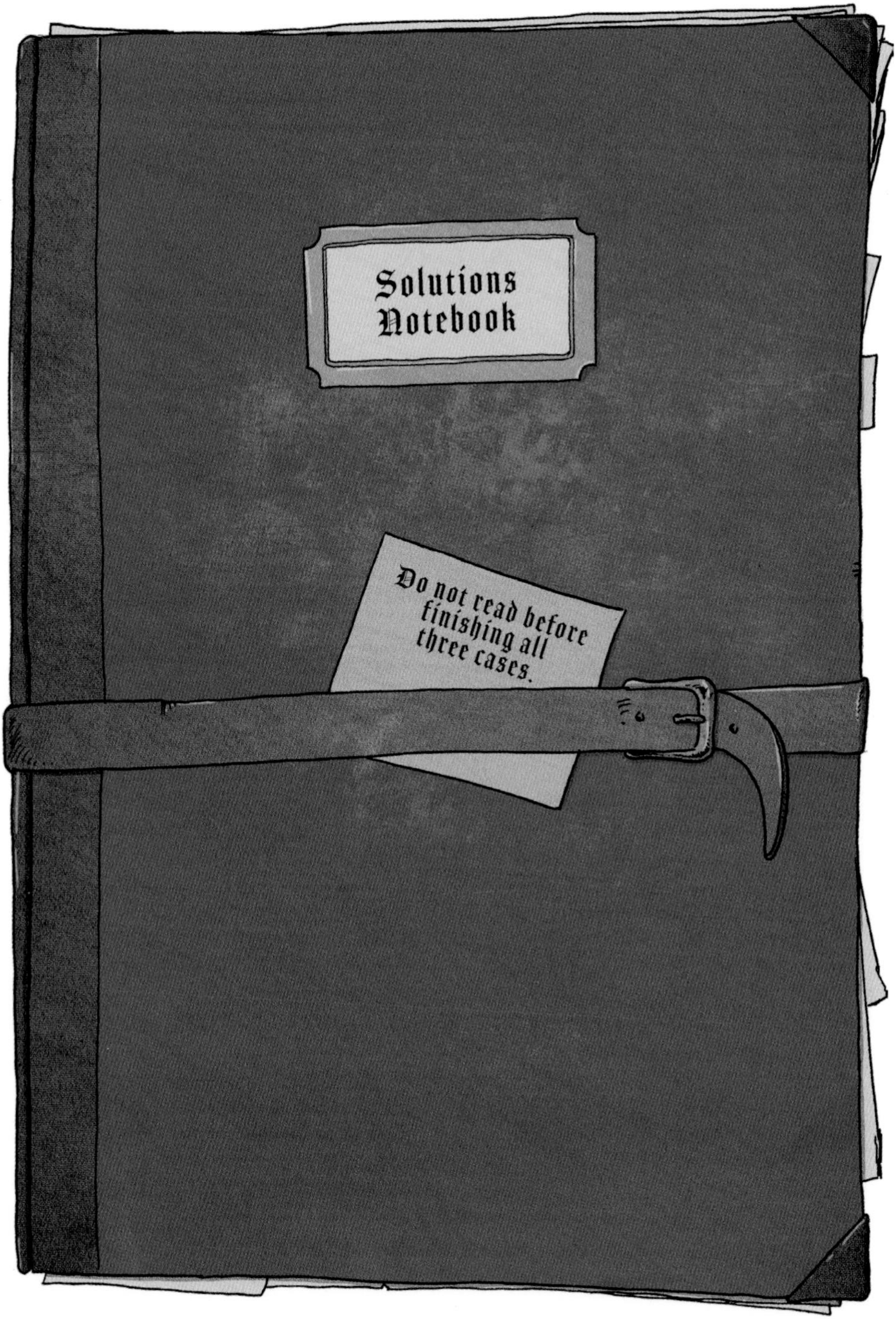
Solutions
Notebook
Do not read before finishing all three cases.

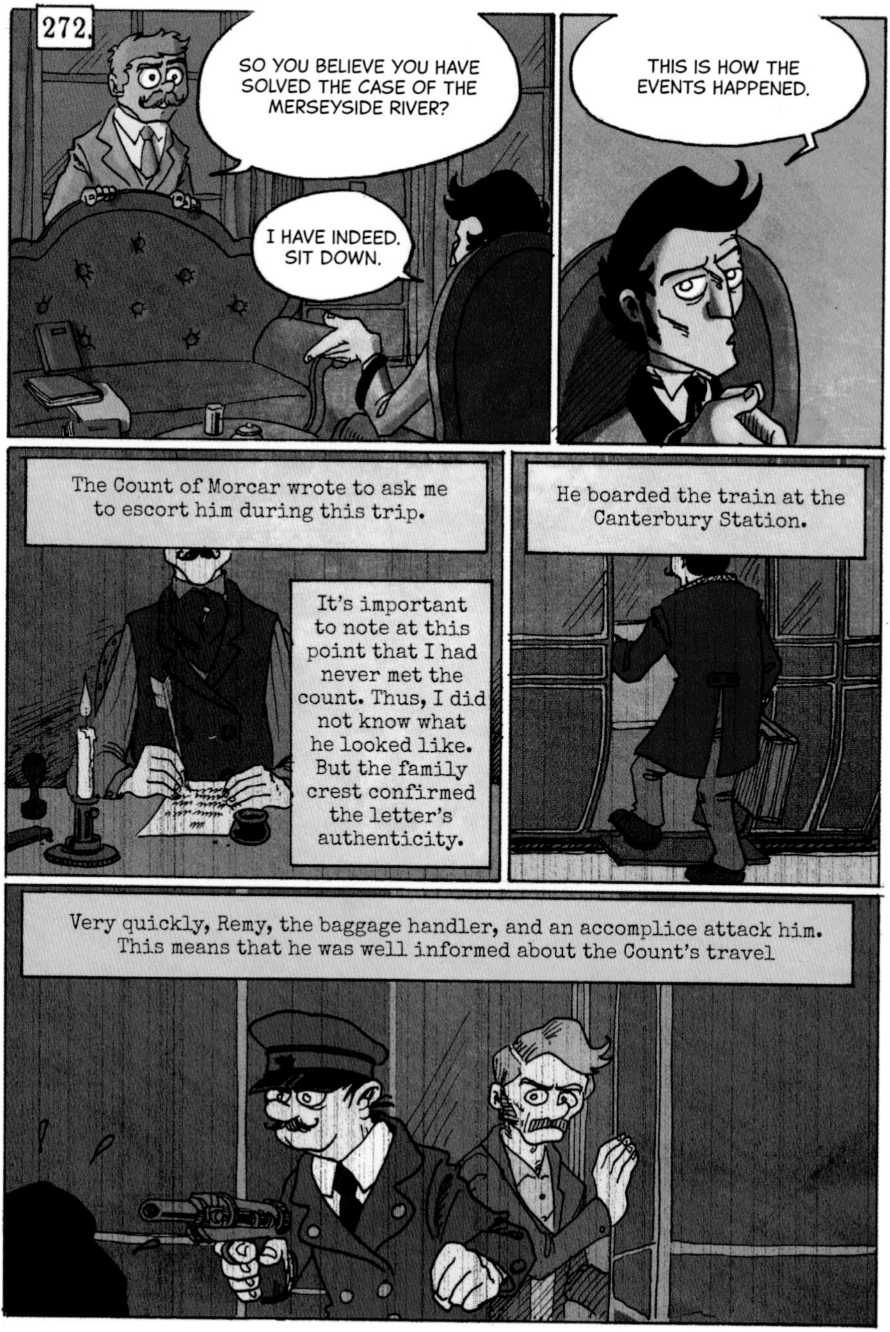
272.
SO YOU BELIEVE YOU HAVE SOLVED THE CASE OF THE MERSEYSIDE RIVER?
I HAVE INDEED. SIT DOWN.
THIS IS HOW THE EVENTS HAPPENED.
The Count of Morcar wrote to ask me to escort him during this trip.
It's important to note at this point that I had never met the count. Thus, I did not know what he looked like. But the family crest confirmed the letter's authenticity.
He boarded the train at the Canterbury Station.
Very quickly, Remy, the baggage handler, and an accomplice attack him. This means that he was well informed about the Count's travel

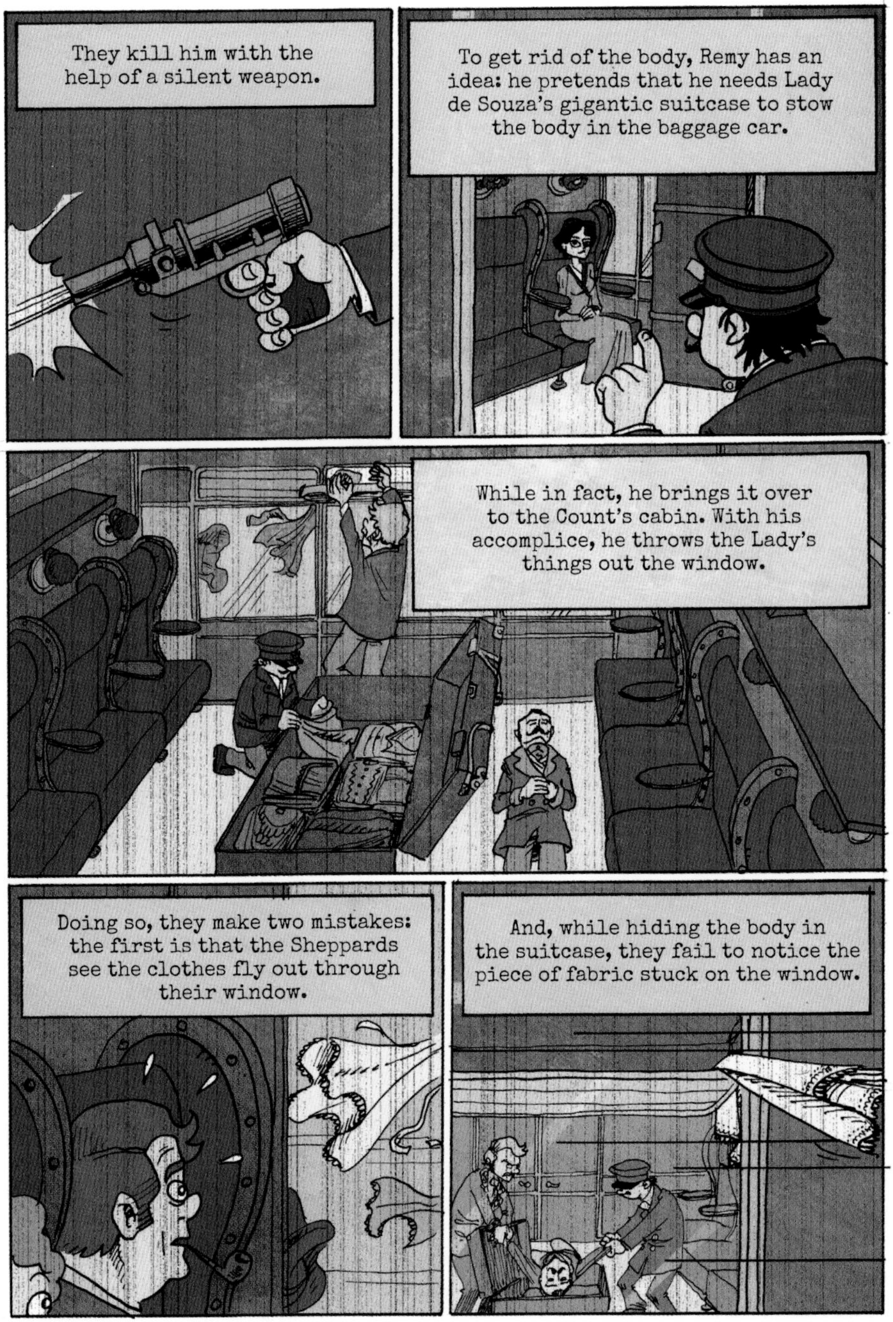
They kill him with the help of a silent weapon.
To get rid of the body, Remy has an idea: he pretends that he needs Lady de Souza's gigantic suitcase to stow the body in the baggage car.
While in fact, he brings it over to the Count's cabin. With his accomplice, he throws the Lady's things out the window.
Doing so, they make two mistakes: the first is that the Sheppards see the clothes fly out through their window.
And, while hiding the body in the suitcase, they fail to notice the piece of fabric stuck on the window.

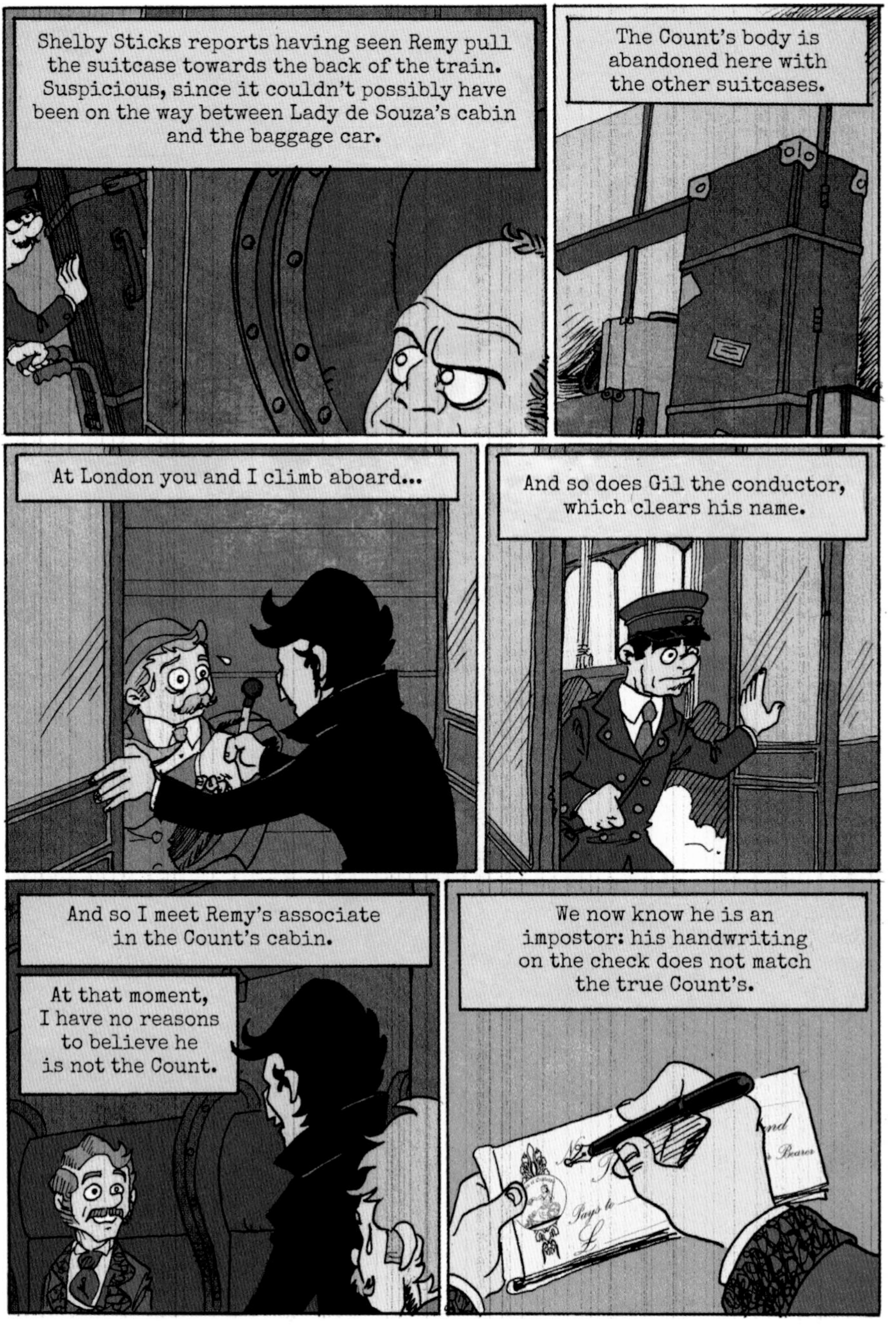
Shelby Sticks reports having seen Remy pull the suitcase towards the back of the train. Suspicious, since it couldn't possibly have been on the way between Lady de Souza's cabin and the baggage car.
The Count's body is abandoned here with the other suitcases.
At London you and I climb aboard...
And so does Gil the conductor, which clears his name.
And so I meet Remy's associate in the Count's cabin.
At that moment, I have no reasons to believe he is not the Count.
We now know he is an impostor: his handwriting on the check does not match the true Count's.

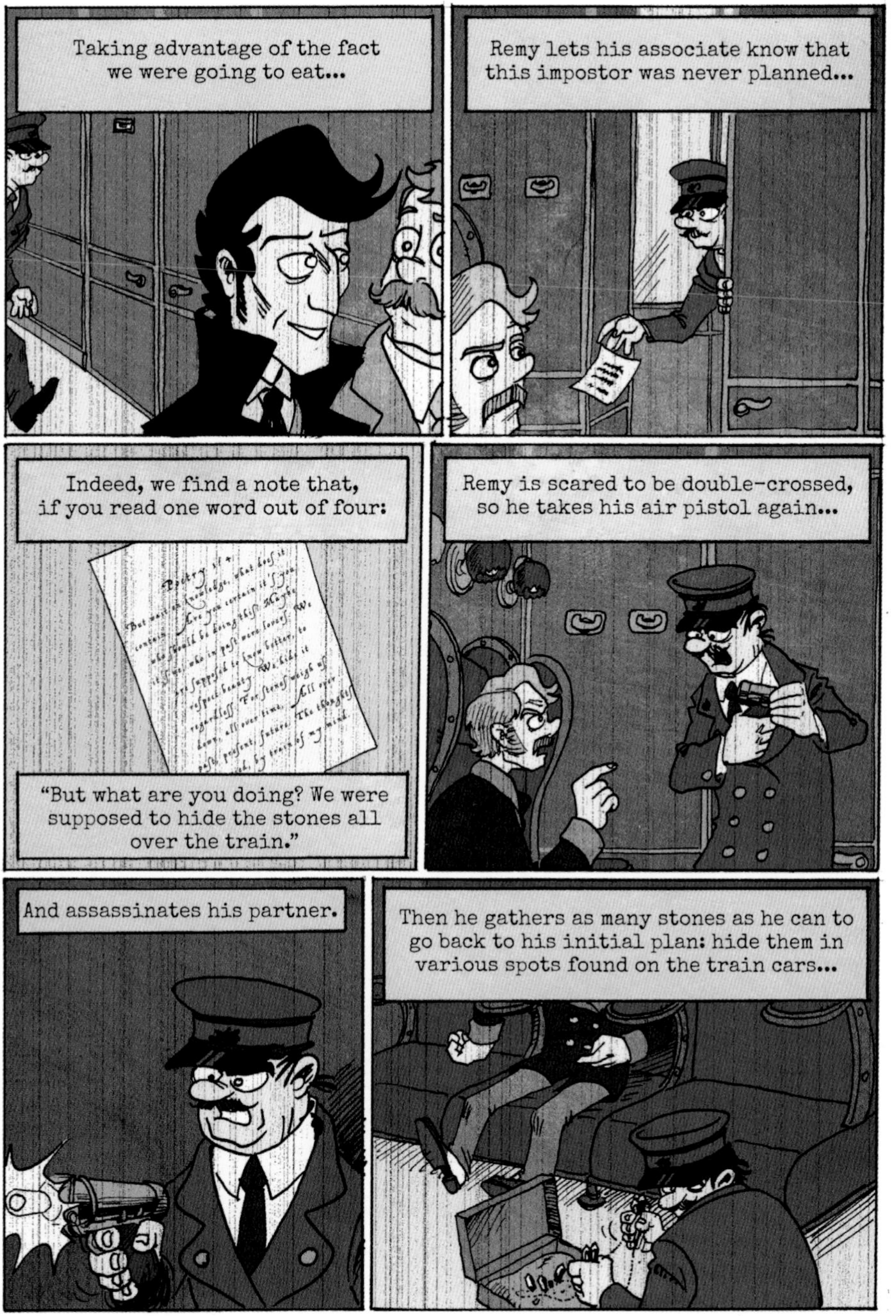
Taking advantage of the fact we were going to eat...
Remy lets his associate know that this impostor was never planned...
Indeed, we find a note that, if you read one word out of four:
"But what are you doing? We were supposed to hide the stones all over the train."
Remy is scared to be double-crossed, so he takes his air pistol again...
And assassinates his partner.
Then he gathers as many stones as he can to go back to his initial plan: hide them in various spots found on the train cars...

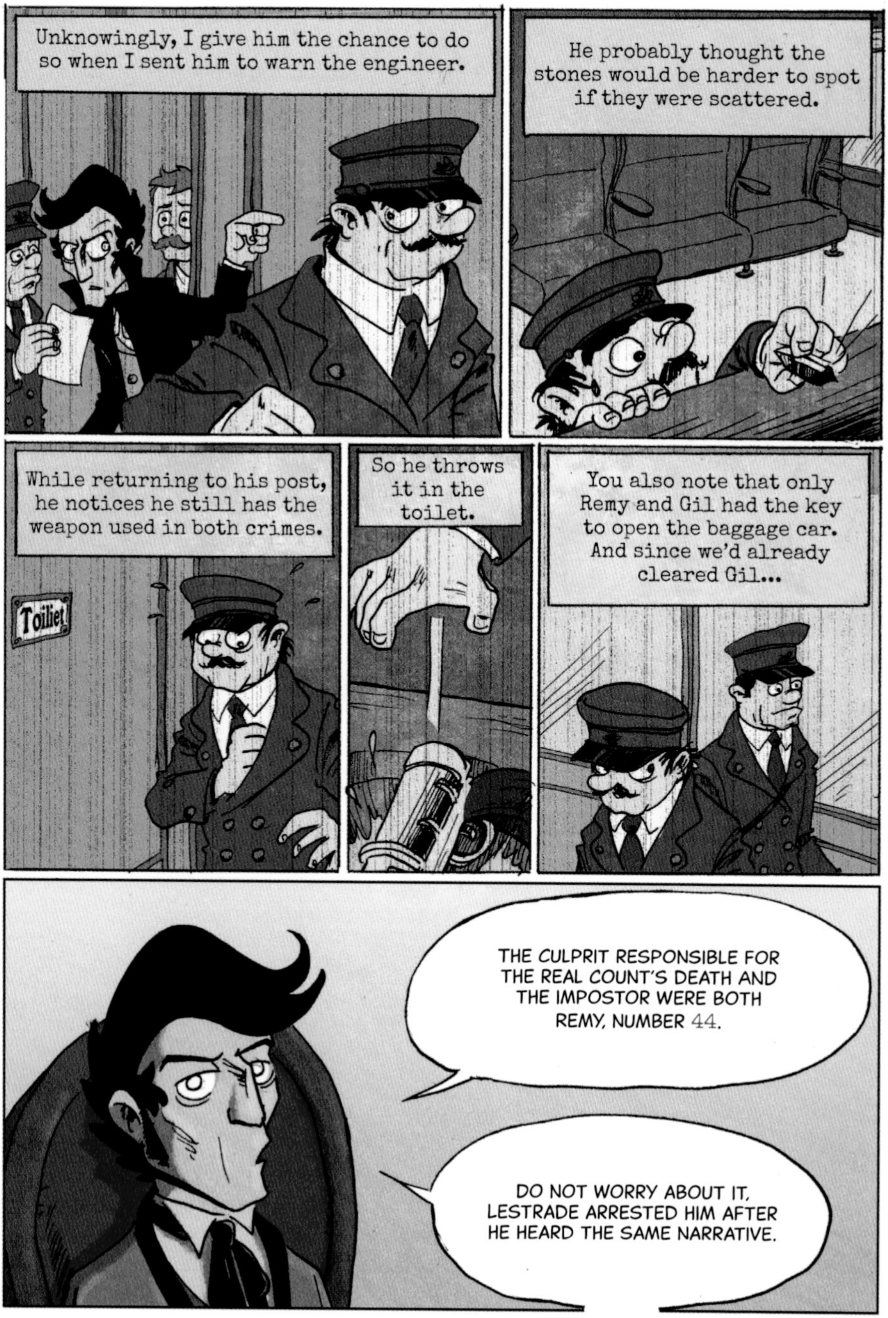

Unknowingly, I give him the chance to do so when I sent him to warn the engineer.
He probably thought the stones would be harder to spot if they were scattered.
While returning to his post, he notices he still has the weapon used in both crimes.
Toiliet
So he throws it in the toilet.
You also note that only Remy and Gil had the key to open the baggage car. And since we'd already cleared Gil...
THE CULPRIT RESPONSIBLE FOR THE REAL COUNT'S DEATH AND THE IMPOSTOR WERE BOTH REMY, NUMBER 44.
DO NOT WORRY ABOUT IT, LESTRADE ARRESTED HIM AFTER HE HEARD THE SAME NARRATIVE.

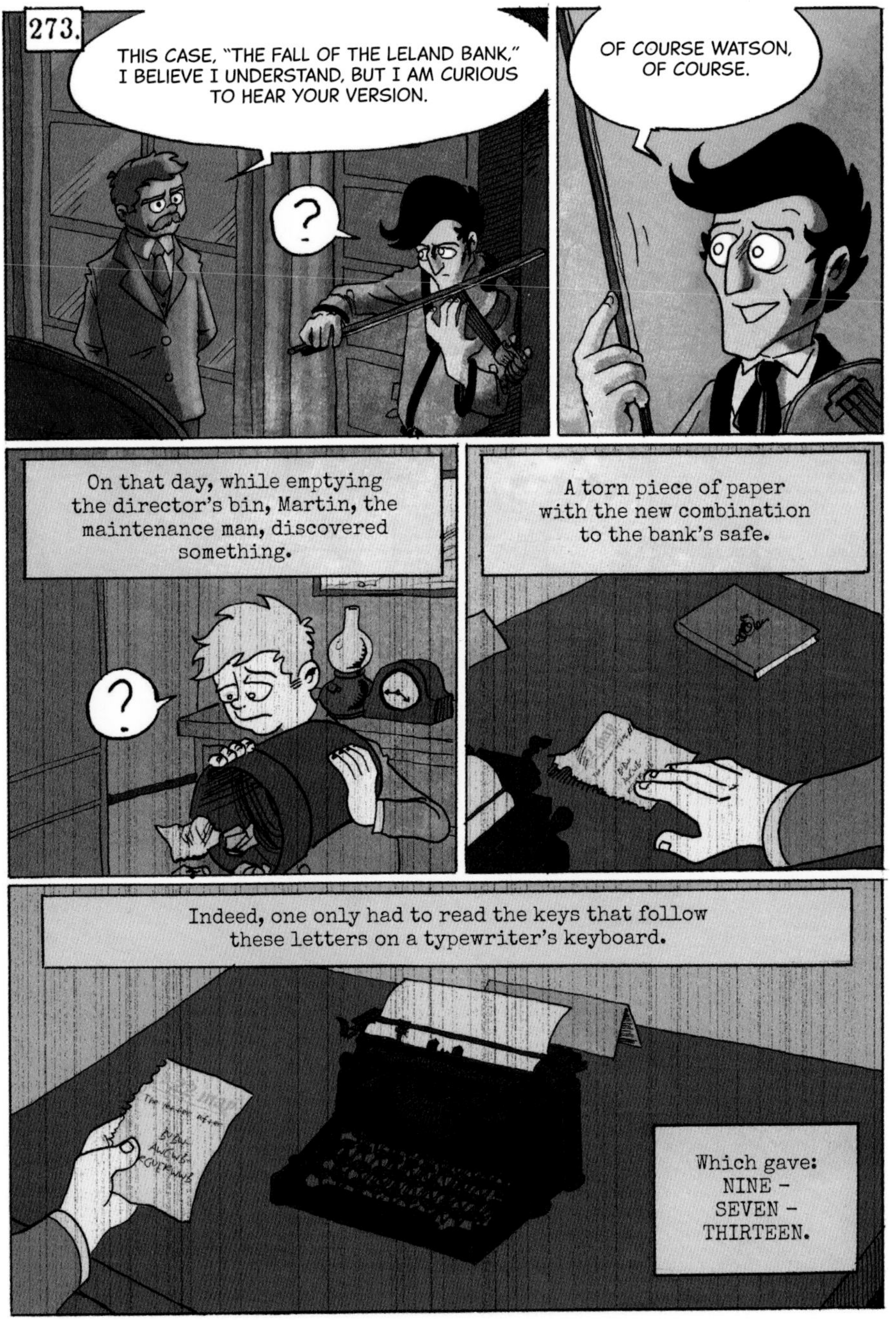
273.
THIS CASE, "THE FALL OF THE LELAND BANK," I BELIEVE I UNDERSTAND, BUT I AM CURIOUS TO HEAR YOUR VERSION.
?
OF COURSE WATSON, OF COURSE.
On that day, while emptying the director's bin, Martin, the maintenance man, discovered something.
?
A torn piece of paper with the new combination to the bank's safe.
Indeed, one only had to read the keys that follow these letters on a typewriter's keyboard.
Which gave: NINE - SEVEN - THIRTEEN.

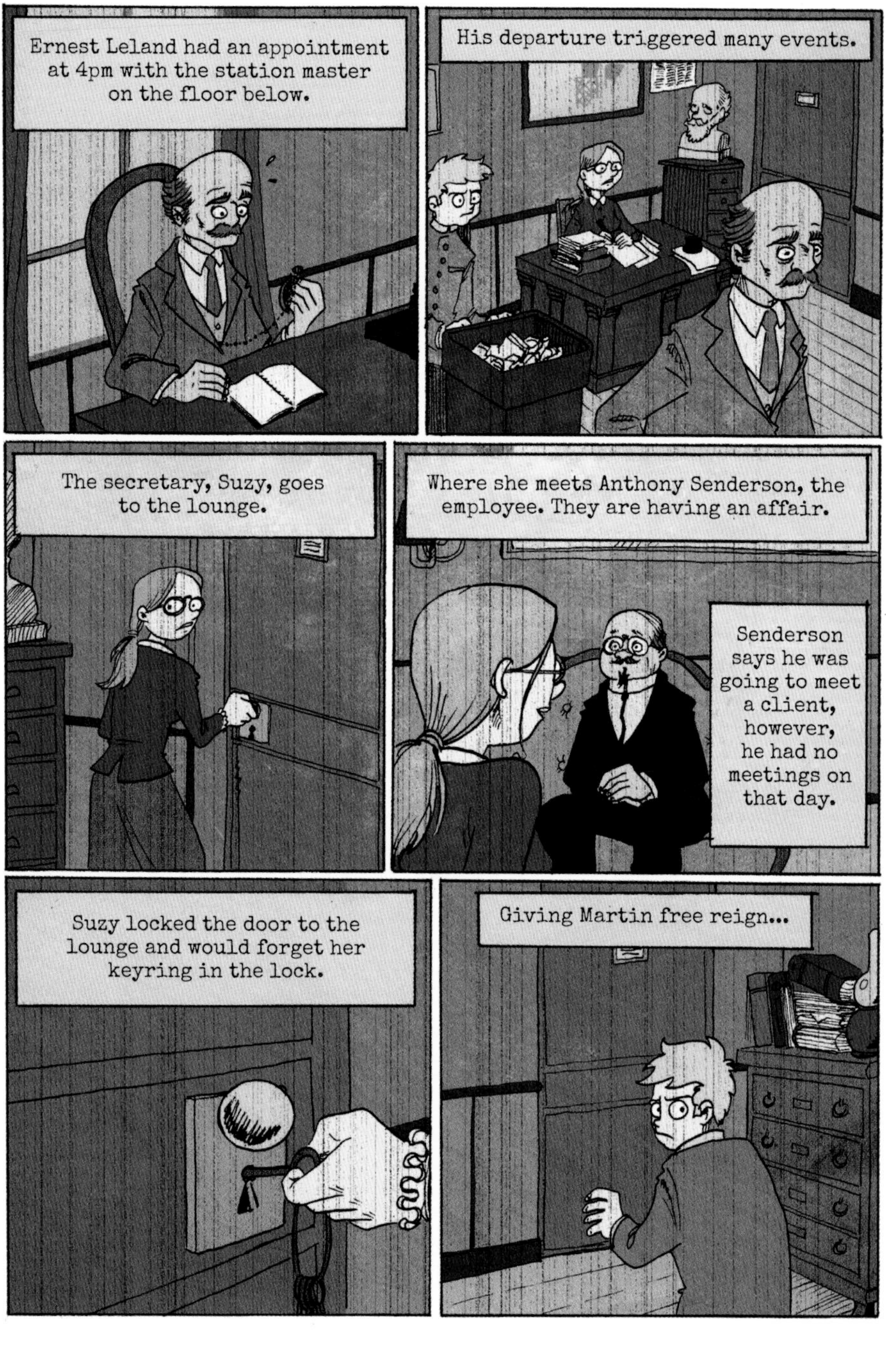
Ernest Leland had an appointment at 4pm with the station master on the floor below.
His departure triggered many events.
The secretary, Suzy, goes to the lounge.
Where she meets Anthony Senderson, the employee. They are having an affair.
Senderson says he was going to meet a client, however, he had no meetings on that day.
Suzy locked the door to the lounge and would forget her keyring in the lock.
Giving Martin free reign...

He goes in the director's office...

And locks himself in.

With his keyring tied to his belt, he cannot leave it in the lock.

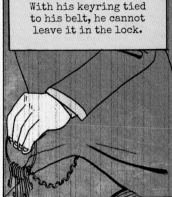

During that time, Ernest Leland noticed that the station master is away. His appointment is clearly canceled.

Out of office all day

He goes back upstairs and finds the door to his office locked.

He peeks through the keyhole and is horrified by what he sees...

Martin opened the safe and he was helping himself to its contents.

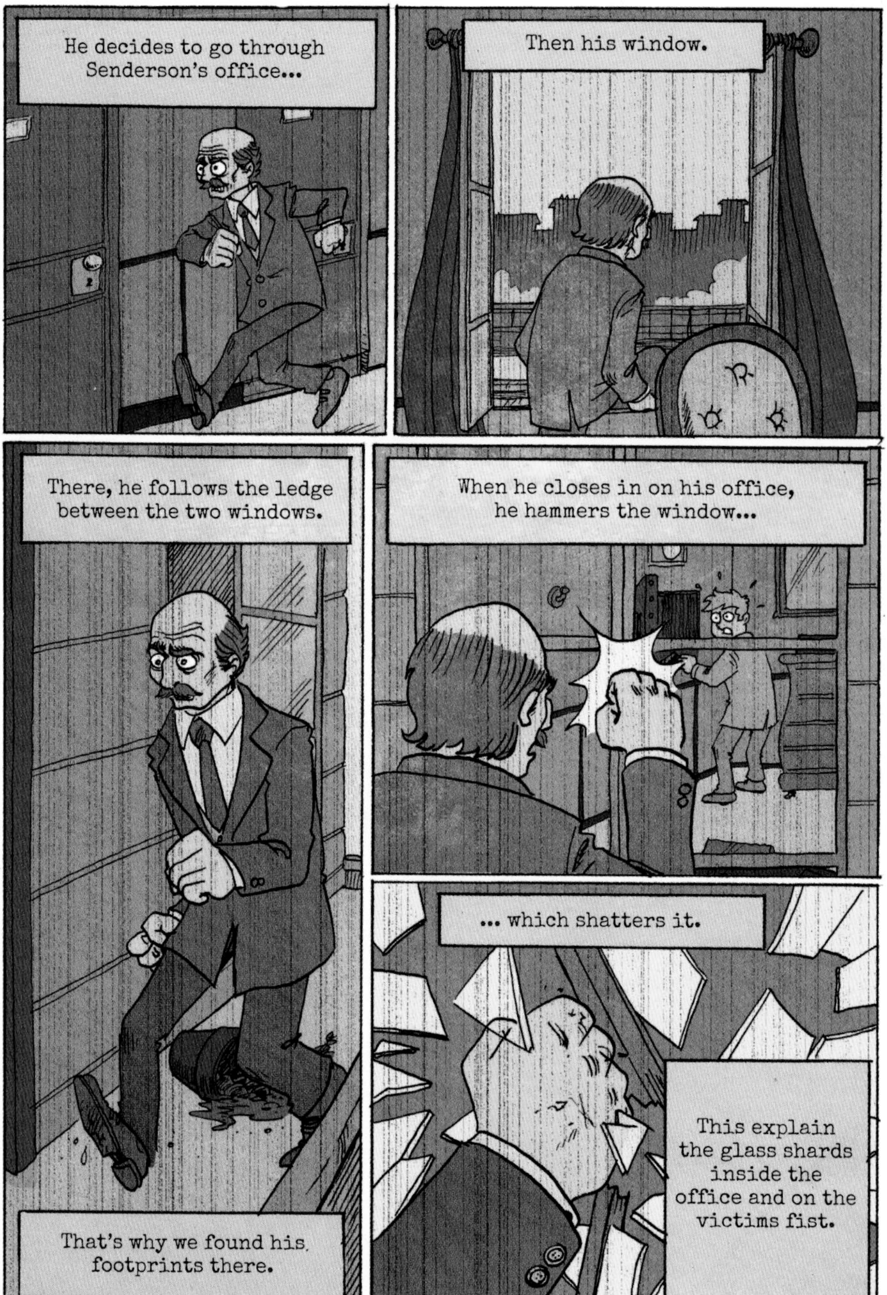
He decides to go through Senderson's office...
Then his window.
There, he follows the ledge between the two windows.
That's why we found his footprints there.
When he closes in on his office, he hammers the window...
... which shatters it.
This explain the glass shards inside the office and on the victims fist.

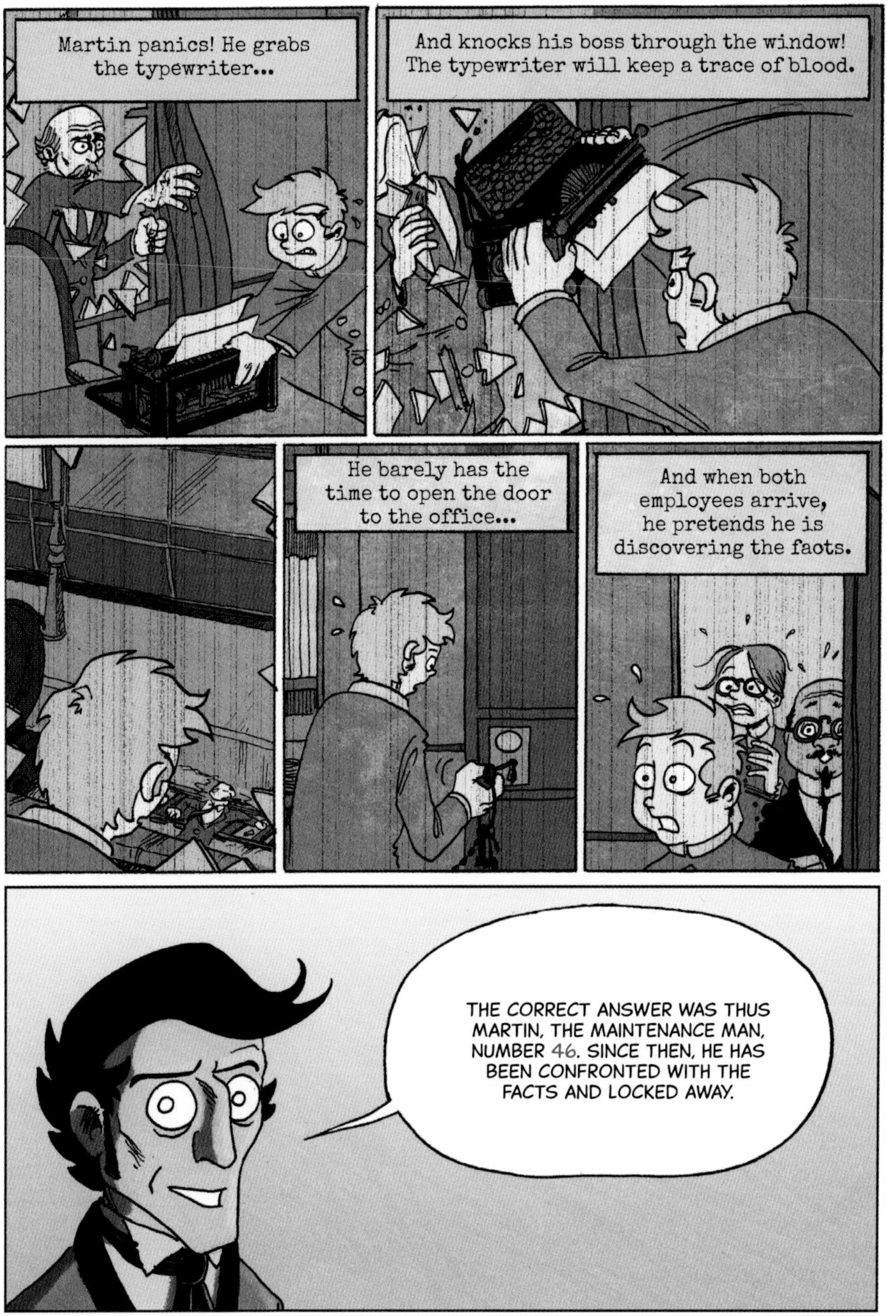

Martin panics! He grabs the typewriter...
And knocks his boss through the window! The typewriter will keep a trace of blood.
He barely has the time to open the door to the office...
And when both employees arrive, he pretends he is discovering the facts.
THE CORRECT ANSWER WAS THUS MARTIN, THE MAINTENANCE MAN, NUMBER 46. SINCE THEN, HE HAS BEEN CONFRONTED WITH THE FACTS AND LOCKED AWAY.

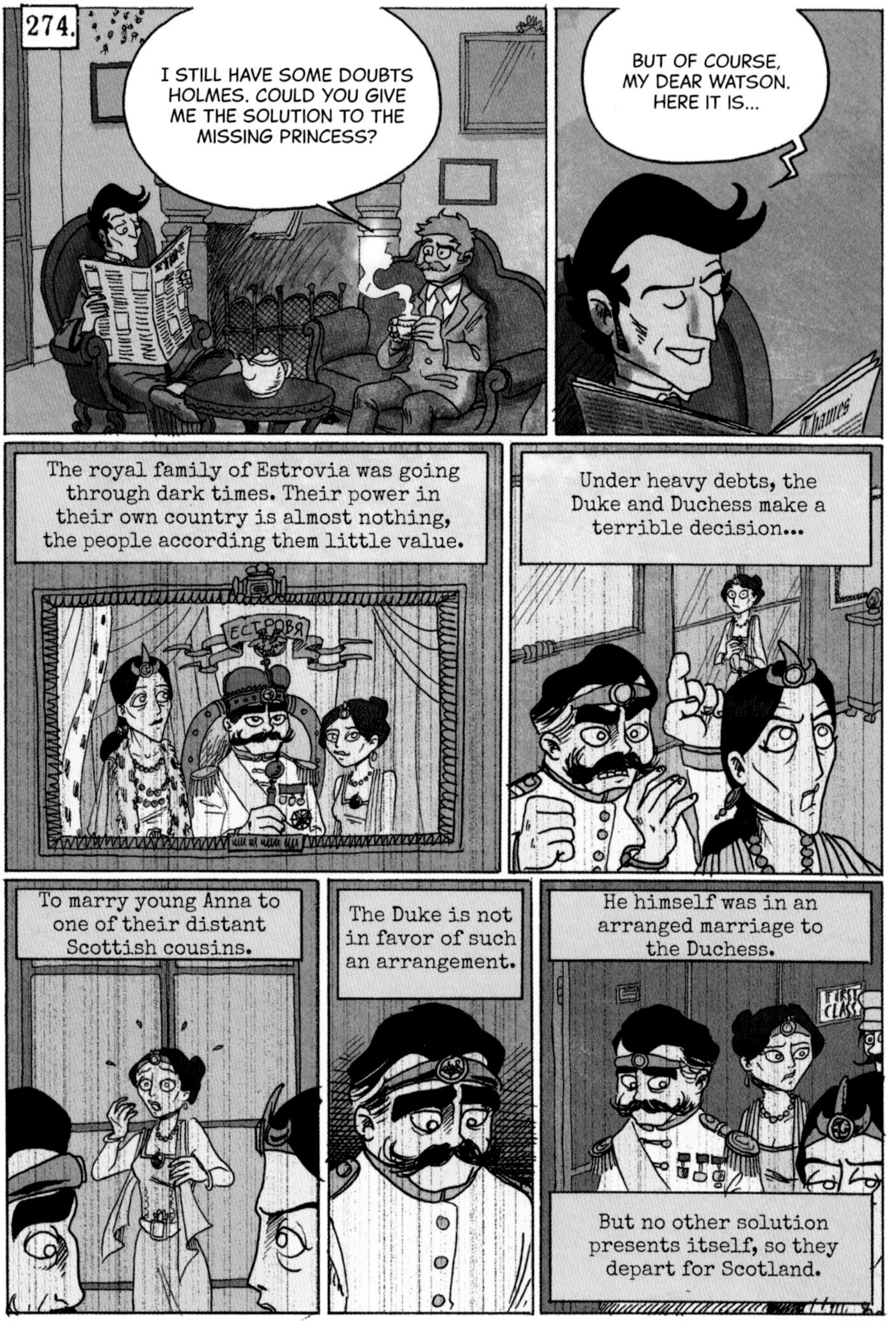
274.
I STILL HAVE SOME DOUBTS HOLMES. COULD YOU GIVE ME THE SOLUTION TO THE MISSING PRINCESS?
BUT OF COURSE, MY DEAR WATSON. HERE IT IS...
Thames
The royal family of Estrovia was going through dark times. Their power in their own country is almost nothing, the people according them little value.
ЕСТРОВЯ
Under heavy debts, the Duke and Duchess make a terrible decision...
To marry young Anna to one of their distant Scottish cousins.
The Duke is not in favor of such an arrangement.
He himself was in an arranged marriage to the Duchess.
FIRST CLASS
But no other solution presents itself, so they depart for Scotland.

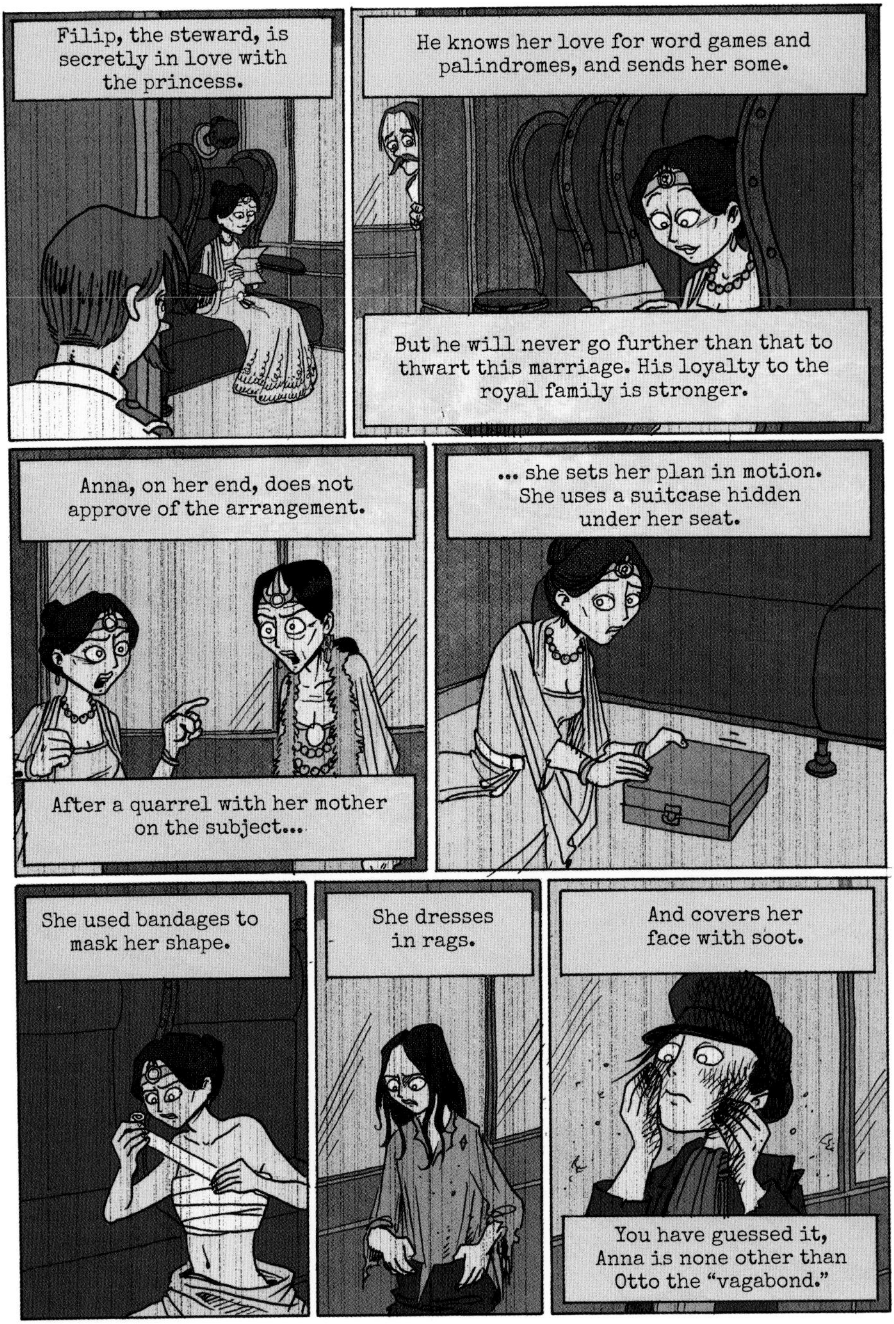
Filip, the steward, is secretly in love with the princess.
He knows her love for word games and palindromes, and sends her some.
But he will never go further than that to thwart this marriage. His loyalty to the royal family is stronger.
Anna, on her end, does not approve of the arrangement.
After a quarrel with her mother on the subject...
... she sets her plan in motion. She uses a suitcase hidden under her seat.
She used bandages to mask her shape.
She dresses in rags.
And covers her face with soot.
You have guessed it, Anna is none other than Otto the "vagabond."

Anna, in her disguise, runs to car where the wood is stored.

She waits for Sid the engineer's break.

Then sneaks onto the locomotive.

Because running away from your family requires money.

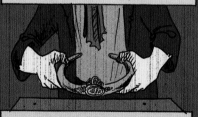

Thanks to Filip, the steward, she knows how to get the gold from her crown.

She used to boiler to heat up the metal.

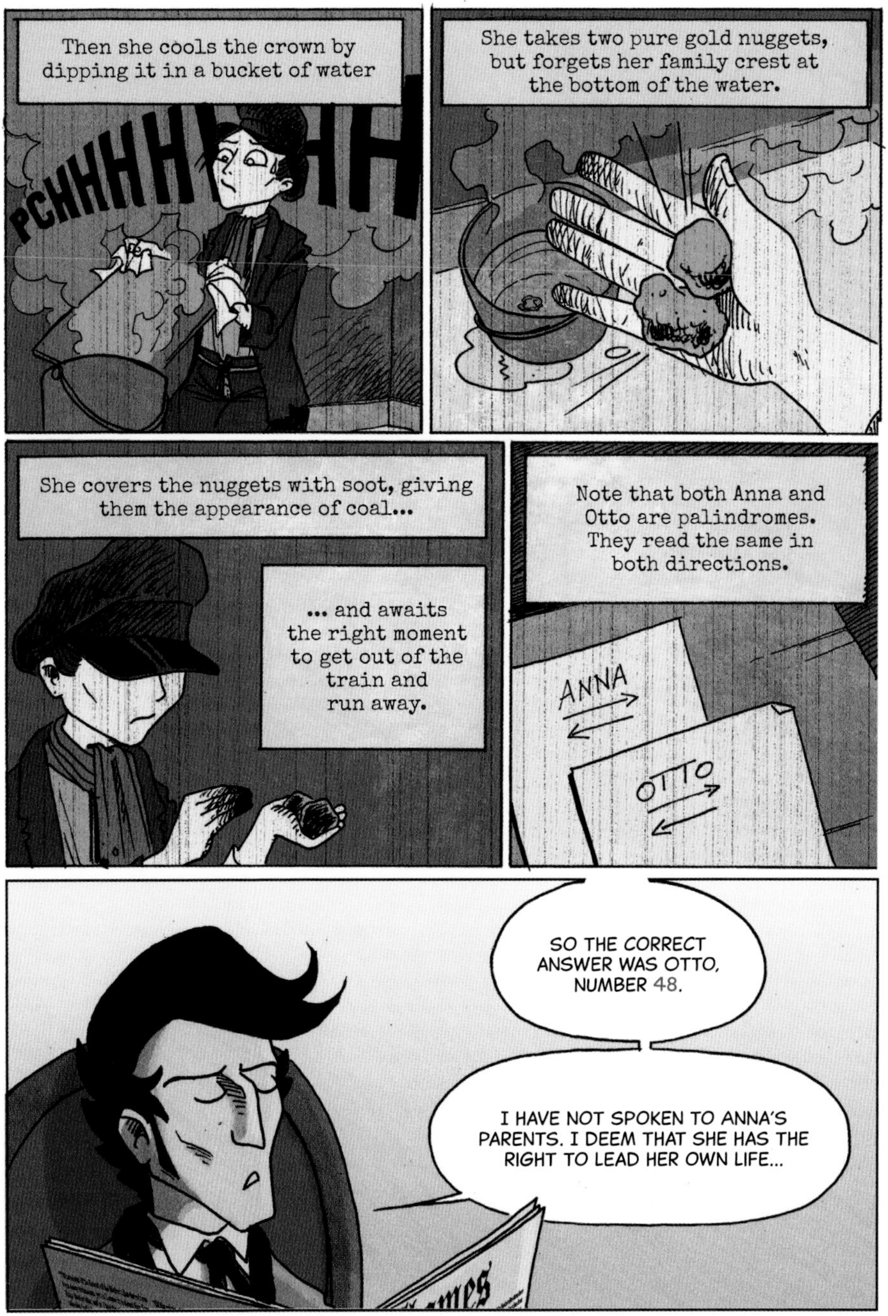
Then she cools the crown by dipping it in a bucket of water
PCHHHHHHHH
She takes two pure gold nuggets, but forgets her family crest at the bottom of the water.
She covers the nuggets with soot, giving them the appearance of coal...
... and awaits the right moment to get out of the train and run away.
Note that both Anna and Otto are palindromes. They read the same in both directions.
ANNA
OTTO
SO THE CORRECT ANSWER WAS OTTO, NUMBER 48.
I HAVE NOT SPOKEN TO ANNA'S PARENTS. I DEEM THAT SHE HAS THE RIGHT TO LEAD HER OWN LIFE...

275.

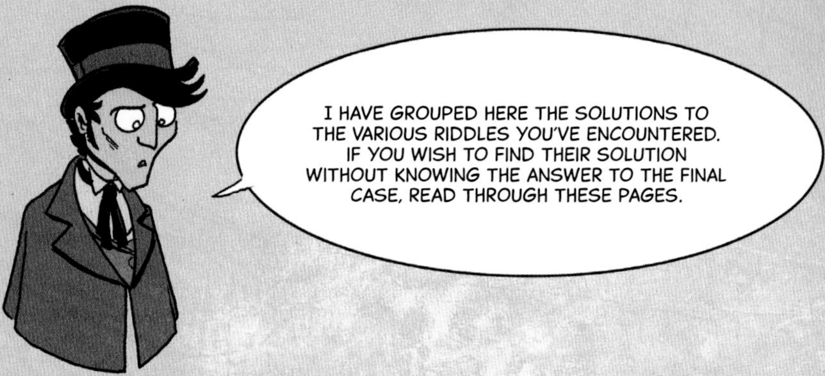
I HAVE GROUPED HERE THE SOLUTIONS TO THE VARIOUS RIDDLES YOU'VE ENCOUNTERED. IF YOU WISH TO FIND THEIR SOLUTION WITHOUT KNOWING THE ANSWER TO THE FINAL CASE, READ THROUGH THESE PAGES.

212. Poetry

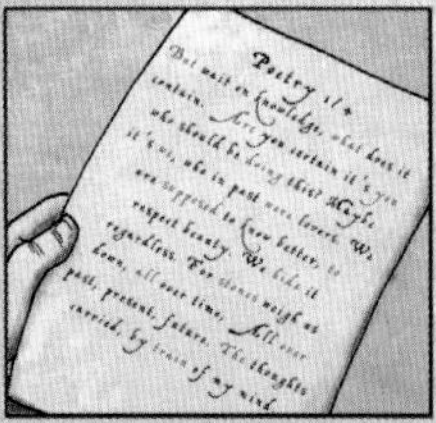
Poetry

You had to read one word out of four, or every fourth word (starting with the first), giving this answer:
"But what are you doing? We were supposed to hide the stones all over the train."

200. Child's play!

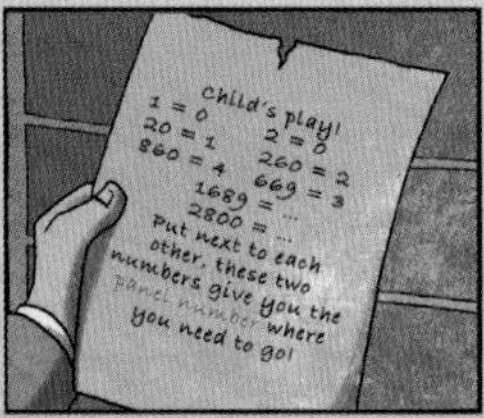
Child's play!
1 = 0
2 = 0
20 = 1
260 = 2
860 = 4
669 = 3
1689 = ...
2800 = ...
Put next to each other, these two numbers give you the panel number where you need to go!

You had to count the number of "loops" in each number. 0, 6, and 9 each have one loop. 1689 has 4, and 2800 also has 4. The correct answer was 44.

178. The Safe's Combination

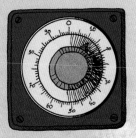

For each letter in the code, you had to find the letter that is directly to the right of it ("the letter after") on a typewriter, keyboard, or any other QWERTY keyboard, giving you:

BUBW—AWCWB—RGUERWWB

NINE—SEVEN—THIRTEEN

161. The Engineer's Riddle

How old is the engineer? Your own age! Sid did say "Let's pretend you're a locomotive engineer." Therefore, the riddle was refering to you. The correct answer was "It depends."

One last riddle, just for fun! LIZ is all topsy turvy! Where is she?

103. The Designer's Riddle

If two trains cross, it's because they are precisely at the same place. So both are as far away from London, Liverpool, Paris, or even New York! The correct answer was "Neither."

SCORING

Score 3 POINTS per case solved as *Watson*.
Score 4 POINTS per case solved as *Moriarty*.
Score 4 POINTS per case solved as *Holmes*.

DIAMONDS

If you found between 10 and 19 diamonds, add 1 POINT.
If you found between 20 and 29 diamonds, add 2 POINTS.
If you found between 30 and 39 diamonds, add 3 POINTS.
If you found between 40 or more diamonds, add 4 POINTS.

If you correctly found Moran's cabin on
your first attempt, add 1 POINT.

ESCAPE ON THE TRAIN ROOF

If you played as Holmes and successfully arrested Moriarty
(without killing him), add 3 POINTS. If you played as Moriarty
and managed to escape, add 3 POINTS.

Add all your points together. This will give you your final score.

If you scored under 10 POINTS, you are a *mediocre detective*.
Fear not! You have ample opportunities to improve by playing the
other Sherlock Holmes Graphic Novel Adventures books.

If you scored between 10 AND 15 POINTS, you are a *talented detective*.
Continue practicing and make your way towards excellence!

If you scored between 16 AND 20 POINTS, you are
an *excellent detective*! Congratulations!